DANCERS
~on the~
SEA

Dancers on the Sea © Gabrielle Samson

All Rights Reserved. Except for private study, research, criticism or review as permitted under the Copyright Act 1968 (Cth), no part of this book may be reproduced or stored in any form or by any electronic or other means including information storage and retrieval systems, without prior permission in writing from the author.

This is a work of non-fiction. The events and conversations in this book have been set down to the best of the author's ability, although some names and details have been changed to protect the privacy of individuals. Every effort has been made to trace or contact all copyright holders. The publisher will be pleased, at the earliest opportunity, to make good any omissions or to rectify any mistakes brought to their attention.

First printed October 2023; reprinted January 2025.

Printed in Australia

Published by Gabrielle Samson gabrielle-samson.com; gabriellesamson3@gmail.com

Edited by Ian Mathieson, ian@ianmathiesonediting.com

Cover Image by Adobe Firefly AI

Paperback ISBN 978-1-7637843-1-4

eBook ISBN 978-1-9231-0109-8

 A catalogue record for this work is available from the National Library of Australia

DANCERS on the SEA

*Stories from Ataúro Island, Timor-Leste
1994 - 2002*

GABRIELLE SAMSON

DEDICATIONS

To the people of Ataúro Island who shared, and continue to share, their lives with me. To my daughter, Freya, who had a distant mother for many years, my son-in-law, Woody, who keeps us all afloat and my grandchildren Zoe, Ruby and Ashton whom I want to know something of their 'avo's' fortunate and amazing life.

ACKNOWLEDGEMENTS

Those friends and family who read my drafts and gave me the encouragement I needed to keep going.

AUTHOR'S NOTE

My story is set in the years prior to 2002, during six of the twelve years I lived and worked on Ataúro Island in East Timor. I was living on the remote island because I wanted, in some way, to help make the world a better place. I was there because I had been invited and had skills that might contribute something to an impoverished, illiterate community. I was there because I'd had breast cancer four years before and thought I might die. I was there, indirectly, because I knew then that I would not live forever which made me eager to be useful in some way, while I could. It also made me curious to understand more about what it is to be a human being. I was on a quest to learn.

My story is not separate from the stories of others with whom I shared this place and time and their stories are interwoven with mine. Many tales of Timor are about the evil oppressors and the innocent oppressed – heroes and villains, black and white. This one isn't. It's about an island in an occupied land, and the lives of ordinary people who lived there; it's a story of wonder, tears, laughter and love during a time of violence and huge change in a remote corner of the world. The events discussed in this book are all real, however some names have been changed to maintain the privacy of individuals. If there are any errors in my memoir, I apologise to my Ataúro friends.

CONTENTS

PROLOGUE 1
Ataúro

PART ONE 3
Satya Wacana Christian University (Uksw), Central Java, 1993
June 1994

PART TWO 7
East Timor: A Brief History
Invaders 1: The Portuguese
Invaders 2: The Japanese
Japanese On Ataúro Island
Invaders 3: Return Of The Portuguese
The Twelve Day Independence And The Civil Wars
Invaders 4: Indonesia
The Santa Cruz Massacre, Dili

PART THREE 14
First Visit
Dili
Seafood Restaurant
Maubara
Ataúro Island

PART FOUR 30

Ataúro: The Genesis Story
The People Of Ataúro
Kupang, January 2 1996
Dili
Ataúro Island 2
Kindergarten
Sea Notes
Ghost
Vila
Sea Notes
Ataúro Houses
Ppsdm
Goat Island: An Economic System
Sea Notes
Religion And Magic
Churches On Ataúro
The Protestant Church On Ataúro

PART FIVE 62

A Seabird And A Rose
Harbourmaster
Family Therapy
Sea Notes
White Yacht
Anton
Boat Pulling
Ataúro Names
Kindergarten
Wedding Party
Dancing Etiquette
Ataúro Isolation

The Portuguese Prison
A Place Of Exile: Jesuina Tells Me Her Story
Solidarity: The Clinic Strike
Sea Notes
Joaquim

PART SIX 102
Anton
Picnic
Sea Notes: Dancers On The Sea
Birthday
Sea Notes: This Sea, These People
Falling In Love
Avoidance
Hotel Turismo
The Visitors And The Spy
The Visit
Akrema
Feet
Ambon
Kupang
An Argument

PART SEVEN 127
Decision
Tipah's Marriage
The Ghost Under The Fig Tree
The Death Of My Father
Lautem
May 3 1998
May 7 1998

May 8 1998
May 9 1998
Viqueque Mourners
Makili Dancing
Alu's Death
Alu's Visits And Release
Music
Ataúro Music
Bakery
Love Notes
Black Pearl
Sea Notes
Guests

PART EIGHT 175
Joaquim
Deaths, August 1998-January 1999
The Shout/The Shadow
Sea Notes: Hameti
Mama Maria
Monsoon Rain
Kindergarten
Fish-Drying And A New Kindergarten
Sea Notes: Grandmothers
Muatan Lokal
Love Notes
Literacy
Books
Library
Sea Notes
Luisa Inan

Love Notes
The Cure
The Shout/The Shadow 2
The Death Of My Mother
Silence
A Sad Wedding
The Shout/The Shadow 3
Two Men (Who've Been Drinking It) Talk About Palm Wine
Violence
Sea Notes: Octopus
Elections
Unexpected Event, 1998

PART NINE 219
Changes
The Library
A Javanese Teacher
High School Muatan Lokal
Sea Notes
Kindergartens
Indonesian Nurses And Traditional Midwives
Broken Windows And Police
Persistence
Sea Notes: Outrigger
Demonstrations
The Gathering Of Guns
Uksw
Preparations
Small Injustices
Stones Through A Window
A Teacher's Fear

Chicken Restaurant
A Truckload Of Students
Liquica Massacre
Visitors
The Rock, February 1999
Ataúro Ghosts
An Opinion

PART TEN 245
Salatiga
Australia
Sea Notes: Australia
The Spy
Back To Ataúro
United Nations Mission In East Timor (Unamet)
August 17 1999: Independence Day
Education For A Referendum
Dili Wedding
Soldiers And Nursery Rhymes
Campaigns
Referendum Day, 30 August 1999
A Party
The Announcement, September 4
Night Sea
The Commandant
Sixteen
Oras To'o Ona; An Unfulfilled Promise
The Nights
Sea Notes
The Knife Edge
Evacuation

PART ELEVEN 284
A Hard Decision
Leaving Ataúro
Kalabahi
Restaurant
The Awu
Bali And Separation
The Monastery
Sulawesi Group
Oxfam And Oxford
Timor, October 1999
Back To Ataúro 2
Conundrum
Eduardo's Story
Oecusse
Border Preparation
Homecoming
Foreign Invasion
Ataúro Chiefs Meet Un New York
Nz Visit

PART TWELVE 320
Bali Christmas
Dili
Roman Luan
Participatory Community Development Program (Pcdp)
Maun-Alin
Airport Denpasar
Ambon Support Group
School Furniture
Back To Ataúro 3

Sea Notes: Six Men In A Boat
Trinkets
Green Mangoes
The Library
Anton
Sea Notes
Tua Ko'in
Adriano Cries At The Gate
Sundays
Lobster Fishing
Turtle
Seven Days
The Last Night
Flag Raising

EPILOGUE 355
September 2022

PROLOGUE

ATAÚRO

This is Anton's blanket I'm wearing, faded now, still heavy on my shoulders but soft with age and wear. When sea breezes turn the evenings cool, I wrap it around me like he did; a traditional Timorese tais cloth, closely woven from hand-spun thread and hand-dyed the colours of indigo and other mountain plants, once it was thick and coarse. It no longer smells of him – his soap, sweat, the sea salt on his skin – but the feel of him is in it still, and still delights me. Like so many other things around me – faces, voices, the pungent smells of sea and heavy rain, shadows cast by the mountains, canoes dancing on the waves – this blanket is filled with memories, familiar things. Here and now, as I am, in this very different present, all around are echoes of the past: sweet, funny, sad echoes, and mysteries I no longer need to understand.

That bougainvillea by the fence – its flame-red flowers remind me of a strange and intimate afternoon tea party. It was September 1999 and teacups for three were set out on a little table under the bougainvillea in the pavilion, then called the "round house", in the military compound. They were fine china cups with matching saucers, patterned with yellow roses and green leaves; I remember clearly the delicate gold rims of the cups. The tablecloth was snowy white with a crochet border. The commandant's revolver was placed on it as a kind of centrepiece.

The commandant loved his revolver. He'd displayed it to us many times before. When he took it from its holster, he introduced it as his "second wife", fondling it suggestively with fat fingers before placing it carefully in a conspicuous place – sometimes pressed against the temples of men – where it would not be forgotten.

'Please,' he said on this fine, sociable afternoon, 'have some tea.'

So we drank sweet Indonesian tea out of fine china cups under the bougainvillea – it was not as large then, but just as vibrantly scarlet as it is now – eating fried bananas while we made conversation with the soldier and attempted to avert our eyes from his second wife resting on the table between us.

While we sipped tea, the commandant talked about his family back in Surabaya and how he missed them. He showed us pictures: "first" wife with her round, serious face and traditional Javanese bun at the nape of her neck; two teenage daughters, pert, short modern hairstyles, bobs, staring proudly out of their military father's much-fingered photos.

It was all very pretty and very civilised. We took a great interest in his family. We thought it best to be polite.

It was four days after the referendum that sealed the fate of Timor Timur and set the seed of independence for Timor-Leste. Just a couple of days before mayhem, murder and destruction at the hands of military-backed militia would devastate the little country. While the outcome of the referendum was yet unknown, our commandant was calm, self-assured and blissfully delusional. Anton and I were patient and polite.

PART ONE

SATYA WACANA CHRISTIAN UNIVERSITY (UKSW), CENTRAL JAVA, 1993

My year of illness and uncertainty was over. My daughter was at university in Brisbane exploring her life as an adult, and I was still alive after a breast cancer operation and all the doubt and medical treatments that went with it: surgery, radiation, chemotherapy. I was alive, for now at least, and so could go out into the world on my quest.

In 1993 I started work at Satya Wacana University's Institute of Community Service (LPM), a small centre tucked away in a leafy corner of the campus in Salatiga, Central Java. I worked as advisor and trainer in the early childhood education outreach program, in poor rural areas. I'd discovered LPM when I was studying the Indonesian language at Satya Wacana and was delighted when my offer to work there for a year was accepted.

My work was initially focused on a large village in the Getasan Sub-district. In Polobogo Village we worked with education department officials, teachers, parents, and children in three kindergartens. I often stayed up there in the mountains and so began to learn about Javanese village life.

In the town of Salatiga, I lived in a tiny house in the working-class kampung of Klaseman, where I shared a courtyard – running water and a washing area – with three other households. My neighbours' children had no access to books, so I started a library in my sitting room and, with the addition of paper, crayons and paints it soon became a lively childrens' centre. Klaseman was an Islamic neighbourhood and, although I worked at the Christian university, once assured that I was no evangelist – not even a Christian really – I was accepted as neighbour and friend.

It was an ever-interesting place to live: the kind of poor neighbourhood where, in the local hole-in-the-wall store, you could buy sugar and oil in tiny 25-gram packs, and cigarettes by the single stick; the kind of neighbourhood where the men were labourers or dokkar (horse-drawn wagon) drivers. We had meetings on Friday nights to discuss local issues, and weekly working bees to sweep our lanes; we had to report to the village head if we had overnight guests and, five times a day, non-synchronized calls to prayer from five small mosques rang through our houses. It was a fantastic place to live and where someone like me, on a quest to understand herself and humanity, had plenty of opportunity to learn. Here were whole new ways of looking at life – at kindness, at expectations, at grief and humour, at conflict, manners, and relationships. It was challenging and wonderful.

My work and home life were everything I wanted, my language and cultural understanding were growing and consolidating. So when I was asked by the university to stay on for another year to continue the program, of course I agreed – I felt I was just starting to be useful. In my second year, our work with kindergarten teachers was extended to the far reaches of eastern Indonesia – to Sumba and West Timor. The program now took me into more amazing places where I worked with extraordinary people in extraordinary cultures. I loved it.

JUNE 1994

On campus in Salatiga I shared an office with Sampurno and Miyono, both enthusiastic Javanese community development workers. Their friends often visited; usually young thinkers, students and academics – they dropped by to discuss ideas, tell jokes, gossip. Sitting on the low, wide ledges of our office windows or dragging up wooden stools, they argued with passion in that safe place about the Soeharto government in the mid-90s, the military, about university politics, poverty, development, who was doing what with whom in the university world.

One day when I came into our room, a stranger was sitting on the window ledge talking with Sam and Miyono. A tall, thin man, he spoke softly, had their full attention and was making them smile. There seemed to be a gentler atmosphere in that small office while he spoke; its usual bustle missing. The visitor, an Ambonese man called Anton, had come from East Timor and was telling stories of his work there. For the first time, I heard of a remote Timorese island called Ataúro where UKSW ran a community outreach program.

From my desk in the corner, I didn't catch everything he said. I heard snatches about fishing projects, people's struggle for survival in that harsh place, the isolation of it, the island's poverty; I heard about small boats and wild seas, the joys and frustrations of working with the island community. The man told his stories with love and laughter, and what I heard touched my heart and my imagination.

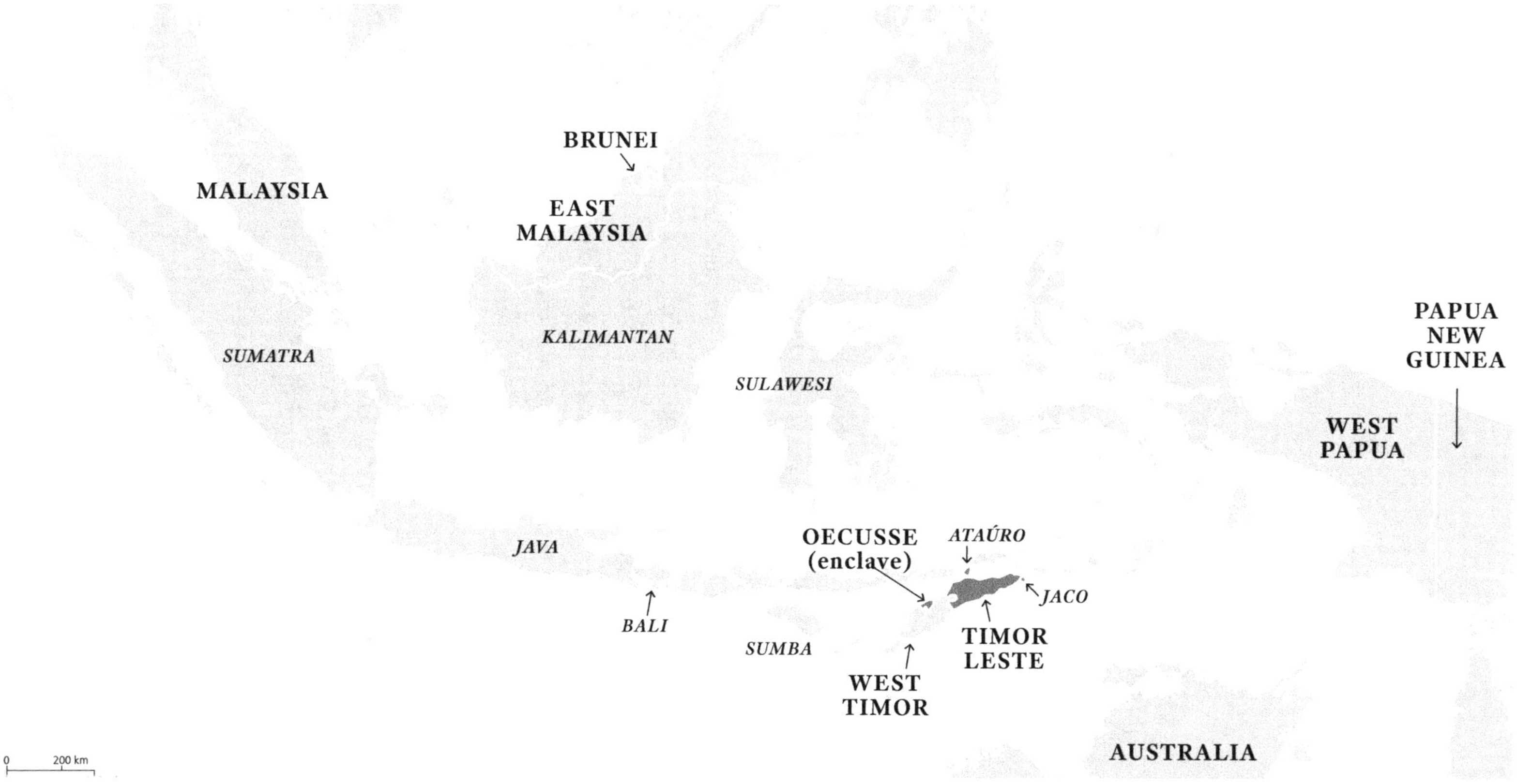

0
200 km

SUMATRA

MALAYSIA

BRUNEI

EAST
MALAYSIA

KALIMANTAN

JAVA

BALI

SULAWESI

SUMBA

OECUSSE
(enclave)

WEST
TIMOR

ATAÚRO

TIMOR
LESTE

JACO

AUSTRALIA

WEST
PAPUA

PAPUA
NEW
GUINEA

PART TWO

EAST TIMOR: A BRIEF HISTORY

INVADERS 1: THE PORTUGUESE

The Portuguese came to Timor around the middle of the sixteenth century and stayed a very long time. For over four hundred and fifty years, they patrolled the coastlines and rugged mountains of Portuguese Timor, cutting sandalwood, planting coffee, extracting taxes from native peoples and forcing them to labour on roads and plantations. Like their English, Dutch, French and Spanish sisters, Portuguese women made sacrifices for their Empires so that their menfolk – seafarers and colonisers – could voyage over vast oceans and toss about in little sailing ships; taking flags to the remote corners of the earth that they proudly occupied, plundered and controlled.

In 1859 the invaders and exploiters of remote eastern kingdoms split up the lands they didn't own. Bending over heavy wooden tables, Portuguese and Dutch fingers traced over yellow maps – 'this for me and that for you; that for me and this for you' – drawing lines that divided peoples, cultures, clans and families forever. The eastern half of the island of Timor remained part of Portugal's empire and the western half of the island, apart from the enclave of Macassar, part of the Dutch empire.

This was decided in 1859, reshuffled in 1893, and finalised by treaty in 1914.

In 1949 West Timor became part of a newly independent Indonesia and East Timor remained Portuguese Timor until 1975.

The Portuguese didn't do a lot for the Timorese over four hundred and fifty-odd years – years that were more about the glory and wealth of Portugal than the development of Timor. Towards the end of their occupation, they brought Catholicism to the animist land and education to an elite group of Timorese who learned the Portuguese language and developed a love for it and the small, fading European nation a world away.

INVADERS 2: THE JAPANESE

During the Second World War, Japan and Australia fought each other on mainland Timor. Part of Australian war legend is that the "kind and goodly Timorese villagers" helped Australian soldiers to hold off the Japanese. Like the "fuzzy wuzzy angels" of New Guinea, the Timorese helped Australian soldiers to overcome their enemies in the mountains of their land, before they could reach the shores of northern Australia.

Poor and powerless in the battle but canny and kind-hearted, the Timorese have been exalted and mythologised in Australian history – making it difficult to explain Australia's turning a blind eye to the invasion and occupation of their little country by our Indonesian neighbour in 1975.

JAPANESE ON ATAÚRO ISLAND

Japanese soldiers came to Ataúro for a period during the war, but I've never heard stories of brutality or exceptional cruelty during that time, only of island people being shouted at and abused in a foreign language, and being forced to do the bidding of new bosses. Having experienced Portuguese colonialism for many years this was nothing new, and people became skilled at following orders in a language they didn't understand.

Elderly Ataúro men laughingly still tell stories of how their fathers pretended to understand Japanese even when they didn't, and how they had to bluff their way into or out of a situation as shouts grew harsher and louder and even more difficult to comprehend. This skill at pretending worked and served the Ataúro people well, right up to their own independence referendum in 1999.

INVADERS 3: RETURN OF THE PORTUGUESE

Post WW2, the Portuguese came back, but it was never quite the same. By 1961, there were political stirrings and the formation of liberation movements in other Portuguese colonies (Angola, Guinea Bissau, Mozambique) and, in the east, their Indonesian neighbours were demanding independence from the Dutch.

THE TWELVE DAY INDEPENDENCE
AND THE CIVIL WARS

Life in Portuguese Timor continued for some time without much change, but by 1975 the wider world had changed, and it was no longer desirable to be a colonial power. The Carnation Revolution in 1974 and the political changes it brought meant that the Portuguese government and its people no longer wanted to own Timor. The decolonisation process moved quickly – too quickly – and, after centuries of foreign rule and years of fierce resistance, suddenly independence was promised. Excited Timorese elites began forming their own political parties, each with elaborate hopes and dreams for their country – and themselves – and competing for control of it

Before the official independent government election was held, UDT, one of the stronger parties, mounted a coup, fearing that their main opposition, Fretilin, was gaining popularity. This led to a battle – later called the Civil War – between the opposing groups of Timorese and sent the country into turmoil. The Portuguese administration, no longer able to control events, fled the erupting mayhem in Dili over the sea to Ataúro, leaving the Timorese on the mainland to fight it out. From the distance and safety of the island, the chief Portuguese administrator tried to rule the colony and bring about negotiations for a resolution, but by this time there was little support or interest from the mother country. In the end, he and his people could only wait, as did the Ataúro people, to learn what was happening in the capital across the sea.

The Fretilin Party won the battle and, on November 28 1975, raised its flag to take what it saw as its rightful place as the rulers of Portuguese Timor… but their newly independent Democratic

Republic of East Timor government was in power for less than a fortnight.

While ambitious Timorese were fighting each other for supremacy, powerful people in more influential countries (even in countries like Australia that may have owed allegiance to the Timorese for their wartime support) watched on and conferred, brows creased in growing concern. Stroking their chins and shaking their heads, these people reached an agreement: a troublesome little *independent* country in that particular neck of the woods, an *uncontrolled* independent country that showed a tendency towards socialist values and was seen to be developing a friendship with other troublesome *little countries* like Cuba, was *not* a good thing, definitely *not* a good thing… so the powerful people of influential countries turned their gaze in the direction of Indonesia and nodded.

INVADERS 4: INDONESIA

On December 7 1975, Timor was invaded again; Indonesian planes and parachutes, ships and soldiers with weapons, arrived. Over the next few weeks they slaughtered, raped and tortured hundreds of Timorese as they 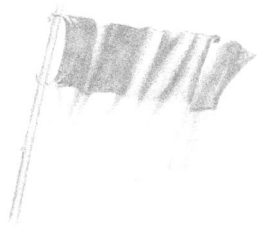 established military control over the country. The Australian government and the governments of other powerful western countries looked the other way. When Australian journalists were killed by Indonesian soldiers in Balibo, they did not seem to see it, nor did they seem to notice the diminishing population of Timor as thousands lost their lives – not only in the first few weeks of the invasion, but over the next twenty-five years.

THE SANTA CRUZ MASSACRE, DILI

The Indonesian invasion of Timor began on December 7 1975, and its brutal occupation continued for many years. Brutal, too, was the determined East Timorese resistance to it. Acts of violence were rife. However, events in the country were largely ignored by the rest of the world until, in 1991, there was one event that attracted attention and changed everything.

On November 11 1991, near the entrance to the Santa Cruz Cemetery in Dili, Indonesian soldiers opened fire on a procession of Timorese mourners carrying flowers to the grave of an activist shot by the military the week before. The procession had left the Motael Church down near the port and the mourners were walking, praying and singing in commemoration and protest of his murder, to Santa Cruz.

Outside the cemetery, armed soldiers waited and a skirmish occurred in which an Indonesian soldier was allegedly stabbed. The soldiers then opened fire on hundreds of unarmed Timorese gathered on the road. People fled through the cemetery; people were shot dead; people were wounded and loaded onto military trucks to be taken away and never seen again.

Max Stahl, a British activist and filmmaker, was filming the procession, and captured everything. He continued to video, burying his film cassettes in the cemetery and courageously later retrieving them and releasing his film internationally. It was then that the world saw and was finally forced to acknowledge what was happening in East Timor.

In December of that year, I searched Indonesian newspapers in the library of Satya Wacana University for reports of this event and found, on page 3 of the Jakarta Post (the English language paper), a paragraph briefly describing a 'disturbance' in Dili. I found no mention of it in other papers; while the world was shocked into outrage by the carnage of Santa Cruz, most Indonesian citizens were kept comfortably in the dark about the event.

PART THREE

FIRST VISIT

In December 1994, I went to East Timor.

Miyono, my Javanese colleague, and I had been working with kindergarten teachers in eastern Indonesia and had set up a network for isolated, unsupported, poorly paid and poorly resourced teachers in Sumba and West Timor. We visited the east twice a year to run training sessions and workshops in such fabulous places as Waikabubak and Waingapu, Kupang, Soe and Kefamanu. This time, after our last training in West Timor, Miyono would return to Java and I was to go over the border to the eastern part of the island (then called in Indonesian Timor Timur) to visit the community development programs run by the university there: an agriculture extension program in Maubara and a small fisheries development program on Ataúro Island.

It was just three years after the Santa Cruz massacre in Dili. The whole world was now aware of what was happening in East Timor: oppression and cruelty under the Indonesian military and strong resistance by the Timorese people to the Indonesian occupation. It seemed a place of incredible sadness and incredible hope, courage, mystery and intrigue. I was glad to go and see for myself.

In those days, foreigners didn't just wander into East Timor to visit rural communities, so the university carefully organised every detail of my trip; my host there would be Roy, an Ambonese man, the university representative and manager of its East Timor programs. I would also be accompanied by Ferry, another university colleague who would come from Java to meet up with me in Dili and Anton, the coordinator of the Ataúro program. Over ten days we would go together to Maubara and Ataúro to visit the projects, talk with people, get a feel for how things were going.

Roy and Ferry were good minders and guides for me. Roy was absolutely the right person for his job. He had already worked in East Timor for a couple of years and knew the ropes and how to pull them. He seemed to have access to almost everyone and almost everything, producing cars and boats and people when we needed them, whispering words in the right ears to get us through sticky situations – and Timor was sticky with situations in those days. Roy was a classic "everybody-loves-him nobody-knows-him" sort of man; bouncy, with a glib and easy tongue, free with jokes and laughter, with grins and winks that may or may not have meaning. Ferry was a dignified, quiet researcher from Minado, Sulawesi; an unassuming academic who people, even armed and uniformed people, took seriously.

In Dili, Ferry and I stayed with Roy and his wife, Annie, their young son, several Ambonese relatives and several Timorese friends and workmates; that gave me lots of opportunity for both observation and confusion. Roy and Annie lived in a small, crowded cement-block house in Vila Verde, just behind the bishop's residence. I was given my own tiny room off the busy sitting room, a small sanctuary behind a thin ply wall with a curtain of faded blue cloth for a door. It was an incredibly active and noisy household and its many comings and goings mostly washed over and around me; people I didn't know, conversations I didn't fully understand, jokes and plans I only half heard.

Because it was East Timor and I was a foreign visitor, a lot of the planning and talk revolved around my visit. There were whisperings, continuous coffee drinking, much serious shaking and nodding of heads, and lots of laughter. Because I was a foreigner and it was East Timor, I watched and listened. This house was full of Indonesians and Timorese living and working together, and it was 1994; as a newcomer to this political context, I didn't fully understand what was going on and thought it best not to ask questions too soon. I spoke Indonesian well, but no Tetun, and both these languages were spoken around me. I tried not to make assumptions about anyone or anything and, as much as I could, to just go along with things as they unfolded.

DILI

I did not expect to see Timorese teenagers playing volleyball in the park in the evenings or families strolling along the esplanade enjoying sea breezes. I did not expect the city to be so full of life, shopping streets to be so lively, the night vendors of grilled corn, chicken and fish on the beach at Pantai Kelapa to be so busy with customers. People of all ages, drawn to the smell of chicken or fresh fish roasting over charcoal fires beside the sea, to yellow lamplight and cheery voices floating over the sand, jostled companionably for service, sharing gossip and jokes.

I saw ordinary Timorese and Indonesian mothers and fathers with their children, talking and laughing with Indonesian and Timorese soldiers in uniform. I did not expect that in Dili in 1994. I expected overwhelming oppression and fear. I expected dark empty streets; I expected hatred and suspicion. I expected,

I suppose, black to be black and white to be white, and what I saw and felt were many confusing shades of grey.

It was not that fear was not there. It was not the total absence of oppression. Everyone now knows the story of East Timor and the Indonesian occupation, and it is not a pretty one. It is dark and ugly. And there was plenty of fear and oppression around Dili in those days. By nine-thirty at night, the streets were dark and empty, and soldiers patrolled. There was no official curfew, but there was a curfew. There was resistance, cruelty and suffering in the districts. But that was not all there was; there were volleyball games in the late afternoon and people strolling by the sea in the evening, there were smoky fires and fresh grilled corn and Timorese and Indonesian boys and grannies and soldiers, mums and dads out for tea.

Before the night grew dark and silent, I heard laughter and affable voices all around me – Timorese and Indonesian voices together. It was later in the night, when families had scurried off home and only shadows moved in the streets, that I felt the other side, the depth of hostility, the tension, the fear. Stealth.

SEAFOOD RESTAURANT

The beachside seafood restaurant east of Dili, where now there are much fancier eating-places throbbing with foreign life and sophistication, was in 1994, the poky, dimly lit haunt of important Indonesians and Timorese. There, you could eat the biggest and freshest fish in town and government and military vehicles filled the car park.

On my first night in Dili, Roy, Ferry, Anton and I went there to eat. As the only foreign person, and the only woman, I felt self-conscious as we entered the restaurant. Conversations stopped.

As we looked about for a table, heads turned, eyes followed us and there was a pin-drop silence. Roy nodded greetings towards the other diners, raised his hand confidently to those he knew (and he knew almost everyone) and gave me a reassuring wink.

Anton and Roy ordered coral trout and a big tuna from the ice tub and we watched the fish sizzle on the charcoal grill, a distraction from the shadowy room that seemed very slow to fill again with talk and laughter. I did not have to look around to be aware of the dark, uniform-clad bodies of men bent over tables, their faces turned towards me, their whispered conversations. The camaraderie of their shared suspicion made me feel, not exactly afraid, but certainly uneasy.

While we waited for our fish, Roy visited each of the other tables, having a joke, a laugh, a quiet word in the ears of people who mattered; people who, I noticed, leaned back in their chairs towards him, interested in what he had to say. There was no attempt to hide the fact that they were talking about me; glances my way confirmed that. But as our meal was brought to the table Roy came back confidently, smiling broadly as the conversations and laughter in the room resumed.

That first time in Dili I was dependent on this man and his apparently smooth, easy friendships with the right people. To run its grassroots community programs in the troubled land of East Timor, the university needed good formal relationships with people in high places in the capital. Roy was the lubricant that kept those relationships running smoothly. I think he took us to that busy restaurant on my first night in town to have my visit brought out in the open, to "declare" me.

It was the end of 1994. There were not many foreigners in East Timor – a handful of International Red Cross staff, a few people working for approved aid organisations, some Catholic missionaries. The Indonesian government and military wanted to know who came and went, and for what purpose. It was just three years since the Santa Cruz cemetery massacre was shown to the world. To the drowsy world that had turned away from East Timor after the invasion in 1975 and to the Indonesian military which had thought its power and dirty secrets secure in that remote corner of the world, it was a shock. The Indonesian government did not want journalists there. It did not want more bad press.

I was working for a reputable private Indonesian university that had good relations with the provincial government in East Timor and had its support to run community development programs there but, still, I was a foreigner and would be deeply mistrusted because of it. I had been briefed by my bosses at the university in Java to leave all planning and negotiating during my visit to Roy and Ferry; being Indonesian, they knew very well how to avoid stepping on the sensitive toes of authority.

My two years of living in rural Central Java and working with local authorities there had taught me a little of how to move without attracting attention; how to show respect in my manner and speech; how, despite being large and foreign, to keep a relatively low profile. My affected Javanese manners were to be extremely useful in East Timor.

MAUBARA

In those days, there was a military checkpoint at the Tibar junction, about eighteen kilometres from Dili and ninety-three from the border. Passing vehicles were stopped and examined there. The military post was a small concrete box but in the hot weather bored soldiers sat with their guns at a trestle table under the canopy of a large fig tree. Some vehicles they waved on and others they investigated and, although they were familiar with Roy and the university 4WD that regularly passed by, with me, a foreigner, on board, we had to stop.

Roy knew the soldiers would have been informed from Dili about me and prepared me. 'Stay in the car. Let me do the talking. Pretend not to speak Indonesian. Be polite and friendly. Ignore their threatening and suspicious manner.' All that was easy. I was nervous but knew how to play that game – to a lesser degree, it was a game you played with authorities all over Indonesia.

The soldiers examined my passport, slowly passing it from one to the other and asking questions about my purpose in East Timor. I smiled at them as Roy, appealing to their sense of national pride, lauded me as an Australian who was there to help Indonesia, a volunteer working with the university to develop education in the far reaches of their land. They nodded appreciatively, returned the passport and smiled back at me. No problem. Showing off their English, they called, 'Goodbye,' and, 'See you later,' as they waved us off.

Pusat Pengembangan Sumber Daya Manusia/The Centre for Human Resource Development (PPSDM), our university's project in Maubara, was an agriculture centre running crop experimentation and agricultural training to improve the lives of local farmers. The university had four or five academic staff – both East Timorese and Indonesian – and a large number of East Timorese training and auxiliary staff working in the program. Willie Toisuta, the rector of UKSW, had set up the comprehensive program as a way for Timorese graduates from the university to work with their people.

UKSW was a non-government Christian university with many students from East Timor. Churches provided scholarships as a way of supporting the Timor struggle, believing that an educated population had more chance of bringing about change. Returning graduates, however, did not always find jobs; political history and affiliation played a major role in who got employment. PPSDM was a non-government program that employed Timorese who had appropriate knowledge and skills to train others. It had genuine community development values and not just pro-Indonesian politics.

I was impressed by the work being done in spite of the pressures under which staff worked. These pressures included: East Timorese and some Indonesian staff feeling they were under constant, sometimes menacing, surveillance by the military; local East Timorese staff being exposed to jealous abuse from Timorese neighbours who hadn't found employment at the centre; senior Indonesian staff feeling the resentment and distrust of junior Timorese staff; senior Timorese staff feeling the resentment and distrust of junior Timorese staff. This was a Christian program with all the best will in the world and many praiseworthy achievements to its credit, but this small neck of the woods was a complicated place. This, I was to learn, was reflective of the whole province.

Fortunately, my job was not to solve problems but to listen and observe. Perhaps my reports would help the university to develop useful long-term support programs for those working at the centre, perhaps not.

ATAÚRO ISLAND

Since hearing Anton's stories when he'd visited us in Java earlier that year, Ataúro had taken on a strong, mysterious persona for me, and I was excited and curious about visiting the island.

Perhaps my expectations were too high. On my first visit, we travelled on a very rough sea. The Ataúro boatman, Guido, was skilled and confident at working boats through all kinds of seas. He took us out of Dili Harbour and gently into the big waves… but soon Roy, the extrovert, the showman, nudged Guido aside and took over the motor himself – before long, his lack of skill had the boat bucking and slapping against the steely grey sea, drenching us with the deep waters of the Wetar Strait.

My knuckles were white as I gripped the side of the boat, a lightweight, fibreglass bath toy that bounced mercilessly over the swells. Roy had cajoled someone in government into lending us the boat and it felt tiny in that great, rolling sea. Ferry, a pale-skinned Minado man and not a seaman, looked very, very pale while Guido and Roy laughed and shouted to each other above the motor, making jokes and attempting to keep their cigarettes alight in the spray. For far too long we seemed to be right in the middle of that rough sea with the mainland way, way behind us and the island way, way ahead; both lands visible and yet too distant. The motor sputtered, coughed and stopped occasionally – Ferry and I exchanged nervous glances – then, after a curse and a rough bang or two from someone's hand, shuddered back to life and went on. It was a long, two-hour journey across the sea that day.

Seen from Dili, Ataúro is magical; crouching on the horizon it's a great curvaceous lizard of an island that's sometimes close and clear, sometimes distant and swathed in mist, hauntingly beautiful. Disappearing into the mist, sometimes it's just not there anymore. On this December day the island was grey and loomed large; too far away as we suffered the cold, rough waves and then as we drew nearer, far too close; too grey, too severe.

Returning from Dili, local boats head for the cliffs and rock terraces at the southern end of the island. From the boat I looked up at dramatic rock faces, their fierce profiles towering over us. It was a harsh, dry landscape. Travelling up the eastern coastline, I swear I didn't see a single palm tree on the island that day. Nor any sand, just rocks and dust. The only signs of life were some grey-leaved, gnarly trees clinging to crevices in the rock faces, and some tiny black goats on a high ledge.

As we followed the coast around the cliffs and past a village – small, scattered bamboo houses with grey thatched roofs, clinging to a dry, rocky slope, narrow paths, rows of dugout canoes on a steep stony beach – I wondered about the choice of human beings to live in such a place. How did they? Why would they? They were poor, subsistence fishers and seasonal farmers trying to eke a living out of one of the harshest places in the world. I found myself recoiling from the difficult grey cliffs,  the brown crumbling rock, the scorched earth, dusty villages and fragile houses exposed along the coast or clinging tenaciously to steep mountainsides. I'd had enough of the rough sea slapping persistently against the boat and the rocky shore; I was cold, wet, bruised and felt no joy.

It was December 1994, and the rain hadn't come. Wet, cold and slightly seasick, I found the landscape overwhelmingly severe and even repellent. And yet I saw tiny human figures with a spring in their step walking around the bottom of the cliff. Dwarfed by its height, then lost for a minute in a shadowy crevice before appearing again, they were dots of blue and red and yellow moving along the path that dangled like a fragile string along the rock face.

We rounded a headland and passed over the reef into a calm lagoon. I finally released my grip on the side of the boat as we headed towards a grey, sandy beach and some dusty coconut palms. Closer, I saw magnificent, aged fig trees, the tall skeleton of a rusted shipwreck on the beach, an old once whitewashed stone house. This was Maumeta Vila, our destination. Maumeta was the original name then it was called Vila – by the Portuguese, I think – and is now referred to by local people as either 'Vila' or 'Maumeta Vila'.

Thin children and scrawny dogs came running as we floated in and hit the shore with a bump. Adults joined them and stood in groups at the water's edge staring at us, not smiling. I hesitated for a moment before getting off. Unused to small boats, I was awkward and painfully aware of being scrutinised closely by a group of agile, seafaring people. I was self-conscious, but also aware of something else – a feeling deep in my belly that had nothing to do with boats. Warily, as I lowered myself into the warm shallow water and my toes sank into the coarse sand, I knew in my heart that this island and my destiny were somehow inexorably linked.

We were to spend three days on Ataúro, and I spent them trying to ignore the nagging in my heart, trying to dismiss the shadowy connection with this island. I told nobody about it and tried to stop the internal dialogue bothering me. I made judgments; judgments that might allow me to distance myself from the island, judgments that might save me from it; the people were not friendly, they stared at me with sad, unhopeful eyes; their lives were hard, too hard; the women were thin and bent under the heavy bundles of firewood they carried in baskets draped from their heads; their faces were grim; it was incredibly hot and dusty; water was difficult to come by; there were no communications from the island with the outside world; no phone, no mail, no ferry.

With the clinic staff, we visited outlying villages that were dry and sad; where I saw the same needle being used to immunise baby after baby; where I heard stories of teacher cruelty and saw gaping wounds on children to illustrate it; where I constantly saw and heard about drought and hunger; where I felt the constant gaze of hard weathered unsmiling adult faces and dirty thin, runny-nosed children. On the second day I was more than ready to leave. The nagging, unwanted call that lingered in my heart was unfair. I was already helping poor people in other remote parts of Indonesia; I was already "doing good" and had plenty of it still to do. Why was this place picking on me? What could I do here to make any difference to this harsh world? After just two days, I desperately wanted to be rid of the inner voice that had met me on the shore. There was a limit to my compassion, to my "goodness".

But Ferry, Roy, Anton, Guido and Baptista were good company. Alu, Guido's younger sister who came to cook for us, gave us delicious coffee and fried bananas for breakfast, and began to overcome her shyness and talk with me. We stayed at the PPSDM office by the beach and I was put in the ply-partitioned room with patches of torn linoleum over the concrete floor, and the biggest geckoes I had ever seen on the walls. Although Anton and Roy played guitars and sang sweet, sentimental Ambonese songs on the veranda at night, although the sky was filled with stars and the sea rolled in beside us as we laughed and sang, I was secretly counting the hours till we left.

But things worked against me. On the eve of our departure, a storm blew in and the sky turned a deep, steely grey. The wind blew fiercely, the mainland disappeared, and the sea produced waves as big as whales that tossed boats on their moorings. Guido announced we would not be leaving the next morning; we'd never get over the reef, and beyond it, the sea would be too wild.

He said we'd have to wait at least another twenty-four hours. I resigned myself.

It was a fateful twenty-four hours.

First, someone gave us some fish! Inspired, Ferry and I searched the unkempt garden and came up with some young sweet potato leaves and a marunggi tree, so we had the makings of a feast: rice, succulent greens and the freshest, crispest, sweetest fried fish cooked over the coals by Alu.

The village head, Sr Vasco, who lived in the crumbling Portuguese house under the huge fig tree just across the road from the PPSDM office, came ambling over to see me.

'You work with kindergarten teachers,' he said in Indonesian, 'and you've been here three days and haven't even been to see our kindergarten.'

It was a mild accusation.

I told him nobody had mentioned a kindergarten, so I was unaware there was one. 'Well, there's not exactly an operating kindergarten,' he admitted, 'but there is a building.'

He suggested I walk with him to see the kindergarten building at the end of the village. I couldn't remember even seeing small children in this village, though I knew they must have been there, so I was surprised by the notion of a kindergarten.

Of course, I would walk with him to see it, although I felt the heavy weight of warning in my heart. It had stopped raining so we could walk up right away, he said. And there it was – a small yellow building standing on a bare rectangle of land on a stony ridge overlooking the sea. The door was locked and the catch rusty and frozen in its place. Vasco, with the casual authority of his position, gave it a tug, broke it free and pushed the door open.

'This is our kindergarten,' he said proudly.

Inside, dust and salt had encrusted the tiny red, blue and yellow tables and chairs, the cement floor was cracked and the few faded wooden toys had fallen on their faces off the broken shelf.

The kindergarten was called the "Rose" kindergarten. Vasco told me it had been built several years before by ABRI (the Armed Forces of the Republic of Indonesia) as part of its social contribution to the island. And there it was – all ready to go but for the want of teachers and an education program.

'What do you think?' Vasco was looking not at me but at the cigarette in his hand.

'Mmm.' I looked out to the sea below. 'Mmm… a pity.'

No mail, no phone, no ferry, no running water, sporadic electricity, poor, sad people.

'What do you think?' he asked again, and then seeing my hesitancy, took a more direct approach.

'Do you think you could come and help us? Do you think the university would let you come and train some teachers, help us start a kindergarten?'

My head and my heart had been in battle since we started our walk. Of course, I had sensed the potential significance of this stroll up the hill with him. We stood at the door looking into the desolate, dusty room and Sr Vasco sucked on his cigarette. I kept cool for a while; detached, comforted by the knowledge that in twelve or so hours I would be on the boat, bouncing on the waves, heading for Dili and adventures somewhere in the rest of the world.

But I am blessed and cursed with a vivid imagination, an adventurous heart, and a susceptibility to need and to being wanted – and when he asked the question again, I heard myself speaking straight from my heart, saying, 'maybe,' and, 'perhaps six months,' and, 'yes I'll ask about it.' Sr Vasco was beaming as if it was all settled.

We walked back down the road in the still evening air and I noticed for the first time the bougainvillea. Brilliant, shimmering white, red and purple flowers in hedges and treetops, and I noticed the soft pink oleanders, the frangipani, the sunlight shining on wet leaves, and the faces of shy children peering from doorways.

Back at the PPSDM office, Sr Vasco explained his proposal to Anton, Ferry and Roy.

'Do you think the university would agree? Do you think she could come here? For six months, maybe?' He was excited and of course, my workmates were also enthusiastic, and I felt again that deep "clunk". This time, the clunk of a decision already made. It was the resounding sound of fate, the sound of certainty. Of course, they thought I could. Of course, I knew I would.

And there was a third fateful event on that last unplanned day on Ataúro. In the late afternoon the sun came out, the wind dropped, the sea calmed and Ferry, Anton and I went into it. We played like children in the lagoon – laughing, splashing, diving, testing who could stay under the longest, scouring the bottom for interesting sea things. The water was cool and very, very salty. We floated on it.

At sunset, the sky above Ataúro was golden and red and we lay on our backs on the water and watched the outline of the mountains against it – the soaring sacred peak of Mt Manucoco, the ridges and steep, dark gullies running down, the stern and ancient grey cliffs, the winding ribbon of sand. And I saw then how beautiful it was.

PART FOUR

On January 5 1996, I came to live on Ataúro to work with the community and start a kindergarten.

ATAÚRO: THE GENESIS STORY

In the beginning, the story goes, there was just a mountain – Manucoco, the Mountain of the Cock's Crow – and it rose up from the sea, sometimes disappearing into the clouds. On the top of this mountain was a huge, spreading fig tree with branches so laden with fruit that some dropped ripe and juicy to the ground.

A dolphin, leaping through the waves below, looked up one day and saw the sun shining on the leaves of the tree and the ripe, purple figs hanging there. It liked the look of these figs and began leaping out of the water in an attempt to reach them. Higher and higher the dolphin leapt till it was finally on top of the mountain beside the tree and, immediately, that sea creature began eating the figs on the ground. After eating all the good ones, it then reached for the figs that dangled from the branches, the plump ones peeping out from the leaves.

Although it ate quickly and quietly, it wasn't long before the spirit of the tree, the god who owned it, saw that a dolphin was eating his figs. This was a powerful god who soon turned the thief, that trespassing dolphin, into a little pig. Being a harsh god, he pierced the pig's side with a spear and placed the squealing animal up in the branches of the great tree, leaving it there to die as a punishment and as a warning to others.

Drip, drip, the blood of the pig fell and stained the earth. It dripped from the branches and dampened the ground where some figs still lay rotting.

The god had no pity at all for the pig but when from its blood sinking into the earth a beautiful girl emerged, his compassion was aroused. The young woman was also fond of figs and immediately began helping herself to the ripe fruit on the lower branches. But this time, the god was gentle and forgiving and allowed her to stay and eat what she would.

It wasn't long, in fact, before the god fell in love with the young woman who ate his figs and he gave her, as well as the fruit from his tree, three strong sons called Lekitoko, Komateu, and Kutukia. They all lived on that mountain, the great Manucoco, which was the whole island then and quite small.

When his three sons were grown men and still living on the

sacred mountaintop, their father saw that the island was not big enough for them all, so he ordered them to take arrows and go out on the ocean together in a boat carved from a tree trunk. He told them to go east and when they reached a certain distant spot towards the sunrise to each throw his arrow – one at a time and each in a different direction – to the west, to the north, to the south. They did this and, following the direction of the arrows, the mountain stretched out from its centre, stretched out to the west, to the south, and to the north.

The rocks and cliffs and earth expanded, and the island became a land big enough for each of the sons and his descendants: Lekitoko and the people of Humangili, Komateu's people of Manroni and Kutukia's Adade clans. It became Ataúro, the island that surrounds the sacred mountain, Manucoco, and is inhabited by the sons and daughters of a powerful god.

This is one version of the genesis story – and the one told by the elders from those who claim to be the descendants of the three brothers but, being an unwritten story, there are several versions of it.

THE PEOPLE OF ATAÚRO

Some say they came from Wetar Island because the languages of Rahesuk, Resuk and Raklungu spoken on the island are dialects of Wetarese; some say they came from the mainland area of Manututu because of the similarity of the languages between them. They have cousins and uncles on the islands of Wetar and Alor and, although Ataúro is only twenty-five kilometres from end to end, the people of the northern part are different from the people of the south – Bikeli people are darker-skinned, heavier, their voices and language more clipped and harsh.

Some clans are descended from the dolphin, some from the turtle and some from the shark. These are their totems.

Some say they fought with each other. Others say they fought with other islands and the mainlanders. There is a story on Ataúro of a powerful magic outrigger canoe that crossed the sea of the Wetar Strait and battled with the people of Manatutu; whenever there was conflict between the islanders and the mainlanders, the boat, un-manned, would fight and win the battles. When Makili people tell you this story, their words come out very fast and their eyes shine.

KUPANG, JANUARY 2 1996

I am waiting in Kupang, West Timor for my friend, Tipah, who is coming from Central Java on her first-ever adventure out of that province.

Tipah is from the mountain village of Polobogo Village where I worked for three years with the university's Early Education Program. I lived there on and off with her family, their two black and white cows, three tail-less cats and an ever-changing number of chickens. Her family is my adopted Javanese family and I love it. Tipah's dad, Pak Mungo, is a farmer who wears a battered straw hat on his bald head and his trouser legs tucked into gumboots when he goes out each day to cut grass for his two tethered cows. Tipah's mother, who I only ever call Ibu (mother) as everybody else does, goes with the other village women to sell vegetables and eggs at the market in Kopeng.

A market seller since she was twelve years old, every day of the week except Sunday she goes off with friends who, like her, haul heavy, awkward bundles on their thin, bent backs. Dressed in clean batik sarongs and fresh kebaya blouses, their hair tied back in neat buns, as beautiful as flowers and twittering like birds, Ibu and her friends arrange themselves and their produce in the dirty, crowded truck that takes them to the market up the mountain. Their life is the village, the road, the market… a small, familiar world that now Tipah, a daughter of the village, is leaving to go to East Timor with me. It's a big adventure for her and a big, big worry for her extended family.

I am waiting for her at the airport and, after we spend a night in Kupang, she and I will be here again in the morning to catch a plane to Dili. It was not my idea that Tipah should come with me. She begged to come and insisted I would need a friend and a helper on the island, and she was the best one to be both. It had been a year since I had agreed to go to Ataúro to start the kindergarten program, a year fulfilling previous commitments with teachers in other places, a year for the university to negotiate with the provincial government to make it possible for me to work there. In that time, Tipah had worked hard to persuade her parents and me to let her come.

Her uncle, a soldier, had served with the Indonesian military in Timor and told us grim stories about the dangers there. He said the situation in East Timor was terrible; the Timorese people were difficult, uncivilised and ungrateful for all Indonesia was doing for them; they would not appreciate our help and we might get killed. But we were not to be talked out of it. It was surprising that Tipah's parents, even after hearing these dark stories, agreed for her to come. For them, new Christians, it was a sacrifice they were willing to make; allowing their daughter to go on a mission to help their disadvantaged East Timorese countrymen was, for them, an act of Christian love.

My assignment was to spend six months living and working on Ataúro, training three local high school graduates as teachers, helping them set up the community kindergarten and developing a curriculum. I expected that living on Ataúro would be a challenge for both Tipah and me, but here we were in Kupang and, with happy hearts, on our way.

Tipah tumbles off the plane from Bali. She is crazy with excitement and kisses me three times, four, giggling and clutching my hand. On the plane she has made a new friend, as Tipah always does, and he is a soldier serving in East Timor. She introduces me to him and says he will be our friend there and will look after us. He confirms this as he shakes my hand and gives me his name and contact details scribbled on a piece of paper. He and Tipah are both very happy about this and I am troubled; Indonesian soldiers are the enemy of the East Timorese people – can this man be our friend there?

DILI

We stayed at the old Turismo Hotel in a twin room overlooking the sea. Roy was working back at the university in Java so we had no middleman and so were instructed to wait in the hotel until Anton contacted us. We'd been there for two days already, and it felt a bit like a prison. We were nervous about wandering too far away – I was self-conscious about being tall and white, a foreigner and the only one at the hotel. And I was nervous also for Tipah, thinking, naïvely, that being Javanese she might be the target of Timorese hatred. But Tipah made friends everywhere – in the hotel garden, on the beach in front, down the road when we finally ventured out to explore; Timorese and Indonesian people all respond to her friendliness. She wants to share her story with everybody and is ready to listen to anyone's story. People are more wary with me, curious but careful. The military watches closely any Timorese seen spending time with foreigners who may be journalists.

One young man we meet in the hotel garden diffidently explains this to us, and Tipah was surprised. It was the beginning of her realisation that there are two sides to the East Timor story. She was uncharacteristically quiet for several minutes, taking it in. Later, in our hotel room, we talk about it again. Tipah and her family, like most Javanese, truly believe that their government is in East Timor to help the Timorese, to integrate these backward people into their country and give them opportunities that will improve their lives. They do not understand why the Timorese are resistant and, of course, hear nothing of the military brutality that attempts to weaken but only strengthens the resistance to Indonesia. She listened quietly and said little.

Finally, on the third morning, Anton appeared. The bottoms of his jeans and the sleeves of his wind jacket were wet, and there was salt drying on his skin. He smelled of the sea. He was embarrassed and apologised for being late – forty-eight hours late – to meet us. There was a miscommunication about when we would arrive, however now that we had all met up, we could leave for Ataúro the next day. He and Guido will come to pick us up at three-thirty am for a four-am start, so please be ready.

And so I learn about pre-dawn departures from the beach in Dili, departures that will become the norm for me. Walking the dark, deserted streets from the hotel to the beach, jumping at shadows of imaginary Indonesian soldiers. Ataúro people, hoping for a lift back to the island, huddled in groups on the cold sand, wrapped in woven shawls against the morning cool; dim kerosene lamplight and muffled voices across the water; boxes and sacks loaded one by one into our boat, the Manucoco. This is our workboat now: a seven-metre wooden hull; white, trimmed with green and grey, a new outboard motor, two wooden plank seats under cover and a small open deck area at both bow and stern. A solid little boat, it's nothing like its namesake, the grand Ataúro mountain, Manucoco, but it's pretty and brave and ready that first morning to take us out into the deep dark sea.

ATAÚRO ISLAND 2

That year the rain came early and in January the island was green in the dawn sunlight. New grasses sprout on the hills, eucalypts and coconut palms are washed clean and glisten, corn grows in brilliant green patches along the beach and up in the hills. Returning to Ataúro was vastly different from my first visit, and this good season was a welcoming, positive start.

The PPSDM office where we will live and work is a converted marketplace down by the beach. Baptista and Anton had lived here for a couple of years and now had to make room, physically and emotionally, for two women in their household. On one side of the main office, Tipah and I were given small rooms separated by plywood partitions. Baptista and Anton moved into even smaller cubicles on the other side. We would all share a tiny dining room on Tipah's and my side of the office and have the "luxury" of two kitchens out the back; one a dirt-floored thatched roof shelter with no walls and a cooking fire in a circle of stones, the other a grey, windowless tiny cement-block cell with two small kerosene stoves and a roof and walls blackened by their fumes.

Our washing-up place was a concrete slab on the ground

outside beside an open tub of water that's filled from the central village water system once a day, if we're lucky. There's another concrete tub of cold water in our cement-block bathroom, and into these tubs we dip for water for washing – dishes, clothes, ourselves. We had no running water except for the hour or so the village system allows it to gravity feed into our tubs, but we are luckier than most people who have to share small communal taps, tanks or tubs.

Wandering chickens sometimes laid eggs in the cool ashes of our open fireplace but food generally was hard to come by, so in the early days Tipah, whose main job she insisted was looking after me, took care of finding our food with a local girl, Alu. They soon became good friends. There's a small market in the village on Fridays but otherwise, it's beans and rice from the local shop (kios) or a search that might yield some cassava greens or papaya leaves and flowers we can eat as vegetables and, sometimes, a fresh fish.

Vila was not really an active fishing village and without refrigeration, food had to be consumed soon after it was picked or caught and cooked. If we were lucky, we might have bananas or papaya to supplement our meals. We cooked and ate together and soon became a happy family consisting of Anton, our Ambonese coordinator, a warm and welcoming man; Baptista, a young Timorese man from Oecusse; Tipah from Java; Alu, a local Ataúro girl; her brother, Guido, the boat driver; and me, an Australian. All six of us – culturally, linguistically, and physically so different – soon found we laughed at the same things, met challenges with the same enthusiasm, and trusted each other, so our integrated household and work life went well.

Ataúro people were not initially friendly. Perhaps it was shyness that made them appear serious and suspicious. They were not exactly unfriendly but in the beginning the women especially kept their distance from me, watching from afar, avoiding conversation and self-consciously going about their own business. There had never been a foreign woman – or indeed any non-Indonesian foreigner – living on the island since the Portuguese days pre-1975, so my being there was a novelty. Tipah, on the other hand, quickly made friends with the Indonesians on Ataúro – the teachers and nurses and their families – and then with their Timorese friends and workmates. Through her, I started to see that, beneath the politics of oppression and resistance, was the complex reality of East Timor, the simplicity and richness of human relationships there.

Working with the community to get the kindergarten running changed things quickly for me. Working together on something people wanted for their children, something I could help them to realise, broke barriers. There was already a primary school and a junior high school in the village and primary schools in the other five villages, but nothing for children under six years old except this empty kindergarten building built by the military several years before. There were no kindergarten teachers and the yellow building on the rise overlooking the sea that Vasco had shown me that afternoon in 1994 had never been used.

KINDERGARTEN

Three young women, new high school graduates, were chosen as teachers for me to train; Teresa, Zelia and Dulce were keen students. After spending a couple of weeks in initial training and making learning games and tools out of whatever we could find or had to hand (shells for threading, feathers for painting, stones and charcoal for drawing, all manner of things for sticking and sorting and counting and building including empty cigarette packets and matchboxes), sweeping off the dust and repairing broken playthings and chairs, we opened the kindergarten. The rest would be on-the-job training, learning and making as we went along.

On enrolment day little children, all scrubbed and dressed up, appeared. Parents, grandparents or older siblings in their very best clothes and good rubber flip-flops came clutching little hands and precious birth certificates. The little ones clung to their elders, burying their faces in familiar laps then peeping out wide-eyed to explore the classroom. Over seventy-five four to six-year-olds were enrolled. They were put into four groups. A parent group was formed. The schoolyard was stony and bare, so we organised the building of a bamboo fence to keep out pigs and goats as the first working bee and a tree planting as the second.

To me it was an advantage that our teachers had not been formally trained – had avoided the Indonesian approach to early childhood education. Indonesian kindergartens at that time often had two teachers – one to "teach" or "lecture" up to forty small pupils who were expected to sit still in their seats and listen, and an assistant who patrolled the classroom wielding a stick and slamming it on desks if children "misbehaved", i.e., moved or spoke. Indonesian-trained teachers were rigid in their approach.

By this time, I had had plenty of experience in Indonesia and knew that Ataúro children, like children everywhere else, would learn best by doing and discovering, trying things out, playing, talking about what they were doing. I saw the island children learning naturally that way every day – on the beach, in the gardens, in their homes – it was our challenge at the kindergarten to provide new and different experiences and opportunities for them. My challenge was to help develop the understanding and skills of the new teachers. For six months, I worked alongside them in that small kindergarten on the hill. It was wonderful.

I was soon asked to teach English to some high school students and adults and so we formed two language classes for evening study in our office. Those students included Anton, Baptista and Tipah and several of the Indonesian and Timorese teachers and nurses. Some time later, Anton and I began to talk about other educational possibilities for the island and, in consultation with the primary teachers, the mostly absent high school principal and several of the keener young teachers, we developed a literacy program for the lower primary school and a local content curriculum for the high school. It was the start of many years of our education work on Ataúro.

SEA NOTES

I learn to live on a small island. Some days the air is rich with sea smells: the sour, salty smell of seagrasses dumped on the shore permeates the village. And fish smells – fresh, sexual scents of red and yellow striped and glossy green fish twirling on the ends of poles, the rank salt smell of shrunken fish-drying, hardening, fading on bamboo racks under the sun – carried through the village on sea breezes and into our houses. There's the wet wooden boat smell, too – fraying anchor ropes, barnacled hulls, old diesel and machine oil, and the scent of sweaty boatmen, their salt-encrusted bodies. The fragrance of all things sea lingers in my nostrils, on my clammy skin, in my hair.

GHOST

On my third night there, a ghost visited me. Tucked up under a mosquito net, I became aware of a presence in the room and woke up to see a face peering at me through the net. I asked myself if I was asleep or awake and sat up when I felt the face close to me. That face is still clear to me years later – a man's face, prominent eyes, nose and mouth, curious rather than either frightening or friendly, a halo of frizzy hair. His eyes met mine for a second or two before the face retreated… fading back from the net into darkness and then disappearing, perhaps through the open window. I stared into the space he left. I don't think I shouted out. If I did, no one heard me and all I heard was the sea pounding on the reef. I was curious but oddly unafraid.

I sat there for a minute or two, puzzled, then went back to sleep.

Although bursting to share the experience of that night, I decided not to tell anyone straight away fearing that Tipah, content by day but still nervous about most things here after dark, would be thoroughly spooked and may even want to go back home to her own familiar Javanese ghosts.

It was some weeks later that, growing more and more curious about Ataúro culture and the beliefs that fuel it, I decided to discuss my night visitor with Anton. Although from a Christian upbringing, Anton is an Ambonese man and will not, therefore, be dismissive of ghost talk. He listened carefully, told me that here, ghosts are to be taken seriously and suggested we talk with Freitas, the shaman, about it.

That evening, for the first time, I met Tiu Antoni Freitas, who soon became a beloved and respected friend. In battered cowboy hat and baggy shorts, his mouth missing teeth and stained with beetle nut, he sat with me on the veranda while I told him about my night visitor. We drank coffee as Freitas listened carefully to my story, asking me questions, nodding, smiling.

'It was one of the ancestor spirits.' He was certain of that.

'They needed to have a look at you, to check you over. There's not been anyone like you here before.' He grinned. 'They want to know who you are, what you're doing here, Ibu. A long, long time ago some Portuguese women came to visit but you've come to live here and the spirits want to know your intentions. They're looking after us. That's what they're doing. They sent someone to check you out, that's all.'

That made sense but, 'How will we know if they think I'm okay? How will we know that they approve of me living here?' I ask.

'We'll know. If they think you're alright they'll just leave you alone and let you get on with things.'

'And if they don't?'

'We'll know that too – they'll keep on bothering you – things will go wrong. You'll probably have more night visits from them. You might get sick. Your family in Australia could even be troubled by them… could get sick or have accidents. We'll know. And then we'll have to try and work it out with them. Make a ceremony to sort things out.'

This man understood the spirit world of Ataúro.

'What sort of ceremony?'

He laughed, shook his head and threw his cigarette stub over the wall. 'I can't explain because I don't know yet, Ibu Gabrielle. We'll have to wait and see. I'll have to listen to them to know what I have to do. Don't worry, they'll tell me.'

The ancestors never bothered me again so they must have considered me acceptable. That was reassuring, but I was hungry to learn more about this place, and was a little disappointed that I wouldn't get to witness a spirit placating ceremony. Not yet.

VILA

The population of Ataúro Island in 1996 was around 4,500 and the organisational structure on the island was the same then as it is now – five villages, each consisting of a central settlement and a number of small, outlying hamlets. The central settlement in each village is the administrative and church centre and, since Indonesian times, each has had a government primary school and a clinic facility for visiting health workers.

Vila, geographically and demographically the smallest village on the island, was and is the administrative centre. It's located in what used to be Maumeta, part of Makili Village, and is "artificial" in the sense that it was developed by the Portuguese as a small port and local government headquarters. Its population of around 1,000 came mainly from Makili but also from other parts of the island, because that's where the few employment opportunities on the island are. Vila is considered a *town,* distinct from a *village* and even in those days it had, to a certain extent, the smug air of a town.

In Vila there was a diesel generator that provided electricity for up to six hours a night if all went well – fuel was sent from the mainland and often delayed for weeks and even months. On Ataúro 'town power' was sophistication. Other villages had no power except for small household solar panels provided by the Indonesian government. In Vila, there is also water, piped down from the spring for an hour daily, sometimes two, and stored in concrete tubs in various parts of the village. Although the population is small, it boasts a staffed clinic, a high school, the sub-district administration office and sometimes water and electricity; all this made tiny Vila the metropolis of the island.

In Vila, a handful of Timorese and Indonesians had paid employment; teachers, police, military, nurses. Civil servants throughout Indonesia could be identified – on Ataúro you know them all personally anyway – by the various drab colours of their uniforms: khaki, grey, pale blue, brown. More often than not, these servants of the people passed their time sitting in groups under trees, smoking, chatting, telling jokes. It was not a busy place.

Vila had no postal service, no communications except a couple of military hand radios and our crackling CB, no public transport to the mainland, six kilometres of road to the next village, and one car, the old white ambulance. It was not a sophisticated town, but it had attitude. And it is where I learned how Indonesians and Ataúro Islanders developed and maintained friendships that somehow, in everyday life, overlooked the conflicts and politics of an occupied territory. As an outsider, how that worked surprised and fascinated me. I soon loved that small world; a slow, peaceful world in the shadow of a larger conflicted one. We all knew each other, our daily lives shared the same aspirations and limitations, the same horizons, challenges, joys and sorrows. The sea, sometimes wild and impenetrable, sometimes soft and milky smooth, separated us from that bigger, complicated, violent world that became easy to ignore.

There was always something to do in Vila. The police (Indonesian and Timorese together) fixed a television set in a wooden box to a tree in front of their station and several rows of wooden benches for viewers. Young men gathered there, especially in World Cup soccer season, and for the finals the generator worked overtime pumping out electricity till the early hours of the morning so that everybody, including women and children, could be there to shout all night. There was a volleyball court, a soccer field, a Catholic and a Protestant Church.

Men's work was mending nets, fixing boats, fishing, building fences and houses; women cooked, washed, collected and carried firewood and water, and gardened in season. Leisure time for young children was playing on the beach or in the sea; for teenage boys guitar or homemade ukulele sessions with mates; for young women evening walks, visiting neighbours and friends. There was betel nut and palm wine, volleyball and soccer competitions, weddings and boat pulling parties. In those times, there were also frequent concerts and dancing to celebrate Indonesian religious and national holidays.

It was a poor but good place to live. On the surface, everyone got on well enough. There were perhaps a dozen or more Indonesian families and single people, including the clinic coordinator, nurses and teachers living there. Most of them, far from their homes and families, are dedicated to their work; a few noticeably less enthusiastic about their postings to this remote island. There are some Indonesian police and military in senior roles and the rest are Timorese, many of them Ataúro men. The atmosphere was relaxed. Indonesians were invited to Ataúro social functions and vice versa. There was always a separate table for Islamic guests – meals without pork and with halal preparation – but apart from that, guests mingled. I was the only foreigner on the island and invited to all social events.

Life on Ataúro was not easy. For people from places like Java and Bali it was isolated and its facilities minimal. Food was monotonous – rice, dried beans, fish and occasionally some greens and seasonal fruit. Communication with the outside world was non-existent. Dili is across the deep and sometimes turbulent Wetar Strait and the only way for people to get there was by hitching a lift in a slow wooden fishing boat or with us when we go each month on the faster Manucoco boat.

A change happened when people crossed the sea heading for the mainland with its armed soldiers, surveillance, and suspicion. Heading to Dili, people laughed too loud. Or grew more serious. People – all of us – carried bribes: island palm wine, cassava, dried fish. A small enclave of Ataúro fishers met us on the beach in Dili. Secrets were passed.

By contrast, returning home there was laughter and singing in the dawn, people falling asleep on bags of rice, rolling with the sea as Ataúro boats danced their way back to the safety of the island.

This was the life Ataúro people knew, eking out a living from the sea, supplementing seafood with corn and beans and any other vegetables the dry soil could yield. Those who had outboard motors could sell their fish in Dili. Bikeli fishermen, more diligent than others, had contracts with the military and were given clunky wooden inboard diesel motorboats that could access distant fishing grounds; other fishermen relied on outriggers and spearfishing close by on the reef. The staple foods were cassava, beans, and corn – one yearly crop grown in the wet season – part of which is eaten young as it is picked, the rest stored for future supplies, ceremonial exchanges, and as seed for the next year's planting.

In some ways, it was a difficult life but while I had friends and workmates like Anton, Tipah, Baptista, Alu, Guido, my work with the teachers, parents and children at the kindergarten, hot chilli and lime to liven up monotonous meals, the sea and the magnificent reef to explore, I was soon as happy living there as ever I could be. On Ataúro the horrors of the Indonesian occupation could fade...

SEA NOTES

As an Australian child I'd had beach holidays – splashing in waves, building sandcastles, running along the water's edge, gathering shells; as a teenager walking on the shore at dusk and dawn, surfing on the waves, perched on rocks listening to their thunder, drenched by their spray. But I've never before lived by the sea and lived with people who rely on it to live by, and, now that I do, I understand that it's more complex, more powerful than I ever imagined; a mysterious entity, the sea is an erratic presence amongst us, a raging or sleepy spirit that demands to be respected, revered though not always understood.

Here, every day you think about the sea, you think about it – not once or twice, but many times a day. You notice that it's calm or it's rough. That it's big or it's small. That it's calmer. Or it's rougher, or it's bigger or smaller than yesterday and that tomorrow it will be calmer or rougher than today. You notice that it's blue or it's grey, that it's green-tinged with whitecaps. People look at it and say that boats will go out today or boats won't go out today. They say it's good for fishing on the reef, or it isn't. They say it's perfect for gathering shellfish, or it's not. When you live by it, and with it, and from it, you can never forget the sea, you can never ignore it; it's there with you, whispering or roaring, its pounding or gentle lapping at the shore as significant as the beating of your heart.

ATAÚRO HOUSES

Most houses have bamboo walls, thatched grass roofs and dirt floors that are swept clean every day. Windows are few and small, closed with handmade shutters – many of them painted bright blue, red, yellow or green. The yards surrounding the houses are bare earth, each decorated with rock-bordered paths and hardy plants in rusting cans.

Grandmothers or teenage girls with coconut frond brooms sweep the yards vigorously every morning, just as grandmothers and teenage girls do throughout Indonesia. There are banana and papaya trees, sometimes a mango or an orange tree in the corner and, in growing season, corn and cassava growing wherever they can.

Public servants, Indonesian and Timorese, live in brick box houses – Indonesian-style cement dwellings with small rooms and bad ventilation – lined up around the centre of town. The administrator, an Ataúro man called Fernando, lived in the grandest whitewashed ex-Portuguese stone house up the hill with a veranda that overlooks the town and the sea.

Bikeli Village is the least poor village because Bikeli men are professional fishers who make a living through their contracts with the Indonesian military. Quite a few of the houses in Bikeli are made of cement blocks – many unfinished – with tin roofs that quickly rust away. Brick and tin, concrete floors, small rooms and tiny windows are "up-market" and are the houses people aspire to.

I prefer the smell, feel and coolness of bamboo and thatch houses and always hope that when I overnight in a village I will be sleeping in one of those – but, of course, as a mark of my visitor status I am often put in a "modern" cement box.

PPSDM

Pusat Pengembangan Sumber Daya Manusia (The Centre for Human Resource Development) was the grand name for our humble concrete and palm leaf office next to the beach where Anton, Baptista, Adriano, Guido – and now Tipah, Alu and I – work and most of us lived. Guido and Alu, siblings, live with their extended family down the road at the back, and Adriano lived with his wife and in-laws in a bamboo house across the road.

PPSDM Ataúro was part of Satya Wacana University's East Timor program. On the island, the focus had been on small-scale fisheries and improving community access to fresh water but now with my arrival, it was venturing into early education.

We had CB radio communication with the university in Java – mostly a bad connection that sometimes at night could reach other nearby islands of Indonesia – and no other means of communication with anywhere else in the world. There was no regular transport to the mainland, and on land a handful of bicycles, a motorbike or two, one car – a rusting white ambulance that rattles along the six kilometres of road between Vila and Beloi and gave rise to the joke that "all cars on Ataúro are white". There were outriggers and some motorised fishing boats in various states of disrepair, and there was our trusty Manucoco.

PPSDM consisted of a dedicated handful of us working with minimal resources and plenty of imagination.

Anton, the project coordinator, contributed fisheries knowledge, management skills, humility, confidence and humour to our life and work. Young and relatively inexperienced to be coordinating such a challenging program far away from the university's guidance, he was a man of integrity, passionate about his work, keen to learn and courageous. I was there as education advisor. but while he was theoretically "the boss" he respected my age and experience, looking to me for advice in general decision-making as well as in designing and implementing programs. We often had to rely on intuition; that was all we had to guide us. Anton and I soon became partners in improvising and stepping out into new spaces. We trusted each other and became brave together. His patience, compassion and humour made working with him a delight.

Baptista, our agriculture and livestock man, came from a mountain village in Oecussi, the enclave that is separate from the rest of East Timor and surrounded on three sides by West

Timor. Since Indonesian occupation, both general and vocational education had been developed and were available to almost everyone throughout the province, so Baptista, initially schooled in a tiny village primary school in the hills of Oecusse, was now a competent graduate from a Dili agriculture high school. Baptista's job was working with village women in small-scale chicken, goat and pig husbandry and attempting to improve vegetable-growing techniques and vegetable-eating traditions. He was an enthusiastic worker.

Tipah, my Javanese minder, was the "sister/carer" of the household. For someone who had never lived away from her Javanese village, she was surprisingly adaptable to life on Ataúro. She was gregarious and in a very short while, everybody was her friend. Young Indonesian and Timorese women and high school girls called at the house for her in the afternoons to go walking. Holding hands and giggling, they'd stroll along the road or along the beach, meeting with other groups of girls, exchanging gossip. This was really no different to what happened in the evenings in Tipah's own village of Blongoran, Polobogo, in Central Java and in villages and towns all over Indonesia and Timor.

Every evening Tipah went out with her new Timorese and Indonesian friends, and when she came home at dusk she always had stories to tell me. I learned a lot about the village from her, especially in the early days when people were much more reticent to share secrets with me, an older, white, foreign woman. Tipah, whose house in Java had an earth floor, whose family kept their two big Friesian cows snorting and stamping inside a room just off the kitchen and did all their cooking on an open wood fire, viewed the Ataúro Islanders as backward and poor. She was amazed that they still used a metal digging stick (ai-suak, a small crowbar) for their gardening work instead of hoes or spades.

She was empathic and threw herself into her own small development projects. While Anton, Baptista and I followed the slow processes of community consultation and decision-making in our fishing, agriculture and education programs Tipah, in her particular areas of knowledge – gardening and cooking – expressed her opinions baldly to her new friends and they either do or do not follow her suggestions. Her way was probably just as effective as any in bringing about change on a small-scale.

Guido and his younger sister, Alu, were Ataúro people and live in their family's house down the beach road, just at the back of our workplace. Guido was married and had a baby daughter. His mother, sisters and brothers, as well as his wife and child, and some of her sisters, some of his cousins and nephews all lived together. Guido and Alu were an important part of our work team, but as island people they had other lives and social obligations as well: family expectations responsibilities, quarrels, and the resolving of those quarrels; clan expectations responsibilities, quarrels and resolving of quarrels, decision-making; church commitments (Catholic), traditional ceremonies and rituals; gardens to maintain, shared communal work obligations such as housebuilding, etc.

They were our entrée into Ataúro life and we relied on them for guidance and for daily information, of which there were different levels and kinds: rumour, which often had to do with the Indonesian military and what was happening in the resistance movement on the mainland, but also about missing boats, fishermen lost, or magical and fantastic happenings; gossip, which had mainly to do with relationships, usually male-female relationships but sometimes concerning disagreements and fights between friends or families; invitations to weddings, baby namings or other celebrations or events; tidings about deaths or serious illness.

Guido and Alu were reliable sources of information. When they were involved in village events there was an expectation that we, as a kind of extended family, should also be present: sickness and death, resolution of family feuds, spirit appeasing ceremonies, group weddings or christenings at the church – we attended them all. It was humbling and fascinating. For Anton and Tipah, both Indonesian Protestants, the traditional events that involve magic and the spirit world posed a moral dilemma but for me, they were eye-opening and wonderful.

Adriano was our caretaker and "security". He was Guido and Alu's cousin, a shy and gentle man, clearly at the bottom of some hierarchy but crucial to our team. His house was over the road from our office and, with guidance from Baptista, he grew fruit and vegetables in our experimental garden on a plot lent to PPSDM by Vasco. In the morning Adriano was there to open up and sweep the office and the yard. Last thing at night, he appeared again to lock up and ensure all is secure. Smoking local tobacco, he often sat silently beside me on the veranda, keeping me company as I worked into the night.

And then there was me, an Australian with qualifications in anthropology and education and some years of experience in PNG, Australia, Central Java and the eastern islands of Indonesia. Older than the others, I was an idealist who wanted the world to be a better, fairer place and believed I could help to change it if only I understood it better. I was a mother of a daughter, Freya, now an adult, independent and out in the world. A mature-age student of life, I was on a quest to understand this extraordinary island, Ataúro.

Later, as our work expanded, we added other Ataúro people – Tomas, Antonio, Marcelo, Domingos, Duarte, Rosa and Julieta – to our team.

GOAT ISLAND: AN ECONOMIC SYSTEM

Ataúro, in Indonesian times, was referred to as Pulau Kambing (Goat Island). You can still see that name on older maps. Herds of goats run wild over the island – not feral goats, but each earmarked to show ownership while they run wild over cliffs and gullies and, in dry times, through the villages. People fence gardens rather than goats and there is no end of trouble about the misdeeds of "other peoples" goats trespassing into corn or cassava fields.

Goats, like chickens and pigs, are a form of currency. They are used when money is needed – for school fees, new clothes for Easter or Christmas, for weddings and funerals. Dragged down from the mountains a goat, selected, described and valued by the length of its horns (its age), is trussed up and, with bleating protest, loaded onto a boat and taken to Dili. There it is sold in the market (or on the beach on arrival if the price was right), exchanged for greasy rupiah notes that would pay for Julieta's wedding gown; rice and vegetables for the party and the tiered pink wedding cake; or grandmother's funeral costs; outboard motor repairs, school fees.

Pigs on the island are tied up by a leg and sometimes kept in a rough sort of pen. Chickens, like goats, are free-range. Baptista's efforts to help the women improve chicken-raising as an income-generating enterprise are mostly in vain; chickens are not penned, are not generally eaten, and their eggs are not collected or sold. If there is a wedding or a funeral, chickens, goats and pigs, are on the menu for the party – and the prevailing logic is that baby chicks are always needed to replace those eaten and if you sell or eat the eggs, there'd be no more chickens. It is an economic system of its own kind; Baptista is torn between his training with the "development" expectation that agricultural enterprises should bring in regular cash income and his understanding of the traditional system which, of course, is the same in the mountains of Oecusse.

SEA NOTES

Sometimes fishermen, bamboo poles hung with strings of multi-coloured reef fish slung across their shoulders, wander through the village singing to the rhythm of the swinging fish.

'Ikan, ikan, ikan se-gar

Ikan se-gar, masih goyang, goyang.'

(Fish, fish, fresh fish)

(Fish so fresh they're still dancing, dancing.)

Quick as a flash, Tipah and Alu are out there bargaining, and we will have rainbow-coloured fish for our dinner!

RELIGION AND MAGIC

Indonesian law says you must adhere to one of the six state-approved faiths: Islam, Buddhism, Hinduism, Christianity, Catholicism and Confucianism. For Indonesians, even if yours is only a "KTP" religion (an official declaration on your ID card to meet legal requirements) and not a practised religion, it is a vital part of your identity. East Timor had seen an increase in Catholicism since the Indonesian invasion; the church, due to its Portuguese roots, became valued as a pre-Indonesian institution that provided support and solidarity for the resistant Timorese.

Guido is Catholic, Alu is Catholic, Baptista is Catholic, I was brought up a Catholic and, as Jesuits might claim, may still be one – of sorts. Anton and Tipah are Protestant; Anton of the relatively liberal, progressive Ambonese Protestant Church, Tipah a member of a small fundamentalist group that had taken root in her Islamic village. Accompanied by guitars and tambourines, her congregation sings their hearts out on Sundays in a tiny white church on the edge of a field.

Tipah and Anton have come to the right place in Timor – unlike any other part of the country, Ataúro Island in 1996 had more than 50% Protestant population, of the born-again persuasion, like Tipah. She is at home here religion-wise and takes enthusiastically to the lively Sunday services with its singing and chanting and hallelujahs, coming home with a wide smile on her face. Baptista returns from the Catholic Mass, shakes my hand warmly and wishes me a happy Sunday, but Tipah takes me in her arms and dances with me, laughing and singing and kissing my cheek. Sundays are good. Anton and I don't often attend church but stay at home, drinking coffee and enjoying the rare inactivity of Sunday morning.

By and large, Ataúro Catholics are closet animists, most of them actively practising a form of animism alongside their Catholicism. There are spiritual "horses for courses" and certain events such as land use – constructing a house, a fence, tapping a spring, launching a boat – require approval and blessings of Ataúro ancestral spirits, and need a traditional animist ceremony to get that approval. Catholicism lends itself easily to a mix of belief systems; rich with symbols and rituals, it speaks to animists, whispers them into a familiar leap into the great unknown through the redness of wine/blood, the dim yellow light of candles illuminating darkness, the glitter of gold implements and the musty, otherworldly smell of burning incense. After Catholicism came to Ataúro some of the symbols, like red wine and burning candles, were adapted seamlessly into animist ceremonies.

For example, when our boat the Manucoco, which had been docked for repairs, was fixed and ready to go to sea again, there had to be a ceremony to ensure we had spirit blessings for its journeys. Chicken blood had to be spilt, ancient words in spirit language chanted, livers read. But it was usual to have two ceremonies. After the chicken had been sacrificed – bashed to death around the perimeter of the boat – its blood mixed with coconut milk and sprinkled over the boat, after its liver had been carefully read and its flesh cooked and eaten, after the shaman had gone, his mystical fire put out and all signs of his ceremony hidden, if the catechist or priest was on the island he was invited to the beach to give a traditional Catholic blessing. Then everyone – including the shaman, hastily washed of blood – came and stood together with heads bowed and prayed. Having it both ways seemed to work for us.

The Ataúro Protestants had certainly on the surface given away their traditional beliefs and customs. It was rare to see Protestants doing traditional dancing and singing to drums and gongs. It was rare to hear of them resorting to magic and ceremony. Not unknown by any means, but uncommon and best hidden.

Anton is the son of a Protestant minister, a man who had preached in a parish and lectured in Theology at the university in Ambon, a man who had brought his family up to be moderate, moral, liberal-thinking Christians. This middle-class, rock-of-earth upbringing gave solidity to Anton but was later to cause him considerable pain. He did not feel comfortable with the Ataúro Protestant service and could not tolerate the hypocrisy of murderous Indonesian army generals and commandants who prayed with him if he went to church when in Dili.

CHURCHES ON ATAÚRO

In the 1950s, down by the beach at Tolorica, under military supervision and the blazing sun, Ataúro men were smashing rocks to mix with sand and ash to make whitewash for the walls of the few Portuguese buildings. Exhausted, one of the men stepped aside and squatted in the shade of a tree to rest – at, unfortunately, the exact moment the administrator, who had come to check on work progress, appeared on the road with two of his officers.

Everyone stopped work to watch the approach of the big man in his white uniform but the young man under the tree did not scramble to his feet as might be expected. His workmates glared at him, warning him, but he remained squatting, watching from his place in the shade. When the administrator saw him, 'Stand up! Stand up immediately and show respect,' he shouted in Portuguese.

At first, the young man seemed to ignore the order and there was terrible silence and nervous glances from one worker's face to another before he slowly rose to his feet. He was taking his time and looking straight into the eyes of the administrator. The administrator, an impatient man, was infuriated by this insolence and rushed at the man, hitting him hard. The force of his fist knocked the young man off balance; knocked him so that he fell back down, cracking his head on the rocks as he fell. Blood flowed over the white rocks and his horrified friends watched as the young man died right there on the road.

Work stopped as they carried his body to his house where his weeping mother, keening sisters and aunts received him: dead brother and nephew, dead clansman, dead son.

After the burial and the first week of mourning the island chiefs, the liurai, came together to discuss this event. They had had enough of this administrator's bullying and came up with an idea; they would capture the big man, take him to Dili and demand justice for his latest murderous deed. It was an audacious plan, and to carry it out they enlisted the help of one of their Makili men whom the administrator trusted. This man, a tall fellow, would often walk with the administrator as he took his morning or evening stroll along the beach. Although he was a sort of bodyguard, he agreed to help the chiefs.

Not long afterwards, the administrator was taking his daily walk on the beach with his Makili companion – strolling along, looking at the sea and stones and shells at the water's edge – when the chiefs and their men approached from behind, grabbed him and threw him to the ground. The big Portuguese man went down with a thud on the sand. He was shocked and struggled in vain, soon he was breathless and his snowy white uniform was soiled and wet. The Makili bodyguard helped his friends to tie the administrator's arms with rope and wind it around him till he was trussed up like a pig. A canoe waited in the lagoon and they bundled him onto it, climbed into the little boat themselves and headed out across the strait to Dili; returning him to his superiors to make the courageous statement that they did not want him, nor the likes of him, on their island.

As satisfying as this was – and Ataúro people still tell the story with pride – it was not, of course, as simple as that. When the administrator was delivered bound and helpless to the authorities with his uniform and stripes and medals all wet and dirty, this act was declared a Crime of Treason. Not an act of violence towards a person, but an act of violence towards A Person Who Was Wearing The Insignia Of The Portuguese Government! The case of the death of the young Ataúro man faded into insignificance against this crime against the empire and the four chiefs and their helpers were all imprisoned on the mainland. To make it worse they were separated from each other, some sent to Viqueque and some to Watilaru… but because one of the chiefs was very old and needed to go back to the island to die, another Ataúro man, Kelimaru, volunteered to take his place. This exchange was accepted. Kelimaru was strong and lived on in prison for a number of years but some of the older Ataúro men died in custody, away from their island home.

On the mainland, Kelimaru met and married a Catholic woman from the mountains and learned from her about that church and its beliefs. When he was released, he brought his wife and Catholicism back to the island, adding incense and candles, the Virgin, the transfiguration of the Eucharist, and guardian angels to the rich Ataúro world of ancestral power, spirits and magic. A Catholic school was opened and two old men, Jakob and Roberto, who I got to know well, were among the first group of students.

THE PROTESTANT CHURCH ON ATAÚRO

The Protestant Church had arrived on Ataúro much, much earlier. In the 1930s, Dutch Protestantism originally took root with evangelists from Alor. Later, the current Assemblies of God church from Wetar and Liran took over the congregation. The Ataúro Protestant Church was always evangelistic – promising the goodies of God's love and eternal life for the simple exchange of animist and other cultural practices like animal sacrifice, dancing and the singing of traditional songs. The people in the north of the island changed traditional instruments for the Jesus-preferred guitars and colourful, if sometimes raucous and bloody, animist ceremonies for church services to which they wore collared shirts and sometimes suits.

The Catholic Church with its rituals, wine, candles, incense, fancy dress and heavenly organ music appealed to some of the island people and the straight, short back and sides, guitar-strumming Protestant Church appealed to others. In reality – as it is in most places – conversion depended on who got there first with their elaborate promises of eternal life. And Ataúro is the only sub-district in Timor-Leste in which Protestants outnumber Catholics.

PART FIVE

A SEABIRD AND A ROSE

The small yellow building perched on its rocky ridge overlooking the sea is called the "Rose" kindergarten, although a search for a rose over the whole island would not produce one. Ataúro Island does not grow roses.

At our first parent meeting, I ask about the name and learn that roses are unknown to the children who attend the kindergarten. I suggest it would be better to have a familiar name for the new kindergarten, a name the children could relate to. The parents, instantly accepting my suggestion, decide to change it. 'Rather than call it the Mawar (Rose) Kindergarten we will call it the Manutasi (Seabird) Kindergarten,' they say, 'Because from this ridge above the sea you sometimes see a seabird: a heron, a tern, a big sea eagle soaring over the water below, and when the children see them, they are happy and jump up and down.' We are all satisfied with this decision.

All, that is, except the military. It turns out that they are not at all happy with it. The day after the opening ceremony which the commandant had gracefully attended, Anton is called to his office and reprimanded. Stung from this experience, Anton tells me later I may have overstepped the mark.

'The mark? Which mark?' I ask.

'It's the name. You changed the name.'

The Indonesian military (ABRI then) had built that kindergarten and had named it the Rose Kindergarten. Apparently, they gave names like that to their community projects – the names of sweet flowers like jasmine and rose, coincidentally the red and white colours of the Indonesian flag. Perhaps they gave these names to overlay a fragrance of flowers over the bloody stench of violence that followed them. Perhaps they thought it fooled people. Anyway, that was the official name given to the kindergarten, they told Ant, and who gave us permission to change it?

'But,' I protest, 'the children don't understand "Rose".'

They've never seen a rose. They've never smelt or touched a rose. Even most of their parents don't know a rose. On Ataúro, flowers are for death, carried with dead relatives to cemeteries so their petals can be scattered over graves lit with candles. Bougainvillea that grows wildly over fences and in corners of house yards they might know, but not a rose. On the other hand, when children see a seabird they run and shout and point into the air; they stand in groups and watch it dip and soar over the ocean.

I ask Anton to explain this to the military.

He tries but they are predictably unimpressed.

'That has nothing to do with it,' the military says. 'You have changed the name without military permission. It doesn't matter if the parents have chosen a new name. We might have offended somebody higher up. We might have trodden on important toes. We might be in trouble.'

It all seemed a bit silly to me, but Anton is surprisingly serious about it.

'A little thing like this could get us offside,' he grumbles. 'There might be all sorts of repercussions. You being here at all is tenuous and uncertain… they can send you away at any time, and they are very sensitive about such matters, the military. If we want to work here, we have to play things low-key and not draw negative attention to ourselves.'

He's right, of course, and doesn't smile about it. He's slightly irritated that I still do and it's the first time I have seen him annoyed. Although I think the naming of the kindergarten is very important for the children and parents who use it, I find it odd that the military, which we all know has a lot of other issues on its plate here in Timor, cares about such a thing. But it does.

The military commandant went to Dili. He went to have a meeting about the kindergarten name with someone at a higher level. Anton was called to the post to be given this information. You must wait for the outcome, he was told. So we waited. The commandant came back. We saw him get off the boat. We waited and became a little nervous. We waited and waited, but Anton was never called back to the military compound and no soldier came to visit us. We held our breath waiting… until weeks went by and the temporary cardboard sign propped up at the gate became sun-bleached and pale.

Nobody ever mentioned the problem again and the parents decided to put up a permanent sign with TK Manutasi painted boldly on a board and hung near the gate. The Seabird Kindergarten was established – a statement made under an apparent turning of a military blind eye.

HARBOURMASTER

Early in the year, we planned to run a training for primary school teachers on Ataúro. The objective was to introduce active learning approaches and bilingual materials, using a guidebook that a team of us at the university in Salatiga had written the previous year. It is a simple "ideas" book and, because Indonesian is the second or third language for most primary-aged schoolchildren throughout the archipelago, the book has suggestions on how to work in two languages (Indonesian and Tetun). This is a first for Timor. I'd consulted Pak Tavaris, principal of the primary school, and several of his teachers, both Indonesian and Timorese, and they were interested and excited about the training. There is not much in-service support on the island and they welcomed our efforts. The education department gave us permission to go ahead; the first training on Ataúro would mean that all local teachers could attend and issues specific to the island could be explored.

Joorst and Dianne, the Canadian education researchers working at Satya Wacana University with whom I had co-authored the Teachers' Guidebooks, were to come to East Timor to trial the books and co-facilitate the workshop. The day before the workshop is due to start, Anton, Guido and I go to Dili in the Manucoco to pick them up.

Joorst and Dianne arrive on the midday plane and we spend the afternoon in the Turismo Hotel garden preparing for the training. Our plan is to make the pre-dawn trip out to Ataúro the next day and, after washing off seawater, begin with the teachers at about nine o'clock.

At five-thirty in the afternoon our planning is done and we fill one of the old Dili taxis with the materials Joorst and Dianne have brought from Java. Guido follows the taxi to the beach to load the boxes onto the Manucoco in preparation for our departure early the next morning. The rest of us go to a nearby café for our evening meal. We are halfway through dinner when Guido comes rushing in to tell us that the military has arrived on the beach demanding that the newly loaded cargo, our training materials, be taken off the boat. They had opened all of the boxes, spread the contents out on the beach for examination and were now insisting on seeing us.

Joorst and Dianne pale and push away their plates. We all look at Anton.

'No rush,' he says, helping himself to more food. 'They can wait 'till we finish eating.' He gestures towards the half-full bowls on our table. Joorst, Dianne and I, shocked by his apparent lack of concern, pick at our food.

By the time we get to the beach it is quite dark but we can see there are no longer any "uniforms" there – just a group of Ataúro people shaking their heads in sympathy and dismay as they look at our things strewn out on the sand. Domingos, one of our crew, tells us that they had left a message: that the foreigners must NOT leave Dili tomorrow morning and must report to the military base NOW.

I'd lived undisturbed on Ataúro for over two months already, so this sudden show of attitude was a surprise, but we decided there was nothing we could do but report to the base as directed. The military building (in Portuguese times, the Chinese Embassy) was just across the road from the beach. Accompanied by Anton, we foreigners walked over and reported to the guard at the front. He professes to know nothing about the incident, is confused that we had been told to report and doesn't know what to do with us. Anton asks him to call someone who we could talk to for clarification.

Because three of us were foreigners and in those days three foreigners loitering outside a military building was an unusual sight in Dili, onlookers soon gathered; our boat crew, various Ataúro people who happened to be in town, and Dili people who were passing by, formed a small crowd on the footpath. The guard became agitated by this fuss and called someone on his radio. We waited. The crowd waited. Until a bevy of young men in jeans, white runners, and with matching short haircuts, arrived on big motorbikes. These boys were suddenly beside us, gesticulating and telling the onlookers to disperse (they don't), attempting to take command of the situation and assuring us not to worry, that they would help us.

Anton whispered, 'Intel.' (Indonesian military intelligence) '… be careful.'

One of the Intel group edged close to me. A tall young man with a scar down the side of his face, he told me his name was Wayan. So I know he is Balinese. His closeness and familiarity add to my nervousness; at our first meeting that day on the footpath, Wayan seemed aggressive and quite, quite scary. He said the harbourmaster had commanded that we foreigners 'tidak boleh' (must not) leave Dili in that little boat, the Manucoco. Not under any circumstances were we to leave in that boat. Not tonight. Not tomorrow morning. Not ever. That was it.

Then I saw a surprising side of Anton. He stood tall (he was taller, though much thinner, than any of them) and addressed those eight or nine, short-cropped worked-out hard-muscled Intel boys in his soft, calm voice. And they listened to him. He explained to them about our planned teacher training and how we were helping their country through our work. He asked them on what grounds they could deprive the Ataúro teachers and children of this opportunity. He pointed out that we had come a long way from foreign countries to help educate their people.

The Intel boys nodded their heads seriously and conferred among themselves. From this new perspective, they were not willing to cause such deprivation – they shook their heads and explained to us apologetically that they did not have the power to cancel harbourmaster decisions. Anton persisted in his quiet way until finally a solution was suggested.

'We'll all have to meet directly with the harbourmaster and ask him to reconsider,' said Wayan.

The crowd listened to all this, nodding as if their opinions had been asked for. We were soon organised onto a cavalcade of motorbikes. Three nervous foreigners clung to the backs of three intelligence officers on powerful machines. Five or so other Intel motorbikes followed, Anton and Guido putt-putt along behind on our much less powerful work bike – and off we go to the port.

It was 8:30 at night when our motorbike procession arrived so, of course, the harbourmaster was not in his office. Someone was sent off to get him and he arrived, not happy, within half an hour. We used the time to work out our strategy: Joorst, a confident western man, thought it would be best if he did the talking; I thought that Anton, being Indonesian and having a better understanding of the situation and being the person responsible for the Ataúro program, would be the best person to talk for us. I, often too naïve and unguarded (which works very well in some situations) would probably be the worst. Diane doesn't want to talk. We discuss all this in low voices in the harbourmaster's dingy reception room in a mixture of English and Indonesian languages; Anton speaks only a little English and Joorst and Dianne only a little Indonesian. The three Intel men who were sitting with us (the rest remained outside smoking on the stairs) begin to offer suggestions as to how we should best go about convincing the harbourmaster. By then, it felt oddly like they were on our side and that it was a joint effort to get us to Ataúro so the training could take place.

'You cannot go to Ataúro in that small boat,' says the

harbourmaster, a portly man with thick wavy hair and a moustache, addressing the men sternly and not once glancing at Dianne or me. 'No way will I allow it! It's dangerous out in that sea. It's not possible. No way!'

Anton explains, 'The Manucoco is our workboat, sir, and it is the boat we rely upon to get our work done around the island. It's a small boat but strong and reliable, and well maintained, and has a good motor, Sir.'

'That's all very well!' shouted the harbourmaster. 'But if something goes wrong? If something happens to these foreigners?' He lit a clove cigarette and puffed on it. 'This is East Timor… the world is watching us here, you know… these are orang asing (foreigners) and if anything happens, if they are lost at sea… oh yes, it's Indonesia's fault. Indonesia will be blamed for sure.'

'But I need to use that boat, Pak,' I protested. 'I live and work on Ataúro… how will I come and go?'

I shouldn't have spoken. Anton glares at me. The harbourmaster turned to me in exasperation. 'That is not my problem, madam,' he said coldly. 'My responsibility is to tell you that you must not go on that boat again, madam. Ever.' He dragged on his cigarette, glaring in my direction. 'And that is that.'

He turned once again to Anton and Joorst. I realised my mistake… and at that moment learned an important lesson about keeping silent, of keeping things uncertain. I learned in that moment that uncertainty in East Timor is generally far more useful than clarity; with uncertainty, there is much more room to move for everybody.

The harbourmaster's office is a big room painted a long time ago in a dirty mustard yellow that has grown dingier and more mustard with the cigarette smoke that constantly fills it. The man lit up again and sighed as Joorst and Anton, now supported by

Wayan and one or two of the others, explained the importance of our training.

Finally, 'Alright,' he sighed in exasperation. And, surprising us, he held out his hands in dramatic surrender. 'Your training is important for our teachers. We care about our teachers. So we will give you the government boat to take you out in the morning. It's a bigger boat. It's a safer boat. It will leave from the beach at eight in the morning… and the foreigners will be on it.' His eyes swept over us. He sighed again. 'We are helping you to help our people, right?' We nod.

Back on the beach – it is now after ten and very dark – we repack the boxes. Ataúro people and Intel stand by, watching. Wayan, the Balinese man, sidled up to me and suggested confidentially that, rather than start the workshop late, we should put everything back on the Manucoco now and leave at 4.30 am as we'd originally planned. 'Nobody will know,' he assured me. I was astonished. This suggestion, in the light of the last four hours, was confusing. I consulted Anton.

'Gabrielle, don't listen to him. Guido and I will take the Manucoco with all the gear at four-thirty,' he says firmly. 'You three go on the government boat at eight as you've agreed. And we start the workshop late.' He was stern. 'Gabrielle, don't trust them. You can't trust any of them. You need to understand that here, or you'll get yourself into trouble.' He means Indonesian military, police and bureaucrats, all of them. 'We just have to play their game,' he said, 'but not fall into their traps.'

And with that, I learned something about how Anton operated here in East Timor; with a sensible respect for the power structure, working with it but not blinded by it. He has learned to work around it in a pragmatic, low-key way. That's what I would do too.

The teacher training went well. The teachers loved the

attention, support and the new ideas we explore with them. At the end of the week we take Joorst and Dianne back to Dili on the Manucoco and, despite the prohibition, I continue to use that little boat for the next twelve years and more. Helped by regular gifts of Ataúro palm wine, yellow cassava and dried fish to the naval base, never a word is said about that boat, or me, again.

FAMILY THERAPY

I'd decided to open my heart to the Ataúro world and that meant learning about its spiritual beliefs and practices. So when we were invited to attend a shamanistic ritual event one Sunday morning, I was keen to go. A prominent family in the village had been experiencing problems: illness (several members becoming sick and neither the traditional healers nor the clinic nurses able to help), general disharmony and frequent quarrelling amongst family members, and the recent inexplicable death of their pet dog. I was told that the dog's death was the final straw and it was then that Faustino, the head of the family, had said he'd had enough. He asked Freitas, the shaman, to help them resolve the issue.

That was all I knew about the event that would start after Mass on Sunday, down near the beach at the house of Ilario, an uncle.

Because it was a shamanistic, non-Christian event Tipah would not consider attending and warned me to be very, very careful. Anton was torn, curious and heavily involved with the community, he was drawn to witnessing the event and learning more about its culture. For eighteen months he has lived on Ataúro but hadn't observed ceremonies like this; always curious, but reluctant because of their non-Christian nature. Now, with my interest and the people's desire to share, he was now faced with a dilemma. Not wanting to pressure him, I suggested he go with me and if at any point it felt "wrong" to him, he could leave.

We left the house that morning with Tipah shaking her head and wringing her hands, concerned that we might be touched, or even taken, by the devil.

When we got there, we saw several people still in their Mass clothes gathered by Ilario's sea-weathered cottage. The sun was high and it was a hot and hazy day. Freitas and another elder, a matan dook (a far see-er) were already busy searching through the dune grasses and digging in the sand. We were told "things" had been buried there; black magic objects that had been used to cause harm to the family. The shamans had already located the area but had not yet found the "things".

I watched as an old man I didn't know and Freitas, whose healing and spiritual skills are known on the island and throughout East Timor, sifted through the sand, now and again raising their heads to "listen" to the guidance of spirits. I watched, as I did for many years at such events, with interest, respect, confusion, a non-troubling dose of scepticism and great fascination.

They eventually found several disintegrating plastic bags that were dragged out of the sand and emptied before us; shells, teeth, some stones, the bones of fish, knotted oily rags, and an animal's jawbone fell out. These items were placed in a bucket surrounded by lit candles. A glass of red wine stood beside it – echoes of the Catholic Church. The shamans bent over the bucket, chanting ancestral spirit words only understood by a few. It was all very mysterious. Everyone was invited to look into the bucket but warned not to touch – the objects had been made less potent by the incantations, but were still powerful and dangerous. Afterwards, we were invited to go to the family's main house further up the beach where the rest of the ceremony would be carried out. We followed at a distance, behind the shaman and the bucket. Anton came too.

Many more people had gathered at the main house, and the yard was busy with preparations. Women with scarf-covered heads were cutting and plucking and cleaning and stirring. Children, dogs and chickens, hanging about for whatever pickings might come their way, were shooed away with cloths and shrill voices, scattering briefly then returning. Fires smoked. Men without specific tasks talked in groups, sitting on logs under trees, squatting on their haunches around the yard. It was big. And what would happen here would amaze me.

I was led into a small, dark room where two aged clan elders were preparing the next part of the ceremony. I squatted in a corner, keeping out of the way. I smelled the herbs, watched their actions, scrutinised the objects, and listened to the hum of mumbled conversations I couldn't understand. The two old men held a long brown curved root – like a ginseng root with two thin outshoots – and muttered incantations as they tied a red cloth around the top of it. As my eyes adjusted, I saw there was a small, black piglet, standing anxiously by the bucket in the corner opposite me. Occasionally we glanced at each other, the pig and I; the pig afraid, and I afraid for the pig.

The next part of the ceremony was outside in the courtyard where a tikar – a woven palm leaf mat – was spread on the ground. The shaman placed the ceremonial objects on and around the mat. The root prepared by the old men was laid lengthwise on it, the end tied with red cloth facing the bucket of black magic items, with the little pig tethered to it. Freitas took his position near the pig and the bucket while everyone gathered around the mat; not one deep, but four and five deep, were the participants now. Anton and I were pushed in among them.

The shaman spoke to the people in Tetum, and Anton whispered a translation to me. Freitas spoke about the "magical objects" and how they had affected the family, causing people to quarrel and fall sick and then kill the family pet. He said he could take away the power of this magic, but the family would be susceptible to more bad magic unless they did something to resolve the problems weakening them and making them vulnerable to evil spirits. He held his hands out to the family members, putting the responsibility of resolving the problem back into their hands.

The eldest son, Faustino, father of three and host of the event, spoke first. He told of the death of his mother and too soon after her death, his father's marriage to a younger woman. With emotion he spoke of the rift that marriage has caused, of his own resentment and lack of understanding. This he told us had influenced his children and grandchildren and their relationship with their grandfather and his new family. He asked for forgiveness and a healing of the wounds. He began to cry and so did several other family members.

The grandfather spoke, forgiving his son and asking for forgiveness in turn. They embraced and cried and everyone embraced and cried. Other people, men, spoke. They all shared about how bad relationships affect them and their lives. A neighbour said that the lack of harmony within the family had affected the entire neighbourhood; this magic and mystery alongside such psychological understanding is deep and wise.

Glasses of red wine are passed around and adults all take a sip. Everyone shook hands and embraced again. The members of the family took hold of the lower part of the root with one hand, and with their free hand took someone else's hand, reaching outwards from the inner circle until everyone there, including me, was connected directly or indirectly to that root. A pledge was made as Freitas cut off the top part of the root – the bad, diseased and dangerous part which symbolised the bad, diseased and dangerous elements in the family – and threw it into the bucket with the black magic objects. He tied the bucket to the little pig, picked up the squealing animal with one arm and faced the group.

'The evil is now being taken away,' he announced. 'I'm taking it to the sea where its power will be destroyed. Now it's up to this family to make sure it doesn't come back. This is your responsibility.'

He walked towards the beach the pig under one arm and the bucket, still attached to the animal, in his other. Each person picked up a fistful of pebbles and threw it after him, spraying his back with stones. Anton and I tossed a handful of pebbles. It was explained to us, that in this way we were all playing a part in getting rid of evil.

'What will happen to the pig?' I asked. I was told it would be thrown into the sea with the bucket but would wriggle free, more than likely swimming ashore to run as fast as its little pig legs could carry it along the beach to find a new home.

'That won't matter,' my informant explained. 'It's done its work. The pig is not evil and once it's shed the contents of the bucket for us, someone else can own it without risking any harm.'

After evil was sent on its way, there was feasting and rejoicing and drinking of freshly harvested palm wine. It was dark by the time we got back home, just a little tipsy, to a relieved Tipah who was waiting stern-faced and anxious on the step.

Anton and I discussed the day's events well into the night, both of us challenged and excited by our experience. We had many questions for which there were no answers. Are the shamans for real? Who had planted the evil things on the beach? For what purpose? Was the ceremony based solely on good intention and goodwill? There were many things to discuss: the unexpected wisdom there had been in the resolution, the power of the symbols and rituals, how very alike were all of we humans yet how very different. The moon came up over the sea and a gentle breeze blew over the veranda where we sat, but Tipah chose not to join us. She saw even a conversation about the ceremony as risky and stayed inside, well away from the reaches of the devil.

SEA NOTES

Sometimes at night the sea roars. In cycles that start outside the lagoon it crashes onto the reef and then rolls in over the seagrasses with a terrible moan. It's on full moon nights, the nights when the boiling foam is lit with silver and the tide comes in high, right up the beach to the dune grasses it *dances wild and ragged. I cannot sleep for the roar of it then, and the bright night calling my soul to watch and listen. I'm alert throughout the night, with salt spray sticky on my skin and the smell of ocean sharp in my nostrils.*

WHITE YACHT

Early one morning, arriving home from a visit to Dili, we rounded the headland to find a fancy yacht moored just outside the lagoon, beyond the reef off Vila. Ataúro boats are small, chunky, wooden, patched and oily, in need of paint; or narrow sea-weathered dugout canoes with bamboo outriggers. This boat was something else altogether; a big, handsome vessel from some different world, it gleamed in the morning sun.

I was surprised to find myself excited that there were foreigners here and asked Guido to run the Manucoco up alongside them.

He and the others aboard were, of course, as surprised and as curious as I. As we slowed our noisy motor and pulled into the shadow of the elegant vessel, a portly middle-aged man came to the rail and grinned down at us. He was big, bearded, hairy-chested, tanned and wore only a cap and brief shorts. Ignoring everyone else, he spoke directly to me, telling me they had sailed in from Maluku the day before. A suntanned woman in tiny shorts and a see-through top joined him and, visibly surprised to see me on the small boat bouncing alongside theirs, invited me to come up on board.

'I'd love to visit later on in the day,' I told them, knowing they could not possibly have any sense of how exciting this was for me after several months without an English-speaking visitor, nor how embarrassing for me among my modest island friends was the scantness of their clothes. It was not every day that a shiny white yacht with two semi-naked foreign sailors aboard arrived in Ataúro waters.

When we got to shore, we learned there were problems. Three of our policemen sat in a row on the beach, brows pinched with worry, eager to tell us their story. The yacht had arrived from the north on the previous afternoon and when it anchored offshore, an astonished fisherman repairing nets on the beach had sent someone to inform the police. The constable, a gentle Indonesian man from Flores, instructed three of his men to go to the beach immediately and wait for the visitors to come ashore and report – the usual procedure throughout Indonesia.

The policemen had waited an hour or so but nobody came off the boat. When two people emerged on the deck the police shouted and waved but the foreign sailors ignored them. The police made beckoning gestures, but they were ignored. The constable ordered his men to take a canoe out to the boat and explain the protocol to the foreigners who, as sailors in Indonesian waters, should know better.

The three Timorese policemen who went out to the yacht were not, they told us with some emotion, well received. From their outrigger, they called up to the sailors. Using the best of the little English they had between them, they explained politely to the visitors that they must come ashore with their papers and report to the authorities. The foreign man, who spoke a little Indonesian, eventually shouted back – yes, he said angrily, of course they would come ashore before the end of the day, now could they please be left alone in peace. He had spoken in bad and impolite Indonesian and was uncooperative and rude. The policemen came back to shore and, alongside the growing numbers of curious villagers gathering there, waited on the beach until it grew quite dark and became apparent that the visitors were not going to come ashore.

The police and military personnel on Ataúro are earnest souls who take their jobs seriously; they are under pressure from above to do so. Understandably, they were getting worried about who these people were and why they were there. They had called an emergency meeting that night. The military was concerned, but the senior military officer considered it best for them to stay out of it as much as possible. They all agreed that the police should raid the boat at first light the next morning and demand to see passports and travel documents.

At dawn, with some trepidation, three nervous policemen, inexperienced in such a commission, had taken an outrigger out to the yacht. Coming alongside they had asked to be allowed on board. Although they knew their shouts must have been heard they were ignored for some time – so they decided to go ahead and board without permission. After all, they told us, they were the police and this was their responsibility!

As they climbed up onto the yacht the big man suddenly appeared from below with a red face and clenched fists. He waved his fists about – the policemen mimed it for us. He shouted. He shouted in what they thought might be German and English and used some very bad Indonesian words. When the police tried to explain that they really must report the man shouted at them again. Quite frankly, they did not know what to do next and were a little afraid, so they left the boat.

They told each other if the foreigners did not report during that morning, they would call for reinforcements from Dili. And they meant it. That was the situation when we arrived, and it was the most dramatic thing that had happened on Ataúro for a long time. Everyone was waiting, and most of the village was on the beach, to see what would happen next.

The police constable asked for my help… as a last effort, could I go to the yacht and explain in English that they must report? It was their legal obligation to do so, and they'd be arrested if they refused. I told him they were no doubt just recreational sailors with no bad intentions just enjoying a holiday. But I knew, as well these visitors must, that the rules of any country, especially East Timor, had to be taken seriously. I told the constable I would talk to them, but I suspected that this was not a language problem at all, but rather an arrogance problem.

In the afternoon as they had still not come to shore, Anton and I went out in a canoe. The scantily dressed sailors, relaxing on their deck and sipping glasses of red wine and nibbling on crackers and smoked oysters, welcomed me on board. They ignored Anton. I was offered wine. Anton was not. When I gently drew their attention to this oversight the yachtsman with a wave of his hand dismissed Anton. 'We don't give alcohol to locals,' he said. Shocked, I begin to explain that Anton is a graduate from Ambon running a development program on the island and is my friend and colleague (as if that mattered) but Anton frowned at me, says, 'No thanks,' in good clear English and turned his back on us to stare out at the sea.

The sailors told me the story of their trip through the eastern islands. They had lived and worked for two years in Jakarta prior to this sailing trip and said, with a smirk, that they knew Indonesians well. They recounted their version of that morning's police raid; amused by the event, sneering as they talked about it.

'We're not going to be bullied by these tin-pot policemen on tiny no-place islands like this,' the man crowed. I was incensed. *Bullied*? I, who had marched against police in the streets of Brisbane in the Bjelke-Petersen times of oppression, felt incensed on behalf of these policemen who were right then waiting on the beach, sick with worry and genuine concern. Referring to Ataúro as a "tiny, no-place island" did not please me either. Anton, understanding bits of it, flashed me a look and turned back to the sea while I attempted to explain things to them from the local police's perspective: the importance of their jobs to them, the fact that they see it as their duty, and they feel a responsibility to report to Dili if they get no resolution.

By now I was quite unimpressed by these foreigners. I was no longer excited by their big yacht or expensive red wine that, tempting as it was, I had refused to sip. Finally, I reminded them that they are in East Timor and if they do not comply they could be sure a military boat would be called out of Dili to visit them. We left the boat.

A little later the foreigners came ashore with their passports and travel papers, and everything was sorted. It was all so straightforward and easy really, and could have been done without anxiety-causing fuss. When they disembarked in their rubber dinghy, they brought with them several huge plastic bags bulging with what was obviously their garbage. Seeing this coming, I suggested to people on the beach that nobody offer to assist them. Instead of helping carry it, we lead them to our burning and burying hole and they drag the stuff up the beach themselves. Tin-pot no-place islands apparently have some use as rubbish dumps to wealthy foreign sailors and after dumping, they sailed off into the sunset.

The next morning the horizon was wonderfully clear of fancy white yachts and troublesome visitors. For several days their dumped rubbish was explored and exploited; among the cans and plastic are useful bits of clothing and batteries, still good slightly cracked plates, an old torch, a working radio, some rope, wire, broken but fixable other things. People walked around for a while in strange bits and pieces of clothing with big smiles on their faces. Tipah and Alu both had fancy blouses that, after downsizing, needed just a button or a darn. They were beaming. Even the policemen wore wide smiles again for days and enjoyed telling their story over and over again.

ANTON

Some Bikeli fishermen and women have come to Vila to talk about the fishing project Anton is helping them set up in their village. I watch as they sit on the veranda discussing it. Anton's interest in these people is deep and he listens closely to their opinions and ideas while they debate among themselves. Their faces are the faces of fishers who spend their days in and on the sea, whose gnarled hands mend nets, wield spears, tinker with oily motors. Anton's is the soft brown face of a fisheries graduate who has learned the theories of the trade but whose interest is much, much more than academic.

To Anton, who is twenty-eight years old, these people are fellow countrymen. East Timor has been a province of his country since he was seven years old. He has had the advantages of education and an educated, middle-class family; these fishermen are poor, uneducated, most of them illiterate. He wants to share his knowledge and skills with them, to help them attain a better and easier life. Sometimes he or one of the other men crack a joke and they all laugh heartily. I watch his face and it beams with love.

BOAT PULLING

The first time I hear the voices of Ataúro "boat pulling", my blood freezes for a second then pounds through my veins, sending shivers up my spine. What I hear is spine-chillingly beautiful. It comes from the beach, the voices of many people gathered into one song; a huge choir. I run, following the sound, and there in the shallows is the big wooden boat, one of the *Tasi Diak* fishing boats, being pulled from the sea. It's pulled slowly, ever so slowly, by two long lines of singers, their arms working together on a thick rope, heaving in rhythm with their chant.

There are a hundred or more people singing and pulling: men pull – men with bare chests and sea-tangled hair; women pull – thin women in sarongs, on their feet worn-out thongs; children pull – small boys and girls clinging to the rope, sometimes lifted off the ground by it, pulling under the strong arms of their parents; there are grandmothers – little old ladies with matchstick legs and shrill voices; grandfathers with salty grey beards; they all pull and I stand, watch and listen in amazement.

Dancers on the Sea

The *Tasi Diaks* are solid boats, great planks of sea-seasoned wood form the hull and the cabin is a heavy square wooden room. This boat could carry twenty passengers or more plus a cargo of fish, rice, cement, metal pipes. This one is an old vessel that badly needs repairs and, to get it up onto dry land away from high tides, had to be pulled manually out of the sea and up the beach. At the waterline, the round trunks of banana trees are placed under its keel as rollers to guide and carry it up, dragged by the two motley lines of determined singers.

An elderly man with a frazzle of wild grey hair stands on the deck directing activities, leaping and dancing and waving his arms; he is the conductor leading the chant, miming the tugging action as he sings. His gravelly voice is deep and loud, and the language he uses is ceremonial language, language for calling spirits, for calling for blessings and strength. I am taken unawares, floods of excitement surge through me. I see Anton among the pullers. Tall Anton, 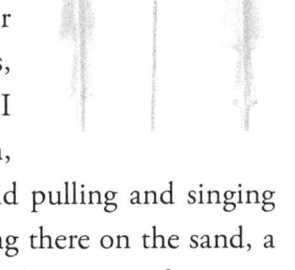 standing out above the rest, is bending and pulling and singing with them, It is a dance they are performing there on the sand, a joyful, determined dance of heaving arms and stamping feet.

They call me to join in and I am suddenly terrified. I am terrified of joining the dance, not knowing the steps, terrified of spoiling it, terrified of breaking the spell – but I do join and the wet, ragged rope burns my hands and I tread back on peoples' bare toes and my big arms have little strength but people laugh and sing and I sing and laugh and we pull and pull and the heavy boat follows us slowly up the beach while the old man dances and sings on its deck.

When, after an hour and more of pulling and stopping, pulling and stopping, and the boat is high and dry on the dune, the cheerleader tosses his stringy grey mop of hair and shouts 'Done!'. There is a huge cheer. The rope is released and people, giddy with the thrill of it, continue to sing and dance on the sand to their own individual rhythms. Waving weary arms, clapping reddened hands, children shout and run about, teasing and laughing and into the sea splashing. Above it all the owners of the boat shout an invitation for everyone to come to their thanksgiving party and drink palm wine.

And such a party it is with gallons of milky palm wine in bamboo tubes and plastic jerry cans and plates and plates of little salted fish and freshly popped corn passed around. People sit on the ground at the edge of the beach and drink wine and talk about the event and the heaviness of the boat and congratulate each other about how well it has all gone. Over a plastic bottle of palm wine, I ask the old man and his group of friends, toughened old men of the sea all, why little children and frail elderly women who wouldn't have much strength also pulled on the ropes. And because to them the answer was so obvious, they stare at me to ascertain if my question is serious.

They mutter among themselves as they do when deciding what or what not to tell me, then one of them explains it: as for the children – 'You know this, Ibu' – they must learn how things are done and they do this by watching and listening and taking part in the work we do; but the women – the women must take part because it's not just brute strength that's needed to pull a boat, it's soft female energy. It's the gentle determination of women that oils the process, that flows into the rope and helps the boat to move. Men use strong muscles and brawn to pull, to bully the boat up the sand, but the energy of women sweetens and smooths the pull and allows the movement to happen.

They all nod in agreement.

I am surprised to hear these old fishermen talk this way, but I understand and we filled our coconut shells with sweet palm wine and drink together to a job well done.

ATAÚRO NAMES

Since my first visit to East Timor, I have wondered about people's names. I hear: Domingas, Maria, Brigida, Elena; Faustino, Guido, Jose, Marcelo – Portuguese names that come from far away. Where had their original names gone, I wondered. Where are the names that belong to this island, these hills, these beaches? And then I discover that they are still here, that hidden behind "Christian" names are traditional names that create links with the past, with ancestors, with each other and the land.

These are some traditional Makili names still given to every child:

Male	*Female*
Kukulou	Ketikia
Mepais	Inakaki
Kaknai	Inakisu
Kurametan	Kosekoli
Kasureti	Kiakuru
Minkara	Kianai

And from Macadade:

Male	*Female*
Kohetia	Kiakali
Kahikia	Kosereti
Kohikili	Kalikaki
Laokaki	Kalitia
Kaikaki	Kiakaki

THE NAMING OF KATALO

The baby girl was nameless; just two days old, she had not yet been given a Portuguese Christian name (Maria, Angela, Francesca or Natalia) or a traditional Ataúro name. But custom dictates that before the end of her third day she must have a name that links her to the island. A name given to her by the spirits of her ancestors who hover about in the trees, cliffs and mountains of Ataúro watching over her. She must have a name that links her to the past and present inhabitants of Ataúro – for her it's the Hresuk-speaking fisher people of Makili. This was her naming day, and she was to be given the name Katalo. I'm invited to attend a ceremony to celebrate the passing of the name.

Luisa and Jorge's small house was crowded. Families on both sides had walked around from Makili bringing gifts of corn and dried fish that are now stacked in piles or hanging in the porch and around the yard. Some people have brought betel nut and others woven tais cloths. There are rules about who gives what and what exchanges must take place at these significant life events; these exchanges will consolidate the giving of the name and confirm the child's position in the complex Ataúro world.

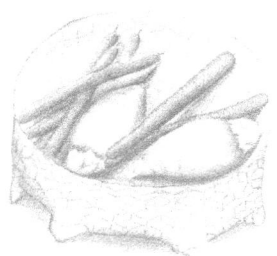

I was ushered into a dark room where the baby, a tiny cocoon swaddled in a cotton blanket, lay on a mat on the sleeping platform beneath the window. She was bathed in soft light from the small square opening. Once my eyes adjusted to the darkness of the rest of the room, I saw there were several people already gathered – grandmothers, grandfathers, aunts and uncles, and there is one younger woman – the wet nurse who has fed her own breast milk to the baby since her birth two days ago.

The ceremony was quick and simple. The wet nurse was given special food – sour fish and mung beans – and put a little of each into her mouth. She chewed the food slowly and purposefully to mix it and, when the stuff was chewed, spat the globule of greenish paste into her hand. With her forefinger she scooped the mixture up and placed a smear of it on the forehead of the sleeping baby. One of the older women, silver-haired and with heavy silver bangles on each thin arm, stepped forward with a greasy grey string of hand-spun cotton. She placed this around the baby's tiny wrist while she gave her the chosen name. Tying the string, the woman sings softly in the Hresuk language, singing words that mean something like: *May you grow into a woman who finds water close by so that every day you can supply fresh water for your family.* They are words of hope and wellbeing, blessings for her life.

And so the little girl had her name, her role, her place. Through the name, she was now connected with all her living and dead clansmen. But if the name is not right for her and does not give her the right spiritual connection she will show signs; she may cry a lot, refuse to eat, be fretful and unsettled. Up until she is three years old, if the name proves unsuitable for her, it can be changed for another. Before she is three it can be changed any number of times until the right one is found – but this day, little Katalo, tiny bundle in her tightly bound wrap, slept soundly through the chewing and spitting, pasting and tying and did not stir through the singing of her blessing. It seemed she was content with the name they had chosen for her. Lucky girl, I thought, to be embedded now in a deeply rooted tradition that places her solidly in position, in relationship, in time and place.

We left Katalo sleeping and went into the other room to eat fried bananas, dry salted fish and popcorn that had been laid out for us. The wet nurse came too and was given bundles of corn and a basket of betel nut as gifts of gratitude. This woman would continue to feed the baby for a week – the birth mother's first milk was still considered dirty and unsuitable for a newborn – and the gifts acknowledge the valuable contribution the wet nurse is making to the child's life.

People tell me that if the baby was a boy the ceremony would be the same, but the naming song would be different, with words like: *May you climb many palm trees and always be able to provide fine fruit for your family.* It would acknowledge his male role and give a blessing for his success in life.

So that was the ceremony and Katalo is named. Some people stay and some drift off. Everyone in the village knows that the new baby is now named and that, long before the church and its holy water sprinkling and its bestowing of a distant Portuguese name, the little girl has become Katalo, child of Ataúro.

KINDERGARTEN

The children come to their new school in clean clothes and leave their rubber flip-flops – a spreading mass of coloured rubber – at the door. They are enthusiastic and becoming more confident with their teachers and less timid with me. Dulce, Teresa, and Zelia are seeing for themselves how a classroom with interesting activities keeps their pupils keen and wanting to learn. With limited resources, our biggest challenge is to provide interesting learning activities and, as their own confidence grows, the three trainees are becoming more creative and are encouraged by the response of their students.

Attendance is high, and there are always one or two groups in rotation, working and playing outside while the others work on the mats or at the small tables inside the classroom. We sometimes take the children to the beach or down into the village and, although these places are familiar to them, we use the excursions to develop language. Back at school, they draw pictures from their walk on the recycled paper that we cadge from the few local offices and the primary school. We make our own books about the village and about village life and the sea. This is something new for both teachers and children and they love it.

Most of the children are well-behaved but, of course, there is the odd one who disrupts and hassles the others, so the teachers and I discuss discipline problems and look at alternatives to "the stick", which is still regarded as an essential teaching tool by most Indonesian and Timorese teachers and parents. There is no stick in our kindergarten. Not only the teachers but also the parents have to be convinced that our gentler approach will work with their children. They express concern that their little ones are just playing and singing and having fun when they should be learning. Learning here is defined as the three Rs (writing, reading and arithmetic); it's supposed to be serious and hard.

Although our kindergarten environment is relaxed and friendly, the children must learn there are rules to follow and expectations that must be met.

Parents and older siblings are welcome any time and we also have special open days for families to come and join in, to learn about and understand the approach we're using in the program. Self-conscious fishermen fathers with stiff fingers and giggling mothers sit awkwardly at small tables and work timidly with puzzles and other educational games, play with red clay, dug out of the hills, and draw with charcoal from their own cooking fires.

They learn why we do things and why we do them the way we do. We have discussions with the mothers and fathers, uncles and aunties, grandmothers; we talk about what they think is important for their children to learn and how we might incorporate those things into our program. In a culture where, in adult company, children are mostly seen and not heard, we have to explain why building children's confidence to talk, ask questions and express ideas is important for their intellectual development. But we also have to manage social expectations and make sure the children understand them too. We are not trying to produce misfits. Achieving balance in all this was very good learning for all of us, especially for me.

The primary school teachers, not understanding about learning through play and exploration, are at first critical of the kindergarten program. They regard the kindergarten teachers' work as "too easy" and say they should be teaching the children to read and write before they come to school otherwise what's the purpose of the kindergarten? It is only in the years that follow when they are teaching the kindergarten graduates, that the teachers see the benefits of our approach and become supportive of our work. They see that children who have been to kindergarten come more regularly to school, are more confident, listen to their teachers, follow instructions and are mostly keen to learn. A couple of years after we have been operating the kindergarten, the principal makes it mandatory for children to have attended the kindergarten program before enrolling in year one.

The daily session start at 8:00 am and finishes at about 11:00 am, five days a week; Saturday on and Friday off. Many of the children have not eaten anything before school and are tired and hungry by late morning. The teachers and I work for another couple of hours – discussing and learning from the events of the morning, planning for the next day, making paints (food colouring, earth colours), games and books and learning songs.

On Fridays, market days, the children don't come to school at all, and we use the whole morning (except for our own hasty shopping trip to the market) for teacher training.

WEDDING PARTY

Our household was invited to a wedding. It would be my first since I arrived three months ago. The whole village would be there and there'd be music, dancing and a feast. We dressed in our best clothes. Baptista carried our wedding gift – a set of glasses in a dented box from the local kiosk, dusted off, spruced up and wrapped in pretty paper by Tipah – tucked under his arm.

In the yard of the groom's family home, coloured lights hung and plastic chairs, two deep, formed a circle. The bride and groom sat in a bridal bower cleverly fashioned out of pink and white cardboard; "thrones" elaborately decorated with woven palm leaves and chains of silver paper show they are king and queen for this day.

Guests – Ataúro people, Timorese mainlanders and Indonesians who live and work here, and me – sit as the local band played through a crackling amplification system. There is an emcee; protocol for the night was formal so the order of things was explained and there would be no surprises. Every part of the night, including the applause for the bride and groom, shaking their hands, and so on, was a numbered item on the agenda. I was reminded of Javanese village weddings I've attended. Women in matching clothes, sewn in the weeks before on ancient treadle machines, fuss and bother over food preparation and drinks; men fiddle with the sound system trying unsuccessfully to get rid of the crackle or reorganise the seating as more and more people arrive. Dressed elaborately, the bride and groom sat stiffly in their bower; the bride a vision in pink froth and frills and the groom wearing a suit and white gloves. They are nervous and self-conscious, communicating with no one, including each other.

After the formalities with the bridal couple and their families – guests lining up to kiss their cheeks and shake their hands – the wedding cake was cut and the couple were applauded as they self-consciously feed each other a crumbly slice, symbolising, as in many other cultures, mutual love and care. A meal was laid out in the yard on three tables: one for the bride's family (on Ataúro they are given special treatment, have their own separate table at the wedding and are invited to eat before everyone else); one with halal food for Islamic guests (Indonesians from Java, Sumatra and some of the eastern islands); and the third for everybody else.

The food was good the best Ataúro has to offer; a pig has been killed, and a goat or two, and every part of the animals have been prepared and presented in bowls of sweet sauce, coconut milk or chilli and lime. There were cauldrons of rice, vegetables (some brought from the mainland), and fresh fish, jugs of palm wine, cans of Indonesian beer, Coca-Cola, Sprite and water. Day-to-day food here was monotonous, but on celebratory occasions, it was varied and delicious.

And, after the meal, it was dancing time! Tables were cleared and carried away, and the band got louder. Like everywhere else in the world, the boldest men and women rose to begin the dance, followed by a rush of eager younger men and women. The dirt floor was filled with moving feet. It soon became soft and dusty but nobody cared. The dance was a Portuguese quickstep – the steps danced throughout the whole night to the same basic rhythm, some extroverts adding their own flamboyant touches.

At first, nobody asked me to dance.and when Anton eventually did and we stand up together, there were loud cheers and clapping. Dancing with Anton was surprisingly lovely and we danced on and off all night, gradually forgetting our self-consciousness, forgetting the heat and the dust. If we took a break someone else stepped in to ask me and always there was a cheer when I go to the floor. It was great fun. But when I danced with Anton my feet and my heart were light — we squeezed into the huddle with everyone else when the floor was crowded and swung out when it was not. We laughed at my mistakes and soon I wasn't making many. I was very happy.

We left about midnight, but the party went on, and when I cycled up to the kindergarten next morning at eight, the music was still grinding away in that dusty yard, and several people were still dancing. I guessed that there would not be many teachers or students at school that day.

DANCING ETIQUETTE

When Ataúro people dance they are serious; there are no smiles, talk, or laughter between dancing partners. It looks like neither partner is enjoying the other. At the wedding when dancing with Baptista, a very good and popular dancer, I ask him about this. In a whisper, he explains to me, 'No, no, no, *Ibu*, you must never talk and laugh with your partner. People are watching – fathers, uncles, brothers, cousins are watching their daughters, sisters, nieces, cousins – and if there's any sign of intimacy like giggling or talking between the dancing couple, the watchers will think they are "planning things" for later. This can get you into big trouble!'

'Oh dear,' I tell him. 'I've been talking and laughing with

everyone I danced with! Has anyone thought I was "planning things"?'

'Oh no *Ibu*, nobody would think of you that way,' he protests.

ATAÚRO ISOLATION

Isolation can be useful for political purposes and Ataúro's remoteness has a history of usefulness.

THE PORTUGUESE PRISON

In Portuguese times Ataúro was used as a remote prison. Prisoners, it is said, were kept at night in a large hole in the ground. People point out the spot that is now a corn and bean field without evidence – no bump or depression even – to indicate the place of underground imprisonment.

From all over the Portuguese world, prisoners were sent to Ataúro; from African colonies, from the mainland of Timor. Thieves and murderers and political prisoners from San Tome, Guinea Bissau, Mozambique, Macau, Dili and Baucau were banished from whatever world they came from to the remote, dry island. Escape was impossible; the sea was deep and rough and the villagers' dugout canoes took many hours to cross the strait.

Ordinary prisoners were put to work by day and at night, the story goes, herded into the hole in the ground, down a rope ladder that was then pulled up out of reach; perfect security. With up to forty men and no light or sanitation, that prison must also have been a perfect hellhole.

There were special treatment prisoners, like Mario Lopes, a political journalist from Mozambique whose writing had offended someone and sent him to Ataúro for life. He was the father of

Vasco, who had originally invited me to come and work on the island. Sr Lopes, the elder, was allowed to live on the island as a settler; he planted coffee on the mountain, started a store and probably no longer wrote articles critical of the Portuguese government. There are a number of families on Ataúro that are, like his, descended from African prisoners who took Timorese wives and are now part of the mix of Ataúro peoples.

A PLACE OF EXILE: JESUINA TELLS ME HER STORY

For several years after the invasion, the Indonesian government used Ataúro as a place of exile for resistance fighters, their families and supporters. Jesuina was one of them.

'I'd never seen the sea before, and the night they brought us to the island was pitch black apart from some lights, I think they were stars, dancing on the waves. Indonesian soldiers loaded us onto the boat. I was with my mother and sister and we were terrified. The soldiers had taken my father away a long time before. He was a resistance fighter and we never saw him again, never even saw his body or found his bones. They took us, with lots of other people from around Viqueque, packed in trucks to Dili where we were kept in military barracks for a few weeks before they sent us to the island.

'I'd never heard of Ataúro. I was seventeen years old, a mountain girl and very frightened. I remember that long night crossing the strait, rocking up and down on the waves; we were clinging to each other, everyone was confused, no one was able to comfort anyone else. There were fifteen or sixteen families on the barge and we were all – even the men – seasick and scared. We got to Ataúro in the early morning, and island people and dogs were on the beach watching us arrive. We didn't know if they were friendly or not.

'The soldiers took us to camps up in the Mutiara area, along the beach from Maumeta. There were long tarpaulins stretched out to make roofs and plastic walls to make separate rooms for each family. We had open kitchens out the back and some containers of water for drinking, cooking and bathing; three or four families shared one container. There were no toilets, so we had to go into the forest at the back for that.

'At first, food rations were sparse – each week about one kilogram of corn for two people – and so we scrounged whatever greens, wild food and fruit we could. The corn was not always good but Ataúro people, whose language we didn't understand, were kind-hearted and gave us vegetables and sometimes a fish. They let us use their land to make our own gardens.

'About six months after we arrived the Red Cross came and set up a kitchen; then we had milk for the young children, mung beans, tinned meat and eggs. We exiles had better food than the Ataúro people themselves then but there was no jealousy. Maumeta was not a town then like Vila is now, so there were not many people around and the ones that we saw were mostly Makili people who were fishermen and had their own gardens up near our Mutiara camp.

'The Indonesians encouraged the children of exiles to attend Vila primary school with local children and the teachers were good to us. I'd never been to school before and even though I was seventeen years old I started in the third class. There was no high school on the island then, but some of the smarter mainland and island children were sent to Dili. Although the exiled parents weren't allowed to leave the island the Indonesians helped their high school children to continue their education:

they stayed at the military barracks (KODIM/KOREM) there and were looked after by the soldiers. The bishop provided food for those students while they were in Dili. I didn't go to high school, instead, I fell in love with Vilanova, an exiled resistance fighter and a hero, and we got married. And even when most of the others went back to the mainland, we decided to stay here on the island away from the troubles.'

In 1983 the exiles were allowed to return to the mainland and most of them did but several families, like Jesuina and Vilanova's, stayed and still live on Ataúro.

Anton's blanket was woven by one of the exiled mainland mountain women. They brought the skill of weaving tais cloth and still weave beautiful cloth on back-strap looms on the porches of their Ataúro houses or under the shade of trees on the outskirts of Vila where they live. Ataúro women have never made this tais cloth instead they wove "rapi hirik" cloth from shredded and spun palm leaves and "folik" cloth from white hand-spun cotton.

SOLIDARITY: THE CLINIC STRIKE

The Vila clinic closed for a week and people with fevers, skin rashes, infections and broken bones hung about outside, waited, shook their heads, then wandered home. All sorts of conjectures grew but the truth was as follows.

Two male Sumatran health workers had been assisting Mama Julietta, who was physically ill and suffering deep depression. Julietta was hospitalised in the clinic for a week or more and these two men had become her friends. They nursed her with medicines but also with care. Friends of Anton, the Sumatran nurses would sometimes visit us at night and debrief about the case with us – unprofessional perhaps, but necessary for them in that isolated place. They trusted Anton and me not to gossip.

Sometime after Julietta was well again, the two Indonesian health workers were savagely beaten by a group of Ataúro men – set upon one night by Julietta's jealous husband. In solidarity with their workmates, the rest of the clinic staff, both Indonesian and Timorese, went to Dili to demand action by health department officials. The clinic was closed. The nurses went on strike and refused to reopen it until Dili government bigwigs came out to the island to sort things out. This left Ataúro in a worse situation than usual but was an effective strategy in bargaining for justice. Even with visits of important people and consultations with police and local leaders, it was a couple of weeks before the issue was resolved, and the staff agreed to come back and serve the island's sick and injured. It was one of several incidents in which Timorese and Indonesians stood together in solidarity in the cause of justice.

SEA NOTES

This sea changes its nature like no other sea I've known before. This Wetar Strait is deep, mighty deep, and overnight can change from a gentle rippling, rhythmic companion into a huge, angry monster tossing unforgiving waves onto the reef, pummelling mercilessly on the shore. I think there's something bothering this sea; stored in its memory is something that stirs its fierce watery soul, something that's whipped up out of its depths by the east winds. And there's no reasoning or understanding it then – you can only let it be – pouring out its fury, pouring out some pain that you can feel in your soul.

I learn to turn my back on the angry sea as others do, as fishermen dragging their nets higher up the beach do, as boatmen pulling their canoes out of its reach do. I shake my head as they do and walk away, to wait. We wait and watch and listen from a distance, watch by day and listen by night as its foaming and crashing roar into our sleep, into our dreams, for a day, a night, a week or more; roaring, pounding, hurling hunks of driftwood, tossing seagrasses, broken shells...

And then quite suddenly it subsides; sea-blue, shimmering with reflected sunlight, it whispers us back then... playfully, seductively it draws us back... whispering and licking at the silver sand along the shore.

JOAQUIM

A good teacher does not have favourites. In my work with the teachers and the children, I was nothing if not fair in showing my love for each of them. Although I still couldn't really talk with the children – they didn't speak Indonesian and I didn't yet speak Tetun – I knew them all and each one soon had a place in my heart. I loved them all. But there was one little boy called

Joaquim who took a special place.

Joaquim lived with his family in a house just past the bridge over the dry creek, in a typical Vila village house, with walls of woven bamboo, a dirt floor, a leaky thatched roof. A couple of skinny dogs slept under the trees outside, and an old man, Joaquim's grandfather, often squatted on the veranda while his grandmother, a strong little woman with a bent back, swept the dirt yard with her coconut frond broom. She swept every morning, shouting at Joaquim's younger siblings or cousins who played naked in the dust, to get out of her way.

Joaquim had the blackest eyes I'd ever seen and the softest and the deepest. He was a shy boy with not much to say but, for whatever reason, he especially liked me, and I especially liked him. Without any words between us that was clear.

He waited for me to pass his house each morning and dismount from my bike so we could walk together the remaining hundred metres or so to the kindergarten. Sometimes he waited for me to walk home too – although that might be a couple of hours after all the children had been dismissed and the teachers had tried to shoo him away from the kindergarten several times. Sometimes he went home when the other children did, but just when the teachers and I were ready to leave, he would turn up at the door again in old clothes, munching a hunk of cassava, ready to walk with us back down the hill.

Often I saw Joaquim on the beach. His skin gleamed with saltwater, jewels of seawater glistened in his hair. He smiled at me, shyly. I don't know what it was we recognised in each other but there was some silent connection between us. Sometimes, to impress me, he did somersaults with the other boys… throwing themselves head over heels into the sea, knees tucked up to their chests, their feet held down, forming little human balls that hit the water with a splash. I laughed and Joaquim's eyes shone. Sometimes he rode a tiny outrigger canoe and showed me how he could manoeuvre it across the lagoon; sometimes he caught little fish with a line or some shellfish with a bucket and gave half of them to me.

If we met at the market, Joaquim would walk behind me, helping me carry my basket of bananas and green vegetables. If I passed his house on an evening walk, someone called him and he came to the front door to smile and wave at me. This was one of my joys.

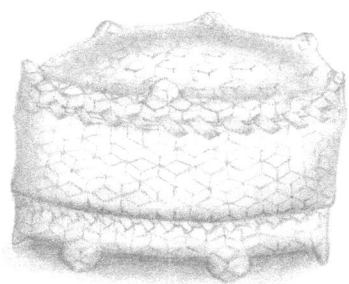

PART SIX

ANTON

Early one morning I looked out my window to catch the moment when the sun rose out of the sea. That great scarlet ball was just peeping over the horizon and the eastern sky – streaked pink, gold and purple – was reflected perfectly in the still water. It was so very beautiful it took my breath away.

And then, in the clear morning light, I saw that Anton was already up and in the garden. He was busy trimming our scraggly hedge, his dark skin and white T-shirt glowing against its green leaves. For want of a better tool, he was using office scissors to trim the leaves, his long fingers holding out the twigs as he snipped. Engrossed in the task he didn't notice me watching as he stepped back the way an artist does to assess his work, head tilted to one side, checking symmetry and balance.

I saw, but couldn't hear, that he was either singing or praying; his work an early morning meditation. Sometimes when he smiled to himself his joy shone into the day as its colours became clearer and brighter. An early morning voyeur at my window, I watched him in the garden and his silent song reached into my heart. Anton in the garden lit by morning light was beautiful; he took my breath away.

PICNIC

We planned a kindergarten break-up picnic for when the school year was to end, in June. Nobody here had ever heard of such a thing but when I explained it, everyone liked the idea. We'd take the children to Lampia – the white sandy beach just around the headland – and have a party with donuts, bananas and horribly sweet orange cordial. And we'd play games. Many of the children are originally from Makili Village and, coming and going from there to Vila, would have walked the Lampia Beach many, many times in their young lives. But they'd never been to Lampia for a kindergarten picnic and in anticipation of that, were wild with excitement. 'Come to my house at seven-thirty,' I told them, 'and each of you is to bring a drinking mug. The teachers and some parents will organise food and drink and, from my house, we'll walk together to Lampia.'

On the morning of the picnic, I was woken at dawn by giggling children and clanking tin mugs outside my window. It wasn't quite six o'clock and such was their enthusiasm for the day that many of them were here already, chatting like parrots. They amused themselves while I bathed and breakfasted and well before seven-thirty everybody was ready to go. Even the teachers and parents were impatient to get moving early.

What a day and what a picnic it was! As a responsible teacher I intended, when we arrived at Lampia, to sit with the children and teachers and discuss with them the plan for the day, explain our safety rules etc. But, as soon as we rounded the headland (along the narrow path we go, the children prancing in a line, singing, laughing, chattering) and reached the white beach, there was no chance of sitting and explaining anything for, in one swift many-legged, many-armed movement the little ones – wild, screaming things, laughing and shouting – stripped down to their bare skins; skirts, shirts, shorts, rubber flip-flops fly into the air and onto the sand as they headed for the sea.

But, but, but… I attempted to bring my kind of order to the day… but it was too late and they were gone. Sixty and more (my goodness, we hadn't even counted them yet!) naked bodies dashed into the water with shouts and splashes and squeals of delight. Nobody could hear me. Nobody cared. The water was cold, and the waves were big enough to leap through. The children dived and swam and splashed and screamed with joy.

More or less sixty naked brown bodies appeared and disappeared in the waves, legs and feet appeared (handstands), shiny buttocks appeared (dives), silver droplets in hair, in the air. And of course, they were safe: this was their life; they were island kids and while they may never have been on such an exciting thing as a school picnic before they are very much at home and happy in this sea. I sat on the sand and laughed. I laughed at myself, laughed at them, laughed and laughed with them. It was pure delight.

Later we had games and races and collected shells and made beads and ate the doughy donuts the parents had cooked as a treat and drank the sticky cordial. In the afternoon, we trooped home along the stony path, chattering away about the day, singing our songs.

SEA NOTES: DANCERS ON THE SEA

The men, on their wooden canoes are like dancers; gracefully, lightly they leap from boat to boat, swaying and dipping, balancing on the small swells. The boats, crude, heavy hollowed-out logs, are bobbing dance platforms from which with sharp eyes the men follow the fish then leap in pairs to dance with spears along brilliant coral beds, *chasing darting fish down, down into the depths and along the sandy bottom: masked aliens they are then, dancing at the bottom of the sea.*

BIRTHDAY

Nobody mentioned it. My birthday. I wondered, did anyone remember? Tipah gave me a kiss in the morning and I thought, hoped, that I saw a twinkle in her eye. Alu glanced at me sideways a number of times. But no one said a word. Perhaps it was wishful thinking, perhaps childish, nostalgic wishful thinking… even if I was turning forty-eight, I wanted somebody to remember my birthday, but it was turning into just a normal workday; apparently everybody had forgotten. Oh well, we had more important things to do.

In the late afternoon Tipah suggested that she, Alu and I go for a walk on the beach as we often did, so with a dog or two at our heels, we ambled along the curve of the lagoon up to the headland.

We returned at dusk after the big generator had started up and lights were just beginning to come on through the village. Oddly though, our place was not lit; there was only a dim glow like candlelight in our front window. Then Anton, smiling and not quite able to disguise his excitement, met us at the door and led me into the front room where, sitting cross-legged on the floor in a semicircle, their weathered faces lit up by the yellow light of a flickering kerosene lamp, were Antoni Freitas and five other elderly men of the village. A jerry can of palm wine, a mug filled with cigarettes and plates of salted fish and popcorn were set out in front of them. Anton gestured for me to sit with them. The old men smiled – wide, betelnut stained cracks in their leathery faces. They had come to make a party, my birthday party!

We all sat on the floor and the men chatted amongst themselves for a while before, quite suddenly, one of them began to sing in a loud, creaky voice. It was the first time I'd heard this type of singing and it made my blood tingle. Ataúro singing has a cyclical form – one person sings an improvised verse, and then the others join in with a familiar chorus, another singer adds a verse and the haunting, gravelly refrain follows. It's a cycle of song that is strange and harsh, music that comes out of a wild, deep sea, music that seeps out of the shadows of mountains and caves; it carries the experience of fishermen, of saltwater and deep oceans, love and sadness, of distance and yearning, of death. It's music from the soul.

I didn't understand the words but the voices of the old men, the songs coming from their hearts, and their weathered faces lit by lamplight, were so beautiful, I cried a little. When they sang grieving songs about lost boats and lost loved ones, of separation from the island and their families, of hardship, they themselves cried openly, pouring out the historical pain of their people in melody, in words and tears.

Sometimes the songs were topical; I heard my name several times and was told they were singing about my coming to the island and the work I am doing at the kindergarten – which made us happy again.

The air was thick and sweet with music and the smoke of clove cigarettes and local tobacco. We drank palm wine and nibbled on the tiny crunchy salt fish and popcorn as the singing went on into the night. Occasionally, a couple of the elders with bowed legs and bent backs, rose unsteadily to their feet to dance in the small space of our living room. Some younger men, hearing the music as they passed by on the road, dropped in to join them. It was lovely. We all got a bit drunk with wine and the pleasure of it all.

Towards the end of the night, Tipah and Alu brought out a cake – a steamed-over-a-kerosene-flame cake – alight with candles! The faces of the ancient singers showed amazement at such a spectacle and now it was their turn to be wide-eyed with wonder and delight as I blew out the little flames. Tipah, Baptista, Alu and Anton sang the Indonesian birthday song and we all tucked into it together.

This birthday celebration became a tradition in our household for several years – until later, when the world changed for all of us.

SEA NOTES: THIS SEA, THESE PEOPLE

I learn that Ataúro people are like their sea: gentle, soft and silent when it's their time for gentleness and silence; fire burning inside, spilling out when it's their time for fire. Unpredictable, they too carry pain and fury as they struggle for survival in this inhospitable land. They are tough people, opportunistic, calculating, innocent, kind-hearted, sweet as honey… like this they survive. Like the sea they roar, like the sea they whisper. Sometimes I think I understand them; sometimes I think I don't. Their laughter is raucous, meant to be heard, rings coarsely through the valleys and over the waves; their tears flood the hot dry riverbeds, splash on the stones; and the sad music from the heart of them enters my heart and stays there.

FALLING IN LOVE

I didn't mean to fall in love. I had no intention of it and a part of me disapproved. This man was too young. He was

Indonesian. And we were in East Timor. Our relationship would be unbalanced; me older, more experienced, not wealthy by Australian standards, but still, *wealthier*. From our first meeting in the Salatiga office the year before, this gentle, wise and funny person had impressed me and now, as we lived and worked together, I grew closer to him but had not contemplated the possibility of romantic love.

It was not love at first sight. It was living and working together, adapting, creating, playing and swimming in the sea, singing and talking and laughing together that grew our love. Then, all the reasons for not being involved romantically didn't matter a whit. I was in love with Anton.

Our work continued slowly, most of it surely; our nights and days were full, we were healthy and energetic, and our household was a happy one. Long before we ever spoke about our feelings for each other I sensed his and feared them. For a time, I denied them.

But indefinite denial was not possible.

When Anton's friend, Conta, a Sumatran government community development worker, single and several years older than him, came to stay with us, I was uneasy. Conta worked with rural women, supporting them to develop small economic enterprises. She came to Ataúro with her team of four enthusiastic young Timorese women. They stayed with us and made our household lively for several days.

Tipah, Baptista and Alu were delighted to have a full house with people sleeping in swags on the floor, queuing at the bathroom door, squealing and laughing together over the cooking, singing and strumming guitars at night on the beach or on our veranda. It was fun. The girls were on an adventure and were earnest, friendly, giggly, and young. Conta, older, trim and creamy skinned, was a serious woman, hair short-bobbed and beautiful. I liked her. We had good conversations, discussed our work, shared experiences and explored ideas about community work. Sometimes we sang Timorese and Indonesian songs with the others. But there was unease hanging in the air between us – noticed in each other's faces, felt in each other's body language. I think we both knew but, of course did not say, that this had something to do with Anton.

Anton was charming, warm and welcoming: an unintentional, natural flirt.

On the second afternoon of their stay, he and Conta went for a walk along the beach together. I watched them leave, deep in conversation, and I was surprisingly restless.

Needing distraction, I went swimming in the lagoon, looking underwater for fish and other sea things, wondering at the coral. When I came to the surface, I looked along the beach toward the headland where the two old friends were walking. I surfaced often, shaking seawater out of my goggles, shaking my head and dipping it quickly again to engage with fish. It was difficult to concentrate.

After my swim, when they were well out of sight around the headland, I walked through the village and talked, perhaps excessively, with everyone I met. Then I went home and sat on the veranda, drinking hot coffee and trying to read. When the electricity came on, I opened my laptop to bury myself in work.

Tipah watched me, her all-seeing, all-knowing gaze occasionally wandering from me to the beach. She had sensed the deepening of Anton's and my friendship and did not approve of it. The questions in her eyes made me ill at ease.

Just on dark they came back, two small dots at the water's edge that grew into Anton and Conta. They pushed open the gate, came up our hedged path, still talking earnestly, shaking sand from their flip-flops. I laughed at myself, greeted them warmly, offered them coffee… More aware of the depth of my feelings for Anton, I was surprised at the sense of proprietorship I felt and hoped my insecurity didn't show.

Anton was twenty-one years younger than me; that's a lot of years. But beneath a sometimes awkward and shy exterior, I knew him to be a wise and clever man. He was mature, had solid values and a sensible but wonder-filled outlook on life. But he was much younger, and we lived in a world that would test such an age difference in a love relationship, perhaps judge it harshly. And then there was the Indonesian issue. Anton was Indonesian and we were living in a country that was Indonesia by force. In East Timor, Indonesians are the enemy and there is a complexity to all Timorese/Indonesian relationships. Anton was dedicated to the people here, he was accepted and respected by them, but he was Indonesian. Although Indonesia was not my enemy, I felt solidarity with the Timorese, oppressed by the military of their vast and cruel neighbour. It was something I could not ignore.

AVOIDANCE

We walk along the beach in the early evening, Anton and I. Children are playing, fishermen cleaning and mending nets, dogs with purpose trotting along the water's edge. We talk about our work while our thoughts wander elsewhere. It is quite impossible; I think, it is improbable and impossible. And then I think it is unavoidable, inescapable, inevitable. We step out along the darkening sand, the space between us taut with uncertainty, our words light and irrelevant, skipping off into the air, our laughter evasive. We kick at broken shells, sending them skittering into the water, we kick at stones. We are sometimes silent, clinging to the silence and the rhythm of our walking to keep things in place for just a little bit longer. Sometimes the thought of being closer to him fills me with excitement. Sometimes it feels just too complicated to be risked.

HOTEL TURISMO

New Zealand Aid, through the embassy in Jakarta, was the main supporter of our education work. The NZ government had supported me with a local salary for several years at the university in Salatiga, and continued to fund our work on Ataúro. Without their funding there would be no program.

In due course, some embassy people came to visit – to see our work and talk about the future and their support. Anton and I went to Dili to meet them; our plan was for me to stay and accompany them on their rounds of meetings with officials before bringing them to the island. The group arrived from Jakarta on the afternoon plane, and we spent the rest of the day in the old Turismo Hotel garden talking about Ataúro, Anton's and my favourite subject.

The next day was to be the Dili day and the morning after that we would head out over the sea to the island. Anton was due to leave with supplies for the island early the next morning and so went up to my hotel room to sleep part of the night there on the spare bed rather than on the beach, his usual practice when leaving Dili before dawn.

Later, in the reception area on my way up to the room, I met Wayan, the Balinese intelligence officer. He was the one we had met the night of the harbourmaster, the man with the startling facial scar. Wayan was now assigned to the hotel and the airport, his main task to watch visitors coming in and out of the country, so we often saw him. Since the harbour master night, he always greeted us like old friends. This night he told me excitedly that he had been assigned to accompany us on our official Dili rounds the next day, and then to come to Ataúro and stay with us while the embassy people were there. He was to be "our spy" for several days and, as he had never been to Ataúro before, and we were "his friends", he was very happy about that.

When I finally got to my room Anton was sitting on the narrow balcony that overlooked the sea. I joined him and we sat there in silence, our feet propped on the bottom rail, watching little waves running in to shore on the lamp-lit beach. There was a strong smell of frangipani from the tree below and people laughed in the courtyard. We could make out the shape of Ataúro across the water, black against the night sky, like a large crouching animal on the horizon. We sat for a long time, the words we were not saying forming themselves in the soft, dark air and floating around us. Suddenly, remembering his early morning departure the next day we simultaneously said, 'You should sleep.' We laughed.

Anton lay on one narrow bed and I on the other. We were very aware of each other's presence in the darkness. We could hear each other's breathing. It was exquisite and painful, lying there watching shadows on the ceiling, hearing voices and laughter a long way away, hearing the sea; the scent of frangipani wafting through the open balcony doors, listening to each other breathe.

Just when I thought he was asleep, Anton spoke. 'Gabrielle,' he said. His voice was quite soft, but the word loomed large in the little room. 'Gabrielle,' he said, 'I'm afraid.' He reached out across the narrow space between the two beds and took my hand. His was soft and cool, his palm smooth. 'I think I'm in love with you,' he said. And his words drifted around us in the dark and played across the reflections of light on the wall.

And… Anton, my brother, workmate, friend, playmate, I think I'm in love with you too, said my heart. But I was silent. There were too many differences, too many complications. Our hands swung gently in the space between the two beds and his fingers stroked mine. I whispered his name but was still held silent by my fear of where this might go.

He came to my bed and lay with me, his lean body beside mine, his arms around me, his face close. We lay nestled together on the narrow bed like small children, awestruck at what possibilities the world might hold for us. We'd never been physically close like this; this new dimension was enormous, feeling the beating of each other's hearts and the rhythms of each other's breath.

In the early hours of the morning he left, brushing my forehead with a quick, sweet kiss, stroking my cheek gently with the backs of his fingers. Then he was gone, and I continued to doze on, images of him heading out over the dark sea on the Manucoco warming my heart.

THE VISITORS AND THE SPY

The deputy ambassador, the NZAid development person and the military attaché from the Jakarta embassy were relaxed and easy company, good-humoured and interested in everything. The East Timor provincial government people were welcoming, and I loved the opportunity to tell them the story of our Ataúro work.

As usual, we were leaving Dili before dawn the next morning, so we ate early and turned in for an early night. The New Zealanders had not brought an alarm clock, so they asked me to wake them at 3:00 am. They were staying in the fancier section of the hotel and on my way back to my own budget room, I again met Wayan, the spy, in the foyer. He told me he was all ready to go and was excited about the trip, but he was worried about waking up because he didn't have an alarm clock. I smiled. Of course, I would wake him too.

I set my alarm for just before three. By now, I was quite used to snapping out of sleep and into action before dawn. I had a torch to help find my way, giggling at the irony of it, through the dimly lit, deadly quiet areas of the hotel – first to the spy's room where I tapped on the door as loudly as I dared, and then on to the rooms of the visitors on whom he was to spy.

In the dark, our group of five walked the two blocks down to the beach to where Guido, Domingos and Ilario were waiting as planned, the Manucoco bobbing up and down on the greasy waters of Dili Harbour. We set out towards the island just before the pale dawn light leeched into the eastern sky.

I was distracted. Once we were on the boat and out on the sea, I began to feel nervous. Not about the New Zealanders' visit. I knew our work, the kindergarten, our plans to work with the teachers to develop early education in the primary schools would impress the visitors and guarantee us their further support. There was no doubt in my mind about that; our program was a good one and had the full support and involvement of the community. I knew also that, although what we could offer in the way of accommodation and hospitality was very basic, our visitors would love their couple of days with us on the island.

I was nervous about meeting Anton. After the night in the Turismo room, after his declaration of love, I was nervous about arriving on the beach and meeting him. The anticipation was intense. I knew that when our eyes met, there would be a confirmation or a denial, a commitment to something that might, in reality, be just a fantasy, that perhaps should remain just a fantasy.

Falling in love was not, for us, a sensible thing to do. Our relationship was a work relationship. We were in East Timor. He was Indonesian, theoretically the enemy of the Timorese people. Our cultures and life experience are very different. He was years younger than I am. And if his eyes confirmed the love timidly declared two nights ago, I feared that nothing would be the same again. It was a big thing, a huge thing. It was surely inevitable that, regardless of embassy visitors and spies, our eyes would connect when the boat bounced onto the beach. I was sure that when that happened the world would change. Anything might happen. Fish might leap out of the sea. The sun might spin across the sky. It felt that big. I was like a teenager in love; it was scary.

My companions on the boat were preoccupied with the smooth blue sea and a pod of dolphins playing around the boat. Thankfully, because the chugging motor made conversation difficult, everyone on this adventure was enjoying their own private reverie while I was trying to calm my thoughts, rationalise, slow my breathing, prepare. Perhaps he had seen sense. Perhaps he hadn't. Perhaps this was folly. Perhaps it wasn't. Where my heart was right now was clear, but where was my brain? Where was his? Did that matter? Where would it go? How would it end? How would it begin? My thoughts and emotions swayed as the boat did on the waves… between danger and safety, love and denial of it.

When we rounded the headland I saw that he was already on the beach, standing tall, looking seawards, watching, waiting. Oh. Our eyes met from a distance, locking as the boat drew closer, tentatively searching. Then we smiled. It was easy, really.

There was the usual scramble on the shore, children and dogs running up to stare as our queasy visitors lowered themselves into the water, splashing into the shallows and stamping their feet on solid sand. As we walked home along the beach that morning, my heart silently singing, a huge school of little fish really did leap out of the water; once, twice, three times – hundreds of little fish leaping, shining silver in the sky. I saw them. We all saw them. And, although I can't be quite as sure of this, I thought I caught a glimpse of the early morning sun spinning on the horizon.

THE VISIT

The New Zealanders were interested in all facets of our work and were good houseguests. They adapted to our simple facilities and enjoyed the adventure of being on this remote island. They adapted to our simple diet of fresh baked rolls for breakfast and lunches, and dinners of rice and fish and local greens – and they brought New Zealand wine which makes our meals grand!

We took them to visit the kindergarten, to Baptista's chicken-raising groups, to the primary school. We arranged meetings with teachers and community leaders. We talked with them about other needs and possibilities for the island. They wanted to learn all they could about what we were doing and were keen to continue supporting our programs and me. Wayan, our spy, went with us everywhere, during the day maintaining what he deemed a respectable professional distance from us, and at night joining us as a friend on the veranda.

It was an enjoyable three days. On the last day we visited Bikeli Village then went on for a picnic at Akrema, a small hamlet on a dazzlingly white sandy beach on the northern tip of Ataúro. Three village heads came with us and Akrema people honoured the visit by bringing us freshly caught fish. We ate it, grilled over a beach fire, with the cassava we brought with us wrapped in banana leaves. We foreigners and Anton splashed about in the warm, shallow, blue water of that northernmost point.

AKREMA

We are returning from our visit to Akrema. The Manutasi, the larger wooden boat we are using is full: the Jakarta visitors, the friendly spy, Baptista, Guido, our local leaders, and Anton and me all crowded in. By chance, Anton is sitting high at the stern of the boat and I am sitting high in the bow. Over the tops of other people's heads, our eyes meet. Our friends are holding onto hats and talking and pointing at flying fish and dolphins; Anton and I are looking at each other.

I look into his eyes, drawn into the depths of them. The motor chugs and the sea flies by, and this time we do not smile. We continue looking as the boat bounces in the rougher sea around the headland. This is not a light-hearted moment; some intense force has hold of us. It is spiritual. It is sexual. And we are caught, have fallen voluntarily into the depths of it and, acknowledging the terrifying connection that is love and lust, we are, at either end of the boat, acknowledging a sort of primordial communion. I feel dizzy with it. My body burns. Perhaps I have had too much sun.

Others laugh and point at the coral below us in the sea, a seabird, a lone fisherman in his outrigger. Anton and I look above their heads at each other. The boat chugs on from Akrema, past the little settlements of Baroana, Pala, Dotan, Beloi. I am facing backwards looking at Anton and he is facing forwards looking at me. The boat is bouncing on the sea and the wind is blowing through our hair.

It is like falling into a huge hole, no beginning, no end, like a dip into the shadows of this world of ancestral spirits, angels and all that is powerful, mysterious and holy and over which we have no control. Surprisingly, the others don't seem to notice, they're busy pointing out flying fish, big bommies and coral ferns beneath the surface, a sea eagle high in the sky. They shout and laugh as the boat dances into waves and seawater splashes over them.

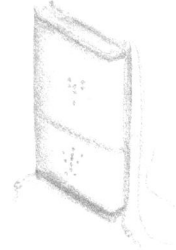

The trance snaps when we arrive on the beach in Vila with a bump. After the usual bustle of finding sandals, bags and hats at the bottom of the boat; getting back to the office and greeting the excited dogs; cooking the fish we'd brought back from Akrema; bathing in turn and eating rice and fish and greens and drinking the last bottle of NZ wine; talking about the wonderful day, then trooping one by one to various makeshift beds; Anton and I are alone. We are alone and no longer fearful. We embrace, feel each other's skin, each other's breath, each other's heartbeat; back in our known world we laugh with the relief and pleasure of it and kiss our first kiss, which is beautiful.

Months of living and working with him, sharing stories, facing challenges, resolving problems, swimming with him in the warm sea, singing into the night and laughing, laughing, laughing with him, have led me to love and a beautiful, fervent lust for this man, this Anton. But we are in Indonesia, we are in a small Timorese village, we have a public profile here. These are constraints to any consummation of our declared feelings for each other. He goes to his bed in the back room that, while our house is full, he's sharing with Baptista and I to mine where Tipah is already sleeping. But the touch of him I carry with me: a sweet, balm on my skin.

FEET

There was a spot in our garden where a large cement water tub reflected the overhanging branches of the neem and custard apple trees that form a small, shady arbour around it. Sometimes little birds dipped into the tub and splashed there, sometimes black and white butterflies flitted above the water. I would go there to sit on a log and watch the birds, or watch the boats drifting on the sea on the other side of the fence, spy on people strolling on the beach road, read; sometimes I went there to attend to my neglected hands and feet.

One Sunday afternoon Anton, uninvited, found me there. He dragged up a log in the shade beside me. Without a word he took my tools – soap, nail brush, clippers, file – and put them on his log. He took my hand and looked long at it, then began to trim and clean it, dipping into the tub for cool leaf-speckled water to wash it.

'My hands are awful,' I protested. He ignored me. 'They are farmer's hands,' I said. He said nothing and continued to trim and file and clean, blowing away the filings with a warm breath, bathing the skin with cool water, patting it dry with my sarong. And then he took my other hand. 'I should take better care of them,' I said.

Silence.

He took a small jar from his pocket and tipped a pool of its contents into his hand. Coconut oil; it was golden, thick, creamy, smelling of the wood fire that produced it. He worked it into my skin until my fingers were warm and soft in his. Each hand, each finger, each vulnerable space between each finger receives his attention and when he finished, he held them up for us both to admire.

'I love your hands,' he said and kissed them, one kiss for each clean finger. He reached for my feet.

'Oh, no,' I protested weakly. 'My feet are worse than my hands.'

But he took them one at a time and washed them, scrubbing carefully with the brush and the soap, with water from the tub. My feet were not beautiful. Broad and neglected, they were but he began to trim and file away the rough skin, holding my foot tenderly, attending to each stubby toe and grubby nail. He worked slowly and methodically. It was Sunday. Children played in boats, and people strolled along the beach; there was time for feet.

When they were done, he rinsed them with dippers of cool water and fondled them dry with the sarong. With the oil he massaged my ankles, the tops of my feet, the heels and soles. His long fingers wove between my toes, one by one, lingering there, oily, warm, gently moving in the cradles between each one. He did not look at me, only at my feet, his fingers moving ever so slowly, slowly between my toes… aware of the changing rhythm of our breathing, we sat in silence and birds return to dip in the tub beside us.

When the job was done Anton held my feet up like a prize, a trophy, and announced, as if to an audience, that these were good feet, that walked through sand and mud and soil, on rocks, through chicken shit, long grass and thorns. 'I have seen it myself,' he said. 'These feet climb rough mountain tracks in rubber flip-flops, they slide down rough, rocky paths. They're useful feet that go to people in faraway places. They may not be as beautiful as some,' he glanced at me, 'but I love them.'

He kissed each of them, and at that moment I loved them too.

AMBON

Anton's stories of Ambon were vivid. Before I had been there, it was already embedded in my imagination, a lively city described through the experiences and adventures of the child Anton: a skinny little boy truanting from school to dive in the warm, murky sea of its bay; a self-conscious teenager flirting with girls in the shade of its fig trees; a lanky soccer and basketball player competing on its sports fields; a keen student studying the sea, fish and fisheries at its university. Anton was the eldest son of an upstanding Ambonese Christian family and before I ever visited, I felt that through his stories I knew his city, his home and his family like the back of my hand.

And when I did visit, everything about his house was so familiar to me: the garden; the entrance; the living room hung with his father's paintings; the beautiful log carved and dragged inside to become a permanent sculpture; the large kitchen with its tiled floor and stacks of tins for the sago cakes his mother made; the small dining area overlooking the garden; the stairway to the second floor and Anton's bedroom with the wooden lowboy and faded patchwork bedcover his mother and aunt had made him years ago. They gave me his room to sleep in and it was like a trip into his past, a step right into all the stories I'd heard from him.

I felt comfortable and was delighted to be there. Anton's mother and father were welcoming. His sister was friendly. The women and I spent hours sitting at the dining table or on the upstairs balcony, talking about our lives and other people's lives and where the world and Indonesia were going. Talking about Timor. His sister had recently been living and studying in Germany, and had an interesting perspective on such things. They asked lots of questions about Anton and about the work he was doing. They were very proud of him and concerned about him being tucked away there on an island in an isolated, unfriendly part of the world.

We talked like sisters and friends, but I didn't tell them I was in love with their boy. Although my admiration for their son and brother must've shone in my eyes and sparkled in my voice, they did not guess at the depths of it. Before I'd left Ataúro, Ant had suggested I talk about our relationship with his mother if the time seemed right. He wanted his mother to know. He wanted her blessing. I did too. But I hesitated each time I was on the brink of telling her... I sensed that although she liked me, and held my hand and laughed with me, her embrace could not include my being in a loving relationship with her firstborn son. Anton's position in the family came with certain familial expectations. So, on that issue, I was silent.

I'd gone to Ambon by ship – one of the big Pelni Line government ferries that each fortnight crossed the seas of eastern Indonesia and passed through Dili on its way to Ambon and Jayapura, West Papua. I was going to the Tanimbar Islands on a university assignment and, although the Pelni ferry sailed past those islands on its way from East Timor to Maluku, it did not call there so I had to go to Ambon first and fly back to Tanimbar in a tiny Summer Institute of Linguistics plane lent to us for this visit. I was to run a teachers' in-service training there for a week. The Pelni boat was, as always, crowded and late leaving, but for the first time ever on an Indonesian ferry I had a sleeping berth and enjoyed a bunk with fresh sheets and silence as we rocked over the waves through the islands of Timor and Maluku. It was an overnight trip and not long after breakfast we arrived in Ambon.

I was to spend two nights with Anton's family before flying

to Tanimbar a precious opportunity for me to listen to their stories of him, watch their faces that showed hints of his smile, look into the same deep eyes as his, hear echoes of his laugh, his humour; it was an opportunity to experience the warmth, the fervent "goodness" of his family. It was a joy for me to see and feel where he had come from, in which nest this beautiful man had been nurtured.

On the second morning when I rose early and looked out from my upstairs window, I saw Anton's father in the garden below – in the pale dawn light under a pink and gold sky, he was pruning the hedge. In the silence, the man's concentration was intense as his long fingers moved carefully over the branches. Every now and then he stepped back to check, as an artist does, the symmetry and balance of his work. As morning birdsong begin to ring sharp and clear through the still air, I saw that he too was singing, or perhaps praying, as he worked.

KUPANG

Anton and I were asked by the university to make a trip to Kupang to visit a well-reputed community-based development organisation and, if we think it's suitable, to organise a work exchange/training placement there for Baptista and Guido. We have been recommending that Baptista and Guido be given an opportunity off the island to broaden their experience in agriculture and fishing and we were all excited about the chance for them to go to West Timor.

For Anton and me there were other possibilities. There would be no Baptista, no Alu and especially no Tipah; we would be alone for five days. When the voice of our boss crackled out of the radio asking us if we'd be willing to go, we exchanged a swift glance across the office, across the heads of the others. Of course, we both agree to go and for a little while can hardly look each other in the eye in anticipation of those other possibilities. That anticipation was delightful and excruciating.

Preparation for the visit to Kupang took a long time. Weeks. The overland trip when we finally left Dili was also long. We were crammed into the small bus with the usual bustle of people, upside-down chickens and rice bags, a couple of bleating goats and one fat pig on the roof. The bus left the Dili terminal in the afternoon and arrived in Kupang about dawn the next day. There was no border crossing in those days, just a security point to check who was coming overland into East Timor.

In Kupang we stayed in a pleasant little hotel overlooking the sea. We shared a room. We sat together on the balcony and looked at the stars. We held hands. We kissed. We laughed. We were timid. We were cautiously and delectably lustful. And, at last, we became lovers.

The five days there were beautiful. We visited the potential host organisation each morning to learn about its programs, in the afternoons we walked on the beach and through the little town; we ate at stalls that sold fresh chicken and grilled corn, at restaurants that sold spicy vegetables and rice, we drank beer on our balcony, we talked and laughed about life, the universe and its possibilities. And we made love.

Anton was not an experienced lover but because he was tender and romantic, imaginative, sincere, warm and attentive and very funny, he was, as I knew he would be, a wonderful one.

AN ARGUMENT

When we returned from Kupang, Tipah, self-appointed guardian of my soul, sensing that her worst fears had come to pass, was not happy. Of course, in true Indonesian fashion, Ant and I were discreet and the actual issue (our changed relationship) was never mentioned or displayed in any way but Tipah was uncharacteristically distant and scornful towards us. One night, bursting with moral outrage, she chose a moment when Anton was alone with her to speak with him, knowing I would hear the conversation from the next room.

I listened for a while, trying to decide if I wanted to be involved in this very Indonesian conversation. I was irritated by the vague and euphemistic terms Tipah was using to scold Anton, and irritated by his seeming inability to tell her to stop. My patience was waning. Tipah was being very Javanese. Anton was being very Ambonese. Two Indonesian Christians of different persuasions, they had the "Christian-connect" and I listened, stunned, to hear our Tipah sinking a fierce arrow of accusation right into Ant's heart. Jesus was, of course, at the centre of it all and although I was shocked at her ferocity, I knew in some way her fears arose, in part at least, from a genuine love for me.

Ant was not experienced in the matter of love or attack and was no match for Tipah that evening. Perhaps he felt his own kind of Christian guilt as her arrow twists; perhaps he even felt, in his old-fashioned way, that he had "done me wrong". He was defensive and virtually speechless. Faced with the barrage of her righteousness he was, perhaps not as cavalier, not as liberated as he had thought he could be.

Eventually, listening to these two discussing me, arguing about what was good for me and what was not, I could stand it no longer. I am older and I am Australian and, though all that biblical and morality talk is not my talk, my own position is a valid one. Sometimes, in my attempt to be culturally sensitive I forget the validity of my own experience and my own culture and bend too far – but not that night.

I strode onto the veranda and told them so. It was a cultural clash but, as I am louder, and took them both by surprise by being totally out of character in my anger, I gained the upper hand and my words ended the dispute. As I turned away from them, I was still angry. None of this was Tipah's business and I really didn't want to see the glimpse of Anton's weakness that had flashed before me. I flounced off.

Alone in my room, I grabbed the "happy moment" photo Anton had taken of me in Kupang and tore it to pieces, tossing the scraps of it into the kitchen wastebasket. I went to bed, seething with the impossibility of ever achieving understanding in this matter, convinced the whole love affair was a foolish mistake. In the confusion, and bruised by Tipah's moral battering, I even resentfully considered the possibility of actual sinfulness in it. The household was quiet.

When I woke the next morning the first thing I saw, propped up on the table beside my bed, was the Kupang photo. The torn pieces had been carefully pieced and pasted back together and my restored face beamed happily out through the cracks in it.

PART SEVEN

DECISION

I don't remember any discussion about whether I'd stay on Ataúro longer than the initial six months I'd agreed to. It just seemed to be assumed – by the university, the Ataúro community and its leaders, and my work family here – that our work would continue and me with it. I had no desire to leave and was excited by some of the ideas we had for more education work with the teachers. But I asked myself, not for the first time, just what I was doing in East Timor; what was my part in this troubled little neck of the woods?

To foreign activists, I might have been seen as working for the enemy instead of supporting East Timor in the struggle to free itself from Indonesian occupation. Significantly though, I never came across a Timorese person who accused me of that. My initial reason for being there was clear and simple: I was invited by the community leaders to help them establish a kindergarten. That initial invitation led to all kinds of other community work to which I could contribute. I had been asked by community leaders to do this and now I was being asked by them to continue.

I believed education would help improve their lives no matter what the eventual outcome of this deadly cycle of military oppression and resistance was. Education nourished freedom.

My purpose was altruistic, but my work anything but thankless. I loved the adventure of living on Ataúro and got enormous satisfaction from my life there. Anton and I worked well together, and I was in love with him. Our Timorese workmates Guido, Baptista, Dulce, Teresa, Zelia and now Domingos, Julieta and Tomas worked well as part of our team. The work was challenging and my position unique. I worked for a well-reputed Indonesian university, but well away from the campus and from the scrutiny of Dili so, to a certain extent, I had free rein to work with the community as they wanted. If I were to stay on, I could not be involved in the politics of East Timor. I had to keep a low profile; any suspicion of suspected political activism would have me out of East Timor immediately and that would be the end of that. And the truth was that although the Indonesian military was despicable in its heavy handedness and strategically foolish in thinking its brutality would ever win their war, I saw the broader picture was not always as black and white as outsiders perceived.

I believed in the work I was doing with the PPSDM team and the Ataúro people, and I truly did not believe it was my right to choose or influence the political future of their country. At PPSDM we nonchalantly bribed the Dili military with palm wine, dried fish and cassava in return for facilitation and regular entrance into the harbour, and we carried supplies of the same Ataúro delicacies for the resistance fighters in the mountains. Our boat, the Manucoco, regularly carried sacks of these goodies for both sides and that worked well for us as we straddled the fence, working away at the grassroots with poor, isolated fishers and farmers and their children.

TIPAH'S MARRIAGE

Tipah's family had agreed for her to come to East Timor for six months. and in June 1996, it was time for her to return to them in Java. She was twenty-six years old and single and both she and her parents were increasingly worried about the prospect of her remaining unmarried and childless for the rest of her life. But not long before we had left Java, she had met a possible marriage candidate and, while she was away, he had asked her parents if they would accept him as her suitor. We heard this by one of the few letters we received from them, and she was very excited. She asked me if I thought the young man would be suitable and I thought he was. From the moment they had met at my house in Salatiga, I had noticed a certain twinkle in his eye and saw he appreciated the rather quirky Tipah. Although conservative in many ways, Tipah was certainly not your average Javanese village girl, and for her to find someone who accepted that in the conservative society of rural Central Java was quite special.

Her prospective husband was a Christian as she was, and that was important for their future. Sad to leave her Ataúro friends (who she would never see again) Tipah was nevertheless excited about returning home and to the next phase of her life.

We all missed her but, to be truthful, her not being part of her household gave Anton and me much more freedom and he moved back to my side of the house where he had lived prior to our coming. We lived together in a more intimate sense, though of course, if not secretly, then at least discreetly. We were aware of the delicacy of the situation and, although our relationship might be common knowledge in the village everyone chose to be tactful about it. That was the Indonesian way. Baptista still lived with us, and Alu and the others were at the house or office each day so, even without the presence of the lively Tipah, we remained a happy family.

THE GHOST UNDER THE FIG TREE

After Tipah went back to Java, Alu spent more time with me. She took over all the tasks Tipah had done around the house and office, and became more confident. She took it on herself to keep me company – often coming for a walk on the beach with me or sitting with me on the veranda at night if I was alone. She would occasionally tell me stories of her childhood or of her family – always in a barely audible voice and only giving me the bare-bones version unless I asked for more detail.

One night when we had eaten late, Alu came to me and asked if I could walk her home to her house down the beach.

'It's late and dark, I'm afraid to go alone, Ibu,' she whispered.

Anton had gone up to meet someone at the clinic, Baptista had gone visiting and I was the only one left, so Alu and I set out down the road. It was about 9 o'clock and the night was dark. In the dull light shining from Vasco's collapsing stone veranda as we passed, we saw a figure – an unfamiliar man – standing under the big fig tree where Vasco's monkey was chained. There was something unsettling about the man. The way he stood? The way he looked at us? His stillness? We both hesitated, nudged each other.

'*Bonoite*,' I called. No reply.

'*Selamat Malam*,' I tried. No reply.

Alu tried both greetings. No reply.

Timorese and Indonesian people do not ignore greetings. Not ever. But this man just stood under the tree staring at us. We hurried past, increasing our pace and keeping our distance from the tree, eyes down. We turned the corner to the road that ran along the beach.

'Who *was* that man, Lu?' I whispered when we had gone a little way.

'I don't know, *Ibu*.' There was panic in her voice. 'I've never seen him before.'

'Me neither.'

'He didn't answer me.'

'He didn't,' Lu's voice was a barely audible whisper. '*Ibu*, I think it's a ghost!'

I'm not afraid of ghosts, so I took her hand and we walked on beside the whispering sea into the very dark night. Then suddenly, sending a shiver up my spine, something dawned on me. 'Lu,' I gasped. 'After I've taken you home, I'll have to walk back alone.'

'Yes, *Ibu*,' she spoke now in a hoarse, urgent horror-movie voice. 'If Edgar or Juliao or Guido are not at home to walk back with you, *Ibu*… you'll have to come alone – back past the tree – past him – in the dark.'

It wasn't that I didn't believe in ghosts I just had never had any reason to feel afraid of them but that night I was spooked at the idea of walking back past the fig tree alone with that unknown man – or ghost – staring out of the shadows. Simultaneously Lu and I whispered, 'Let's go back to the office and wait for Anton.' And we turned and started running back towards the corner and the shadowy fig tree.

As we ran in the dark, I scanned the area around the tree to see if the ghostly figure was still there. He seemed to have disappeared but was perhaps still watching us from behind the broad trunk. In my concern I became disoriented, miscalculated the junction of the roads and turned too soon, flew over the 50 cm high culvert and into the deep concrete drain that takes floodwaters when it rains, into the sea. I screamed as I flew and landed with a thud; Lu kept on screaming when I stopped.

People came running out of the dark; Guido arrived first. I was lying stunned and sore and had to be helped out and supported while I hobbled back up to the office. Alu kept close by my side as they laid me down and examined my wound – a gravel rash, bruising and a cut on my hip where I'd hit the concrete edge on the way down and the base at the bottom of my fall. Anton bathed it gently with warm salty water and a cloth. I fainted. They rubbed some ointment over the broken skin. I fainted again. I came to with Alu and Anton beside me. Alu handed me a glass of sweet tea.

'What about the man under the tree?' I asked her.

She shuddered. 'No one else saw him,' she said. 'It was a ghost, *Ibu*,' and her voice still wavered.

I looked up at Anton whose face remained concerned but unconvinced.

'You stay here and drink your tea and I'll walk Lu home,' he said, stroking my forehead.

Alu and I grew closer after that night and had many whispered conversations about it. Whenever we did, her eyes would become big and her voice small. Perhaps mine did too. Sometimes we laughed about it, but it was never completely a joke. I still have a little scar on my left hip to remember it by.

THE DEATH OF MY FATHER

My father died the first year I was on Ataúro; I heard that news out of our crackly radio. It was Jenny's voice calling me from Satya Wacana that afternoon, and she told me as gently as she could. My father was dead.

Our work stopped. People embraced me. Guido got the boat ready to go to Dili and we left at dusk. I felt so very far away from my family, and from Dili I could at least phone and talk with them. I had spoken to my dad a couple of weeks before and he had told me confidently he would be waiting for me when I came home for a holiday in December. He had been ill but had reassured me he was getting better…

It was already dark when we reached Dili Harbour and we hit the reef on the way in. The crew didn't usually take the *Manucoco* to Dili after dark and in their concern to get me closer to my family with a phone call they had rushed and miscalculated the tide. There was no damage to the boat, and not much to the reef, but we were wedged. We sat in silence and waited for the water to rise so we could rise with it and push the boat back into the channel. The sea all around us gave me space for grieving. It gave breadth and depth and whispered its songs into my soul. Wedged on the reef that night the waves rocked us gently. Stretching out to the stars, the trillion lights of eternity, the sea took my tears, succoured my sorrow, sang my pain.

I did not go back to Australia for my father's funeral. Although the ceremony was deferred as long as possible so I could be there, it would have been difficult. If I was to retain my Indonesian work visa I would have had to go back to Java while the university organised my exit permit in Semarang. It may have been possible in the time we had, but I felt strongly I wanted time to think about my father and his passing, spend time with him and not haggling with bureaucrats and hanging around airports. Perhaps it was selfish not to be there with and for the rest of my family, but I knew my five siblings and their families would be there for my mother and each other.

The day of Louis Edward's (Ted's) funeral was a beautiful one. In the morning I went up the hill above the headland where there was a forest of gum trees overlooking the south-eastern part of the strait. I took woven cloth, shells, seed pods, three cigarettes, three coloured stones, candles, my sketch book and pencils. I made an altar at the foot of one of the white eucalypts. I spent the day there high above the sea, close to the spirit of my dad. He was a recreational fisherman, a lover of boats, a lover of the sea. I faced the direction of Australia and his sea and spent the day in prayer, tears and song – his songs – laughter, drawing, writing, recollecting. It was a beautiful day that is etched in my heart forever.

For many years after that, on the anniversary of my dad's funeral I went up the mountain to celebrate. Sometimes Anton came too but when up there, he chose another copse, another outlook and spent time in his own contemplation, giving me space.

Note: it is customary in Timor and around the islands to add cigarettes to the offerings in ceremonies for men if they were smokers, as my dad was.

LAUTEM

Anton and I took a trip to the east, to Los Palos in the Lautem District and to the very eastern point of East Timor, to the village of Tutuala. We'd both been in East Timor quite a long time but mainly on Ataúro; we'd hardly seen any other parts of the province at all. At Easter we took four days off and travel overland, passing through Manatutu and Bacau and along the coast to Lautem. An Indonesian doctor friend organises a lift for us with a medical team going from Dili to Los Palos for the Easter break.

The coastline from Dili to Bacau is beautiful. As we wound around cliffs and travel the coastal lowlands, we see Ataúro across the sea. It was fascinating for Anton and me to see different perspectives of the island that was our home. It was good to see the mainland coastal villages and towns along the road too, but until our island was out of sight, we were preoccupied with it – its shape from this angle, its line from that.

The others in the van, a Timorese doctor and several Indonesian and Timorese nurses, were good company, returning home for Easter celebrations in high spirits. We stopped for fresh grilled fish and palm wine at the stalls along the road. We explored the market in Bacau. In those days, foreigners were rare and people followed us to stare at me. Timorese children and teenagers were curious, but still friendly and polite; white foreigners were still the "good guys" then. Soldiers and police took an interest in our group too; white foreigners were not considered to be the "good guys" by them and they trailed us around the market. A policeman asked the doctor who I was and where we were heading, but did not approach me directly.

Along the roads we saw "hidden" military camps, perched high above the road on hills that afford good views along the coast and into the villages. These camps were "hidden" from view, but water drums waiting to be filled on the side of the road below usually gave them away. You saw the drums, you looked up, you saw a path through the grass that led your eyes to the thatched or tin roofs of a camp. They were not really hidden at all, and sometimes you could even see a flagpole with the red and white cloth fluttering in the breeze. There were dozens of camps. They were part of the serious game being played out on the mainland. People were being watched and the watchers were making sure that people know they were being watched. There was a level of fear and intimidation on the mainland that was not on Ataúro. Our Timorese and Indonesian companions made jokes about the military as we drove along. Laughter was a way to connect. It was a way for ordinary Timorese and Indonesian friends to cope with the grim reality of what was happening in this land.

We reported to the local police, a requirement for travel in all of eastern Indonesia and more especially in East Timor. They were tight-lipped and officious behind their desks and then lighthearted and friendly when they come outside. We spend a night at a homestay in Los Palos town. Surrounded and stared at by curious onlookers, we ate at a small food stall in the main street. We wanted to see traditional Los Palos houses and that district's famous tais – back-strap loom weaving – so we wandered around the small town looking and talking with people who were friendly and helpful. They were always inquisitive about me and about my relationship with Anton. We were reminded by them that, while we were there, we were being watched by the military. Life in this part of the country was like that for everyone.

The next day we took a lift with the local ambulance driver to the village of Tutuala. Our plan was to visit Jaco Island on the eastern-most tip of East Timor. We'd heard about the white sands, the magnificent reef and the dugongs and turtles that lived in the sea grasses around this sacred island. We were lucky because the ambulance driver, Agusto, was a Tutuala man, going home for a couple of days. He was happy to take us with him.

The ambulance was old and rattled along the dirt roads, while above the noise Agusto shouted explanations and pointed out places of interest: the Lake Ilhalaru; the transmigration villages (settlements of people from other parts of Indonesia); deserted "ghost" villages from which, Augusto told us, the local people have all been killed or "removed".

We arrived in Tutuala in the late afternoon. The village sits on a magnificent cliff overlooking the sea and, in the distance, Kisah Island. Jaco Island is hidden under the ridge and out of sight. Jaco and Ataúro are the only East Timorese offshore islands and, unlike Ataúro, Jaco is uninhabited. Tutuala was eerily deserted.

Agusto, once there, was tense, anxious to be rid of us. He dropped us off unceremoniously at the Portuguese guesthouse on top of the hill. The building was a relic of former days – a storybook house made of white stone held together with thick brown mortar and surrounded by a wide, white-tiled veranda. A gnarled tree had grown through its stone fence and the wind blew up and whistled around it. At the edge of the cliff, under an old climbing rose entwined trellis, were garden seats overlooking the sea far below. It was beautiful, but eerie. Doors and windows were closed. There was no sign or sound of life, just the wind around us as we sat on the arbour seat looking at the sea and wondering what to do next. We were puzzled and apprehensive. This was Indonesian military territory and we naturally thought of disaster.

But after a while, some children appeared; a small group came chattering up the path from the village. They told us everyone in the village had gone down to the beach for the festival of the sea worms and only some old people and a few children had stayed behind. They'd be gone all night and would, perhaps, be back tomorrow. I was familiar with the sea-worm festivals – they are celebrated on many islands at this time of the year – and I had attended the amazing Pasola ceremony that celebrates the sea worms in Sumba at this same time and had tasted the harvest of green worms that were a delicacy there. It was too late in the afternoon for us to go down to join people at the beach, the children tell us it is a five kilometre walk down the steep hillside.

Anton and I had a packet of biscuits and a bottle of water each. We had sarongs and toothbrushes. We could survive till the next day. We sat with the children watching the sea darken as the sun goes down. A couple of teenage boys appeared and warned us to be careful. They said the military was aggressively active in this area and people were afraid of them. Just before dark, the boys left us and we moved to the veranda of the guesthouse to make our night nest on the tiles.

'Fried chicken,' said Anton pointing to the first two plain biscuits when we sit down to our meal. 'These next four are fried noodles with pork and egg. The next spicy beef then chicken coconut curry – what would you like?'

As I reached for a biscuit I saw movement in the trees just below us, and a tiny red glow in the dark. The light was moving towards us – then there was another – not two but three, four, five, six glowing cigarettes coming our way.

'Soldiers,' Anton said. 'Be careful.'

They were young, uniformed soldiers and they came up to us out of the darkness as friendly as you please. Inviting themselves to sit with us, one or two of them began asking me questions in English. Where did I come from? How did I get there? Who was Anton? Could they practice speaking English with me? When their English ran out, they said, "You speak Indonesian, don't you?" And so, we knew they had been informed. Even speaking in Indonesian, they directed most of their conversation to me. Though I made attempts to include Anton, neither he nor they had any interest in talking with each other. Ant was decidedly disdainful and disinterested.

My way was to chat. I found out where the soldiers came from – from Bali and Java, one from Sumatra – and talked with them about their home provinces, asked them questions about their villages and their families back home. Although it was dark, I could see their faces when they were lit up by a puff on a cigarette. They were young. I listened to them talk about their homes and could imagine them in their villages. They were village boys, with mothers and grandmothers like the Javanese and Balinese mothers and grandmothers I knew; village boys who dress in beautiful Balinese temple clothes or clean sarongs and white jackets for the mosque.

I wondered if they were murderers. Killing and torture happened in this area. Were these boys part of that? I'm sure the old village women who are their grandmothers consider their boys heroes, here in the outpost defending their country, their flag. Didn't all grandmothers of soldiers believe that? And armed, in uniform and in enemy territory, aren't soldiers and grandsons conversely all murdering nationalists? I looked closely at the faces of the boys in the glow of their cigarettes. They had nice faces, soft, gentle Indonesian faces.

When they left us, I asked Anton if he thought they were killers but he didn't answer. We went back to our biscuits and to watching the magnificent inky sky light up with stars. We had a small torch for emergencies but apart from that, there were no lights except the millions, trillions of stars and their reflections dancing in the sea below. We sang some songs. We talked. Anton reminded me not to trust people who come to speak with me.

'We're not on Ataúro,' he said. 'You don't know who anyone is here, and they don't know you.'

It is true that I am often not wary enough. I speak openly to people; trust is a habit of mine that I like. But recognising the strategic line between openness and stupidity in certain circumstances is sometimes not easy for me. Here, I have nothing to hide really – except that my Indonesian work visa only gives me permission to teach at a university in Central Java and shows no official permission for me to be living and working in East Timor. Sometimes, according to Anton, I was careless with my words and he, who had grown up in an authoritarian military regime, knows better.

We spread our sarongs on the veranda, rolled spare T-shirts into pillows. Anton began to sing softly and I snuggled onto my bed of tiles. I had just begun to doze when a bright white light swept across my face, across the veranda and back again. I sat up, confused, shielding my eyes, unable to see anything but the brilliant light shining straight onto me.

'Military, Gabrielle,' Anton whispered. 'Careful.'

Men's voices apologised as the spotlight swept aside. Searching the area around us again, they told us not to worry. When the light was turned off, we were left with a gas lamp and a group of uniformed men staring at us. Some of them began opening the doors of the guesthouse, others watched as we tried to compose ourselves after the shock of their intrusion.

'Please come in,' a soldier invited us, opening the guesthouse doors. More lamps were lit. 'There's no problem,' he said hospitably as if he was the guesthouse owner. 'We can let you in. We've just come up to meet you and have a chat.' He giggled.

They were arranging chairs and lamps and I felt uneasy regardless of their assurances and their smiles. They were here to interrogate us and in no time at all Anton and I had been separated into different rooms, sitting in easy chairs across from smooth-talking senior soldiers. They spoke to me in Indonesian and were ever so polite. They asked the same questions several times: where did I come from and why was I there? I remembered my Indonesian good manners and used them exquisitely, I hoped.

I dropped the names of important people in Dili whom I vaguely knew and perhaps vaguely knew of me. To keep the interview conversational I used my usual tactic of asking my own questions: where do the soldiers themselves come from? Have they been long in Timor? Do they miss their families? Of course, I knew the towns some of them came from and could say a few things about them; Indonesians always have strong bonds with their villages (their kampungs) and if you have been there or even nearby, you have a tenuous link with them. I did not pretend the link was strong, but it was useful in forming momentary and difficult relationships. It did prove, at least, that I had spent a lot of time in Indonesia. Anton and I had nothing to hide – we really were just sightseers to this area – so I knew that telling the truth was the best strategy and knew Anton would agree.

The soldiers attempted to make their visit a friendly social occasion and it was almost midnight by the time they left. They departed with the doors still open and us inside, so we had access to big room and a comfortable bed with clean white sheets. They sniggered a little at this, of course. Anton was annoyed and still muttering about it as I fell asleep.

In the morning, the guesthouse and the village were still deserted. It was odd being the only ones there but just as we were about to tackle our remaining dry biscuits and water, a man appeared and introduced himself as Agusto's cousin. He invited us to breakfast at their house.

Agusto's house was a typical village house, with thatched roof, dirt floor, neat front room with artificial flowers on a sideboard and small, hard upholstered chairs for guests. Store biscuits and two warm cans of Coca-Cola were set out for us as a special treat by Agusto's wife, and his children sat in the doorway giggling shyly behind grubby hands. We were there only five minutes, still making introductory talk, when a messenger came to the door saying the military commander wanted to see Anton. Ant, surprised, apologised to our hosts and, muttering, left.

Agusto's family and I soon talked about our lives. They were careful to let me know about the dominance of the military here. It gave me an idea of what secrets, fear and caution they had to live with every day. As I sipped on warm Coke I was distracted by thoughts of Anton and what was happening. When I expressed my concern, one of Agusto's brothers was sent to find out.

'They're just talking,' he told us when he came back. 'He's alright. They're just asking him questions.'

After our night visit and interrogation, I couldn't imagine what questions there could still be left to ask. Obviously, our jovial and hospitable military friends did not trust us as much as they pretended to, and were pushing Anton harder.

'They probably think you are journalists, looking for stories,' suggested Agusto. 'They don't like that. There are too many things here they want to hide.'

Almost an hour passed and, in spite of the warmth of the family, I became more and more on edge. I decided I had to go and find Anton, so Agusto took me down through the rows of empty houses to the village centre. A sort of court had been set up there under some pepper trees. The commander and his right-hand men (some I recognised from the previous night) sat at a wooden table at one end, several soldiers (I couldn't see the Balinese grandsons among them) sat on plastic chairs down either side. Anton sat at the far end, facing the commander. Some villagers hung about to listen.

It was extraordinary. A shady courtroom set up in the middle of the village on a sunny Sunday morning and there was Anton at the centre of it, somehow looking cool, relaxed and dignified. The commander invited me to join them, and another plastic chair was put beside Anton's. At that stage, the conversation was about our work on Ataúro and I was amazed to see how much it was actually Anton who seemed to be directing it. He was name-dropping, talking about military personnel "friends" on Ataúro, telling jokes that made the commander laugh. My joining them somewhat spoiled the dynamic; the commander tried to include me in the conversation by asking questions about my work on Ataúro and about my relationship with Satya Wacana University. He obviously already knew the answers, but we made small talk for some time until there was nothing left to talk about. Everyone had become restless and nobody seems to know what to do next. It was like a social occasion that has ended but nobody was going to make the first move to leave. I could see that Anton, at least, has had quite enough and to my surprise, it was he who finally drew the session to a close.

'Well, sir,' he said with a subtle balance of politeness and disdain. 'If you have finished with us now, we would like to go. Thank you.'

I think the commandant and everybody else was taken aback by Anton's audacity. 'Thank you,' the big man said getting to his feet and taking control again. He nodded at me. 'There's one more thing Ibu. Now that you have seen this place it would be best for you to head back to Los Palos today. There's no need for you to go into the other villages in the area. No need at all. There's nothing to see. Some people here are still rebellious, and it could be dangerous for you. I'm sure you understand.' We didn't reply. 'As it happens,' he added, 'one of my men needs a lift back to Los Palos today. We would appreciate it if he could go with you. He could keep you company. He could practice his English.' They all laughed.

That afternoon we bumped back along the road to Los Palos, accompanied in the old ambulance by a soldier and his gun. As it happened, he had needed a lift back to the town. As it happened, he could make sure we got there without any diversions and as it happened, he could make sure our conversations with Agusto and his cousin were limited to chitchat.

In an overcrowded bus on the way back to Dili next day, I made up a not-very-clever ditty:

'We went to Lautem (the district of Los Palos)
To look in the sea
And what did we see?
We saw ABRI.
We went to Lautem
Just you and me
And who did we see?
The TNI'

The TNI (I/i is pronounced "ee" in Indonesian) – TNI is the more recent name of the military that previously was called ABRI.

Anton sat beside me, wedged tightly into place on our broken seat by a woman with a basket of dried fish and a man with a flea-bitten puppy. He stared straight ahead, unmoved by my song.

'You were a bit of a hero, Ant.' I squeezed his hand. 'You were brave. All those soldiers and guns… and you, as cool as a cucumber.'

He continued to stare straight ahead. I knew that his disdain, his hatred of the military went deep. He had no illusions and was deeply ashamed of their actions, not only in East Timor but also in other parts of his country.

'Of course, they're killers,' he said, finally answering my question from the night before. 'That's their job.'

MAY 3 1998

The *Manucoco* picks me up and cradles me as we cross the sea, rocking me gently as the sun rises over the mountains, over the city of Dili, over the water. I've been away in Java for two weeks and am returning to Ataúro. I find a spot on the narrow bench and wedge myself between the wall and the lumpy tarpaulin-covered boxes and bags piled up on the floor. I have a lifejacket for a pillow and an open window near my head for fresh air. The sea is rough and sprays of saltwater spill through it and onto my face; nevertheless, I sleep almost the whole journey. Drifting out of sleep, I open my eyes and see the familiar forms of the crew, hear their familiar teasing and their jokes: Guido, Metan, Freitas, Domingos; each with his own role on the little boat; each with his own social position in the village; each with his own distinctive style and character. Rough, seafaring men – my friends and workmates – they fit easily into my sleepy awareness, as does the salt spray, the tossing of the waves, the hum of the motor. It all feels normal and comfortable, ordinary even.

But as we near the island something stirs my soul. I am suddenly wide-awake, excited, impatient to see everything, wanting to smell and hear everything, absorb it: familiar rocks and beaches, tall palms, hidden houses; our quiet, green, wet world. Because the current is too strong today, we can't get over the reef at Vila so, regardless of my impatience to be home, we leave the boat at Makili Village and walk home over the rocks of the headland and coves. To friends, excited dogs and Anton.

MAY 7 1998

There's shouting out on the reef; it sounds like there's a boat out at the 'pintu masuk', the door – the deep channel that forms an entrance to the lagoon. It's the boys bringing a boat back from Dili: Nusantara 2 or Ekmotain or one of the Tasi Diaks. At low tide, they sometimes can't cross the reef and shout out for a canoe to come out and pick up passengers.

Men's voices call. They're calling, 'Oy! Oy!' It's eight-thirty pm. I'm making hot chocolate for Anton & me. I wonder if anyone's taking any notice of the shouting. Is anyone taking out a canoe or are the passengers having to wait till the tide rises? I'm getting ready to read my book. I put the milk on the bedside table and notice that voices are still calling. It seems a long time… is it low tide?

Suddenly it dawns on me and others Everyone is running outside, to the road, to the beach. Guido and Mingos, Anton, we are all running outside. Something is wrong out there – they've been calling out too long! They're calling for a different kind of help those voices, they're screaming for help! Anton tells Guido to get the *Manucoco*, take the life jackets, take the petrol; run! Guido and others are in and out grabbing things, we all run to the beach. The moon must be covered with cloud, it's dark. We can see the whites of waves breaking on the reef, it's high tide and the voices are still shouting over the water. They're close – at the entrance – but they keep shouting and shouting. Men's voices are screaming. I don't hear a woman's voice, not one.

'Anton, get someone to shout! Tell them help's coming! Let them know quickly!' I yell. But there's no loudhailer, and no reassuring voice reaches them or us. Only the waves and the terrible screams.

Alu is on the road, she's crying. She clings to me.

'They're all in the water, the boat has sunk. They're drowning, *Ibu*! They're drowning!' She is sobbing, her head is in my chest. She thinks it's the Nusantara! She thinks it's Edegar and Juliao, her brothers. No, this can't be true. The boat can't have sunk. We stand there helpless, listening to the voices, listening to the sea, seeing the white caps, not seeing anything else. Oh God Guido hurry! For God's sake get out there! Get the motor going! Why haven't they got the motor going? Get out to them!

The entrance is about 100 metres to our right. The *Manucoco* is anchored two hundred metres along the beach to our left. That's such a long way tonight. Alu and I stand holding on to each other. 'Pray,' Alu tells me. 'Pray.'

We see the shapes of the men down on the beach in the moonlight, preparing the boat. They seem to be moving very slowly. We hear the screaming voices to our right but see only the caps of waves; no boat, no people, nothing.

People come running down the road to the beach. Someone says, 'It's Ekmotain!' Januario's wife, owner of *Ekmotain*, is there with a bare shoulder and a terrible face. 'It's Ekmotain,' she repeats and starts running along the beach… then runs back and up the road. '*Maromak*!' (My God!).

The *Manucoco* boat is moving at last, a dark shadow on the sea, heading towards the entrance. The administrator's car comes down from his house above… it's all in slow motion.

'Go, quickly, shine the lights on the entrance. Give them some light.'

We run along the beach in front of the entrance. The lights of the car shine out on the sea but are too low, far too low. You cannot see a thing out in the waves. Fifty or so people have gathered on the beach now, around the glow of the car lights. Nobody knows what to do. I don't know what to do. Women on the beach are moaning, some are crying out, 'Maromak! Maromak!' (Oh God, my God!)

Two men stagger out of the sea and into the light, and drop to the stones. They're immediately surrounded by people rubbing their bodies, their legs. 'Clear the light path, clear the light path!' Nobody has a torch. 'Give them light on the sea!' Guido and his crew have thrown lifejackets into the sea and the *Manucoco* has gone out beyond the reef, beyond the light. On the boat, they have only my small dynamo hand-pumping torch and the moon is behind the clouds again. What on earth can they see out there?

Our orange lifejackets are floating in the sea. Some have dark bodies clinging to them, some float empty. The waves are big and the current is strong. The entrance is so close. So close! Not more than one hundred metres from the shore. The Ekmotain is out there. The *Manucoco* is out there. A large battered and broken cupboard washes in to the shore. There are no more shouts.

We stand gazing at the sea, praying. We hold on to each other. Small children see me, '*Selamat malam, Ibu,*' they say smiling and greeting me in Indonesian as though it's an ordinary night. They are happy to see me there on the beach. They watch adult faces. They follow adult eyes searching the sea. *Ekmotain* has sunk just 100 metres away.

For a long time – perhaps an hour – we watch as if in a dream, pacing up and down on the sand as men are washed in or struggle to shore. People are at the water's edge to pull them in. Seven, eight, nine men come out of the sea. Some still can make the sign of the cross before collapsing on the stones. We check their breathing, we turn them over, make the water run from their lungs. We are running up and down the beach. We are counting.

'How many passengers came from Dili?' I ask.

'Seventeen. Twenty. Twenty-two.' Too many.

'Who knows? How many women?'

'Five. Five women!' someone says. And not one of them has yet made it to the shore. In my heart then I know that the women will not be saved. Women do not know the sea, women are afraid, women are not strong in the water, women will surrender, the women will drown! They are a hundred metres from the shore and the water is black and rough; they will drown. And all I can do is stand there. Maromak! Maromak!

The *Manucoco* has gone back down the beach to anchor. They can't do any more. People call for the lifejackets to be brought back. People say some of the women passengers are from Vikeki; they wouldn't know the sea! People say one is heavily pregnant, someone says they had children with them.

Anton tells me that several people have been brought back to shore by the *Manucoco*. One is a young girl who has drowned. We run along the beach, stumble on the stones. The moon is brighter. The girl is on the sand with a group of people around her. She's not breathing. We turn her on her side. We clear her mouth of water and vomit. I breathe into her mouth. Her chest rattles. More vomit and water. I breathe into her body and Anton pumps her chest. But she's already dead. She's about fourteen years old. A man holds her upside down and shakes her roughly to get the water out. She is dead. Anton and another man carry her body along the beach and up to the clinic. There is no sign of the ambulance vehicle. I spit and spit and cry for the dead girl.

Guido and Metan brought in six people. One was a tiny baby floating on a jerrycan that was supported through the waves by one of the *Ecomotain* crew. That baby is alive! A distressed and badly injured man is carried up to the clinic. Anton sees another young girl there who he thinks is dead. He tells me another young woman in jeans is dead, but later we hear that she isn't.

Three women are still missing. Down on the beach, *Pak* Camat tells people to go out and keep looking. We can't see anything; the waves are big and the current is strong and three women are still out there in the sea. There is no bright light. Someone says if people go out into that sea searching, more people will drown. We stand there, helpless, looking at the sea.

I taste the dead girl's vomit in my mouth. I spit and spit. The car still ferries exhausted survivors to the clinic. We go home and sit at the table and don't know what to do. I bathe and change my clothes. I go out to the beach again. Some women tell me the second young girl is alive, not dead, and the injured man has badly cut feet and is in a lot of pain. It 's his baby boy who's survived, but his wife is still missing. She's a Macadade woman and they were coming to Ataúro to visit her family. The dead girl's missing mother is seven months pregnant. They came from Vikeki to visit family here. They are all Maria Lisboa's family and that pregnant mother is still in the sea.

At eleven o'clock Anton and I walk up to the clinic. People are sitting in the dark and in groups around the clinic lights. Some are crying, some softly moaning, some greet us in normal voices. We are all in shock. The nurses, surrounded by a group of spectators, are treating the injured man. There's no doctor. There's blood all over the white tiles. The man is moaning and groaning crying out, his foot and shoulder badly cut and he's in a state of shock. He knows his wife is still missing in the sea; he calls out for her.

In one of the two small clinic wards, the young girl who survived is wrapped in a dirty sheet and cradled by a young man sitting beside her on the bed. On another bed, Justino is sitting, shocked, exhausted, wrapped in a blanket and being given sips of water from a plastic cup. On the third bed is the body of the drowned girl wrapped in a striped sheet, her cold, blue feet sticking out.

Augustina, the Indonesian nurse, is calm. She tells me what she has done to help the survivors. She says shouldn't we call (radio) Dili and ask for help. What! Hasn't anyone called Dili? Surely the people in charge of this place have called Dili! Someone says they have and it's too late anyway… Augustina takes me to see the miracle baby – a three month old boy wrapped in bright pink cloth and lying in a glass case with a lamp to warm his little body. His eyes are bright and brown and search our faces through the glass. The nurses suck liquid from his chest with a thin white tube and feed him sugar water from a cup and spoon. We feel his plump arms and legs. They are growing warm. He has spent half an hour in the sea tossed about on a plastic jerrycan held by a half-drowned man and he is alive and calm and warm! His father is being stitched up, without anaesthetic, in the next room and his mother and two other women are still out in the sea.

We walk back down to the beach. It is almost deserted and bright now in the moonlight. We can't see or hear anything apart from the crashing of waves. No matter how hard we look into the water or how hard we listen we can't see or hear anything but the waves. Back at the house, Anton tells me he's never carried a dead body before, and the girl was very heavy. His arms are still shaking. His whole body is shaking. After a time, we are so exhausted we go to sleep.

MAY 8 1998

The next day the sea was calm and blue. The wreck of *Ekmotain* was clearly visible as the waves washed over it. It looked so close now, upside-down and hooked there on the reef – with my fins on I could've swum to it in two or three minutes..

They found the bodies of the three women at four that morning, washed up on the rocks at Lampia, the white sand beach; just a hundred metres down the coast from Vila. One is a Macadade woman, mother of the miracle baby; one a Vikeki woman, aunt of the drowned girl, and seven months pregnant; the third, a Makili high school student. They carried them back to Vila and in the morning borrowed our generator to begin making coffins.

At 9:30 am the navy patrol boat came and waited out beyond the reef. Two bodies wrapped in red tais cloth were carried from the clinic, along the road, across the field to the beach. The woman, I learned, was a resistance hero, well known and respected throughout the movement; her death is a huge loss. People gathered to watch as the corpses of the aunt and her niece from Vikeki were carried to a *Tasi Diak* boat and laid out side by side on the deck. *Ibu* Maria Lisboa and her family go out in a canoe. They will accompany the bodies back home. They are all taken out to the waiting patrol boat, which will take them to Dili and back home to Vikeki. It was the end of their first, and only, visit to Ataúro Island.

That evening the statue of the Blessed Virgin Mary was brought in procession to our house. It's the month of May and every evening the plaster-of-Paris Virgin is taken to different houses, in turn. This night was our turn. Mary's month. Mary; blessed of all women. Patron of all women. The children in their good clothes accompanied her with flowers and candles and sang her songs, her praises, with pure voices and pure hearts. Adults and children said the Rosary together. 'Ave Maria… Santa Maria. Ave Maria.'

On the other side of the fence the calm evening sea lapped over the upside-down hull of the *Ekmotain*, showing glimpses of its yellow and red paint.

'Blessed art thou among women…'

That night, I could not sleep.

MAY 9 1998

Alu, Atita and I walked to the white beach; other women walked and searched the rocks. Alu told me they were looking for things washed up on the beach from the *Ekmotain*. Some have found coffee, still good in plastic bags, and others have found soap. Alu herself found some packets of shampoo early that morning and there was still the possibility of these little gifts from the sea if we looked hard. That's the sort of place Ataúro is… and God is great, isn't He?

VIQUEQUE MOURNERS

Not long after the naval ship carrying the bodies of the Viqueque woman and her niece headed across the sea to Dili, an unfamiliar wooden boat appeared around the headland. After gathering with the others to send-off the drowned women, Alu and I were still down on the beach and we saw the boat coming in. It was clearly not an Ataúro boat – we could see that from the tentative way it crossed the reef. There was something menacing about its approach. The men on the deck glared at us across the shallows. Two of them jumped into the water and wade ashore. Guido and a couple of other Ataúro men go to greet them but were rebuffed with an angry demand; these are Vikeki people who have come to take the bodies of their women back home. They demand to know where they are.

Guido explained that the women had been sent back to Dili on the naval ship that they must surely have just passed on the sea. The Viqueque men were not happy about that. They were understandably devastated by the deaths and they were also angry with the Ataúro people who they blame for the accident. They shouted at Guido. He tried to explain what had happened but they didn't listen. Shouting, they waved their arms and threatened the group of island people that have gathered. A couple more men leap off the boat and join into what looks like might become a nasty fray.

I remembered Guido's bravery the night before, going out on that wild sea to try and save lives. I thought of the young girl and how we had tried to revive her – I wanted these Vikeki people to know they were yelling at the wrong people. I wanted them to know we understood their pain, that we were all shocked and saddened by the deaths.

'They have lost a loved one, *Ibu*.' Alu put her hand on my arm, restraining me, while we listened to the angry shouting and angry demands for compensation. The men demanded coconuts, dried fish, corn and cassava and Ataúro people rushed off to get these things.

Sitting under the fig tree with Alu and Terzinha – the Viqueque men were sitting on the beach with their backs to us – I tried to understand the reaction of these men and the acceptance of it by Ataúro people. Everyone except me understood the anger of the Viqueque visitors and quietly accepted the blame for what had happened. They are Timorese. I, an Australian, still traumatised by the tragedy, am the only one disturbed by the blame. I think it unfair, I want clarity, want acknowledgement of those who were heroic. But the Ataúro people, understanding the pain and rage of those bereaved visitors, quietly accept it.

Bags of coconuts, dried fish and cassava were taken out and loaded onto the boat and without a word, the visitors left. We sat in silence, watching them follow the bodies of their hero, her unborn baby and her niece, back across the sea.

MAKILI DANCING

On the night of the full moon there's dancing under the sacred mountain Manucoco at Makili; two hundred or more people gathered in a circle, dancing around and around to beating drums and singing.

Single voice (a woman's, high-pitched):
'Tama sai saie
Tama sai saie-e-e-e…'
The dancers respond:
'Remai anan sai lolo
Remai anan sai lolo
Tama sai saie…'
Single voice:
'Tama sai saie
Tama sai saie -e-e-e…'
[In and out… In and out
Hold hands together to make our circle strong
Hold hands together to make our circle strong
In and out… In and out.]
… the circle moves around and around.

Anton and I were invited to join. The step was simple, the constant body sway and repetitive chanting mesmeric. It was hard to stop. Hour after hour we danced as the moon rose over the sea, shone on the mountain. This night was a preparation for the coming visit of the administrator from Dili and, although he is pro-Indonesian and would come accompanied by the formal Indonesian rigmarole, the practice was wholehearted and great fun.

It was almost impossible to stop dancing, even when we were tired. It was trancelike and people on either side had a firm grasp of our hands. Being part of the dancing circle, moving to the beat of heavy drums and gongs was also magical; it was magical singing under the mountain Manucoco, its great peak above us lit by the moon. People of all ages danced and sang – young children danced until they dropped off one by one, falling asleep in heaps, limbs intertwined, on the edges of the field.

At around midnight, the dancing suddenly stopped as word went round that some teenage girls had fought and one had been hit with a stone. They said she was going to die. Some said she was already dead.

Everyone went home or to the village head's house. We went back to Fernando's where we were staying and drink hot coffee under the mango tree. Fernando told us that traditionally people always danced like this on moonlit nights and it was the recognised time for finding a partner… but the church forbade it, saying it led to sin. Now it was reserved for special occasions like the coming *Bupati's* (administrator's) visit. People avoided talking about the girls and their fight.

We spent the night in Fernando's and Maria's little house beneath the mango tree. They insisted on sleeping outside on mats under the tree so we could have their bamboo beds. We brought bread, eggs, sweet potatoes, and coffee to Makili but Fernando's family gave us a meal of corn, beans, fish and fresh oranges from their tree. They put out their best plastic chairs and a table with an embroidered cloth for us. We didn't talk about the injured girl. Fernando talked instead about his good fortune in having this big mango tree right beside his house – apart from the fruit, it was a place that was always cool even in the middle of the day, and a good spot to sleep on hot nights, or to eat a feast at midnight as we were doing.

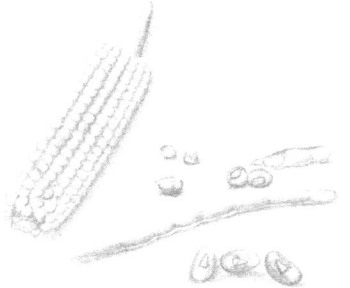

I slept, but was troubled by thoughts of the injured girl and puzzled by the seeming lack of concern about her. But it turns out that it wasn't so bad after all; the next day, crossing the mountain on our way back to Vila, we met a woman and two girls on the track, and somebody whispered to me that one of them was the girl who they said had died last night. Apparently, she did not and everything was sorted out before dawn. To everyone's satisfaction the aggressive, bigger girl was beaten by her father, or so we are told, as the injured girl skips along the steep track ahead of us.

Under the mango tree at midnight, I was taught another Makili love song – the sad song of a wife calling to her wayward husband:

Roi mose topo nga hon
Taa nge kema aun klaa ham mne
Tuli peun klaa aso peun hne -e-e-e
Taa nge kema aun klaa ham mne
Tuli peun klaa aso peun hne -e-e-e
[I am tired weaving my baskets
Weaving baskets makes me weary.
I am tired weaving baskets, waiting, waiting
Wondering why don't you come to me
Instead of to that proud, dishonest woman?
Weaving baskets makes me weary.
I am waiting.]

ALU'S DEATH

In Bali, on route to Java for meetings at the university, I received a call from Anton. It was still very early morning when Anton told me that our sister, Lu, had died. Stunned, unable to believe it, I sat on my friend Leo's veranda, staring at rice fields and swooping white herons. Just the day before I had left Ataúro, and Timor and Alu. I had taken her hand when I said goodbye and reminded her that we had made an appointment for her with Dr Dan in Dili and, although reluctant, she must go with Anton the next morning. This was the next morning, still three hours before the appointment time, and Lu was dead.

Ant told me they had all risen early to get the *Manucoco* ready for the Dili trip and Alu, too, had prepared her things early. She had put on her best clothes for the trip and, with Mama Sara and various cousins who were going to the beach to see her off, had started out from the house. Alu then remembered something she had left behind and went back alone to get it. The others waited on the beach. Anton, Guido and Ilario waited on the boat. They all waited too long so Mama Sara sent one of the cousins back to hurry Lu up. She found Alu in the house, lying on the floor, dying.

My head spun. I could not get back to Timor in time for Alu's burial that evening and could hardly believe that our dear Lu would be laid in the hard, red earth on the cemetery hill this very day. I thought of Mama Sara, Lu's sister, Domingas, her father and her brothers; the shock and grief they would feel for their beloved Lu. I thought about our house and office without Lu. I thought about Lu's gentle manner, her soft voice and downcast eyes, her shyly told funny stories, the basket full of goodies she lugged home for us each market day. I thought about the night we saw the ghost under the fig tree and our frequent ambles along the beach together. I thought how upset Tipah would be when she heard. And I feel sad and guilty because we had not made Lu go to the doctor earlier.

I stared over rice paddies as herons cruised the early morning sky and felt her passing. In my mind and heart, I could hear the chanting of the Makili women who would soon come, clutching their sticks as they hobbled around the headland on thin, frail legs to gather beside Lu's body; the terrible weeping and wailings of grief that would fill the air at Tolorica today as her family came to touch her and kiss her and call her back to them. I cry for her too, and whisper her name to the white birds flying over rice fields.

They do not conduct autopsies on Ataúro. People die, sometimes quite suddenly without any warning; they are wept over, and buried. Flowers are put on their graves – after the first week "bitter flowers", and then a week later "sweet flowers". Tears of their grieving loved ones wash the soil. And unless the dead person is old and ready to "go back" those who are left behind discuss at length the possible reasons for the early death – in the end, whatever story persists the longest becomes the true reason for the death.

Alu most likely died of tuberculosis. When I rang Dr Dan, he told me she had probably haemorrhaged internally. We did not know for sure she had TB and should have suspected it when she was unwell with a cough for some weeks. We were so busy doing our other *good works* we didn't see Lu fading in front of our eyes. She was, as Ataúro people often are, unwilling to go to Dili for medical treatment. It was when she told me she was coughing up blood that I became alarmed and made arrangements for her to have a medical examination in Dili immediately. Immediately was too late for her.

When Lu was still alive and coughing, and even after her death, there was another story related to her illness that went like this: when she was a little girl, Lu and some other children had killed a cat. They had found the cat on the beach, tormented it, as Ataúro children often do, and eventually killed it. Then, the story goes,

Lu did something that was very, very wrong. She tied a string to the dead cat's tail and dragged it along the beach. This act, Freitas told us, angered the spirits who held their revenge until an appropriate time – they were now punishing Lu with illness.

I had problems accepting this story for several reasons.

(i) I couldn't believe the spirits would be so mean.

(ii) I couldn't believe they'd carry their anger around for fifteen or more years and only now take their revenge on Lu.

(iii) You hardly ever saw a cat on Ataúro and the ones you did see were wild and wary, skulking at night through long grass and bushes, never hanging around long enough to be caught and tormented by children.

(iv) It seemed odd that the act of dragging the dead cat by the tail was deemed worse than the act of killing it.

But then, who was I to say?

Many other people believed the cat story though and when she had begun to get ill, a ceremony involving Lu, Freitas, another shaman, the spirits and anyone else who had a connection with Lu, had been arranged. As Lu's good friend and "sister" I was asked to be part of it but as it turned out, that week I was called to Dili so Anton had to stand in for me. Ant was still trying to come to terms with animistic ceremonies and how to reconcile them with his Christian upbringing. He had only reluctantly agreed to it, more out of his growing curiosity than any sort of belief in the process.

When I came back a couple of days later, he was still grumpy about the whole thing. Sitting on the front step drawing circles in the dirt with a stick, he told me about it. 'It was awful,' he said, 'I had to eat raw intestines, Rae (his nickname for me). Freitas killed a chicken and he and I… it should have been you… had to eat some of it. Lu had to eat it, too.'

He lit a kretek cigarette. 'It was awful, and I can't see how any of this stuff is going to help Lu.'

'Perhaps it'll all be okay now that they've done the ceremony,' I suggested. 'Perhaps now the spirits will leave her alone and she'll get better.'

Anton stared at me. 'You don't really believe this has anything to do with Lu's cough, do you, Gabrielle?'

I shrugged. 'I don't think so... but I don't know. Not really.'

Exasperated, he shook his head. 'You should have been the one to eat the raw intestines,' he grumbled.

Lu didn't get better after the ceremony, though for a while she said she did and even stopped coughing. It seemed to all of us that she died too suddenly on that Saturday morning. We could all keep asking and wondering, but would never really know why this happened to our good Lu.

ALU'S VISITS AND RELEASE

In some ways, I was almost more aware of Lu's absence than I had been of her presence. Anton said the same thing. We felt some shame in that, but that was the kind of person Alu was; a carer for her family, friends, me. She made no demands of her own. She didn't voice opinions, didn't draw attention to herself in any way or much express emotions. She just *was* and after her death when she *wasn't* anymore, the space she had so unobtrusively filled became a gaping hole and we missed her terribly.

But Lu didn't leave us entirely. She came back in the form of a large gecko that hung about on the veranda posts and rafters of our house and office, listening in to our conversations and chatting away in a loud lizard voice, 'Tok-kay, tok-kay, tok-kay.'

It was Guido who told me the gecko was Lu and when she was

there on a post or in the rafters, he would chat to her in their Hresuk language. More often than not, he would just be telling her to be quiet and let us get on with our work. Lu as a lizard was beautiful – green with iridescent orange spots – and as a lizard she was much bolder than she had ever been in her human form. We could be in the middle of a meeting – discussing some important point, or a proposal to a donor, say, when the toke would interrupt loudly, screaming, 'Tok-kay, Tok-kay. Tok… kay.'

'Don't listen to her, Ibu,' Guido would instruct me. 'She just wants your attention.'

And he would tell her in no uncertain terms to leave us alone. Sometimes she would and sometimes she wouldn't; it never really bothered me. I couldn't understand what she was saying anyway and I liked her company, as I always had.

Alu was not the only Ataúro spirit that came back in the form of a gecko. Lots did. Having them around was just something you had to put up with. Or enjoy.

It was more worrying to everyone that Lu was not cooperating when the time drew close for her *kore metan* ceremony, the time one year after a death when mourners take off their black clothes or unpin their black cloth, as in the case of Lu.

Freitas announced that Lu was being difficult and, as the problem concerned me, he came to talk with me about it. He'd heard from his spirit sources that she was refusing to go back to the family house for the *kore metan* ceremony and that she would only agree to come to my place, our house and office, to be with me. This was quite serious and, if it couldn't be resolved, would upset her family, the community and the whole applecart of ritual as practised by Makili people. Freitas came to ask if I would agree to persuade Alu to go to the family house for her ceremony. Of course I would, but what would be involved? What would I have to do?

It was this: (i) prepare a suitcase of my favourite clothes to be given (symbolically) to Alu. This seemed to be an act of friendship, but perhaps also a sort of bribe. (ii) Prepare an offering and call her spirit and, when she came, I was to talk seriously with her and persuade her to do things properly in the traditional way. Freitas would help with the offering and would interpret from Tetun to spirit language and back again for me. If she agreed to go, we would then accompany her to her family home where everyone would be waiting for the send-off ceremony.

It did not sound difficult. I could do that. But on the arranged night, as things were being prepared, and the witnesses started to arrive I felt nervous. I asked myself how honest I was being in taking part in this ceremony. I started to have doubts – was I a fraud? Did I believe what I was about to do? And if not, could I sit among her people and talk sincerely to their dead loved one in a spiritual ceremony? Could I *not* do it?

As chairs for Freitas, Alu and me were set out on the veranda and plates of dried fish and corn and glasses of palm wine were laid out on a mat between the chairs I experienced something like pre-performance nerves. In desperation, I whispered some kind of prayer to the universe and before long it became clear to me that of course, I *could* talk with the spirit of Lu – in the same way I often chatted to my father's spirit, and my mother's, feeling their presence there with me. It wasn't that I was unused to talking with spirits, I just wasn't used to doing what was usually a private thing with an audience of listeners eager to hear the whole conversation and with a personal interest in its outcome.

I sat opposite the empty chair and Freitas sat next to me. Through him, I invited Alu to come and after a short time, he indicated that she was there. I spoke with her as naturally as I could, explaining that her family was waiting and that, as it really was her time to be released from this earth through the ceremony, I hoped she would cooperate and come with us to her house. From the corner of my eye and with some relief I noticed the witnesses, sitting in a row at the side, nodding their heads in approval and support. Freitas translated both ways in a loud voice so the other spirits around would also understand what was going on. Finally, we shared the food with her – the corn, the fish, a sip of palm wine – and Alu agreed to go with us.

Holding candles to light our way we walked in procession down the beach road, the same one where Lu and I had encountered the ghost under the fig tree. Her spirit really was with me as I remembered that… and now she too was one of those wandering beings from the other world. But she was not a bit scary. Her presence, as always, was gentle and mild. It was a sacred procession that meandered along the beach road that night and I felt honoured to be a part of it.

Alu's family house yard at Tolorica was packed with people – relatives who had walked from Makili, neighbours, friends – their faces glowing in the dull light of a couple of lamps. They celebrated as our group arrived, bringing the spirit of Lu. Freitas explained to the crowd what had just occurred, and everyone cheered. The bag of my clothes was unpacked and each item held up for viewing; people gasped and cheered again. My clothes were not very flash – even my good ones – and were many sizes too big for Alu but that didn't seem to matter. People commented about my generosity, demonstrating such love for Alu. Everyone gasped again as masticated betel nut was found in the bag amongst my clothes – unknown to me – and held up by Mama Sara. In a ritual of inclusion, she smeared a dab of it on each family member's face, including mine. Then Alu was released into the spirit world… free at last.

The bag of clothes was returned unceremoniously a few days later and the beautiful big gecko would frequently return and natter away in the rafters until Guido sent it off with waving arms and an exasperated shout.

Each anniversary and on All Soul's Day, Lu is remembered with the burning of candles and the laying of flowers at her grave. On her second anniversary, I was asked again to speak with her, this time at the cemetery, and I did. Twice each year her mother, sister and brothers weep for her, and their tears wet the dusty earth as do the tears of all families in East Timor as they cry for their many dead. Victims of war and political strife, victims of illness and black magic, victims of accident, gang warfare and revenge, victims of poverty. Timor was known as, among other things, as the land of tears.

MUSIC

My life was filled with music. On weekend nights we sat on the veranda and sang – Baptista, some of his Indonesian and Timorese friends, Anton and me – playing guitars, singing Indonesian, Ambonese and Timorese songs. The nights were velvety and lit by stars. Backed by the rhythms of the sea, our voices floated into the sky, along the beach. Sometimes I played my own CDs and the voices of the Three Tenors, cello and piano concertos, Maria Callas, string quartets, filled the night. I turned the volume up loud and the beautiful, incongruous sounds of my own culture formed a soul-stirring juxtaposition with the Ataúro night. Through silhouettes of palm trees, squawking bats in the fig tree, over the crashing sea, the sounds of strings, piano and classical voices soared into the dark tropical sky, brought tears to my eyes and astonishment to my Ataúro friends.

ATAÚRO MUSIC

Ataúro has its own music and many songs that are magic to my ears and my heart. Songs for working, praising and celebrating, and sorrowful songs that stir my soul. I hear:

Singing on Boats: the coarse voices of men fading over the waves as they go out to sea singing fish-hunting songs. And their voices returning, growing louder as they pass over the reef into the safe lagoon, celebrating the catch and giving thanks.

Singing of boat commuters: people passing by in outriggers as they travel from one village to another, mens' and womens' voices harmonising in song as they move up and down the coast visiting family, friends, taking gifts.

Fish herding: large circles of men out on the reef splashing and beating at the water; shouts and high chants cajoling the fish into their circle, herding them towards waiting spears, shouts of success when they surface, spears full of shiny, writhing, colourful fish.

Boat pulling: at boat repair time the heave-ho chants of men, women and children; breathless, hard work chants, voices rising in unison as people tug rhythmically on thick, wet ropes that pull heavy boats up from the water to dry land.

Story songs (usually sung at night with palm wine): the wonderful sung stories of current events, of sad and happy things, relationships, love, deaths, fears and magic

Mourning: the high pitch of grief and despair. Keening chants that reach into the spirit world, cry out for explanation, for reason. 'Why did this boy, this girl, husband, this mother, this baby, die?' 'Why have they left us?' 'Why gone, just like that, from our houses, our beds, our arms?'

Wine harvesting: in the early morning or at sunset, the gravelly voices of men high up in palm trees singing thanks as they collect the sweet juice that has dripped all day or overnight into their bamboo flasks.

The music of children: bobbing up and down on the waves in small canoes – sweet, sharp voices, high and clear, of children playing on the sea and singing the songs of their ancestors

Kindergarten songs: Indonesian nursery songs we have translated into Tetun – songs about flowers and birds, fish and geckoes, counting and shape songs, market songs sung with actions and body percussion. Natural singers, these kids sing with gusto everywhere – on the sea, on the beach, along the road.

Dancing songs: with traditional instruments; *Keklanguk* (the mouth harp), Tihak (drums), *Dedir* (gongs). Dance steps, groups, in *tais* and feathers, circle dancing, ancient songs – single voices soaring into the night, choral voices following.

The songs of old women: oh, the songs of old women – mothers, grandmothers – betelnut chewing, tipsy on palm wine, rocking, raunchy, flirting, teasing songs with risqué words young girls could never sing.

The songs of teenage boys: in the evenings in groups at the beach, at the clinic, walking along the road – boys with guitars and homemade fiddles strumming and picking and singing Indonesian and Timorese pop songs. Loud, happy voices, laughing, slapping shoulders, shouting to friends.

Church music: glorious hymns and harmonies from the Catholics – keyboard accompanied music straight from heaven on the wings of angels; vigorous songs with guitars and alleluias from the Protestants, passionate in their determination to be God's people, singing their way to heaven.

The Indonesian National Anthem: sung every morning at the primary school beside us – poignant with layers of meaning and emotion as children and teachers sing a song that stirs their hearts in different ways. Listening, my eyes fill with tears. It is so serious, it is sad. But the little children shout out the anthem with gusto as children do – making it a happy prelude to their school day.

BAKERY

At night, but not every night, about ten o'clock or sometimes later, when most of the village was already sleeping, the warm smell of fresh, baking bread drifted over to us from the old *cantina* across the road. This meant the bakers were at work and we paused to inhale the delicious, warm aroma that floated over to us. We waited ten minutes or so and then, mouths watering in anticipation, crept over past the big fig tree (the ghost tree) to where the team of ancient bakers was at work in the crumbling stone building that housed the big wood-burning village oven.

We climbed the broken steps into a Dickensian world; the light was dim, sounds muffled. The five bakers were little old men who might well have been baking together for a hundred years in this very room, on this very wooden table, in this very aged and grey charred oven, on this very crumbling cement floor.

The walls of the room were scorched brown, once white tiles now yellowed and broken. A little boy and a yellow dog slept in a corner on a bare mattress. The room was stifling hot and unventilated. Two of the grandfathers were at one end of the table kneading dough with stiff, calloused hands; at the other end, two more rolling the dough into balls and placing them in rows on a wooden tray that goes onto a shelf to rise; the fifth man carried already risen rolls on his paddle to the oven and slipped them deftly into the ashes at the side of the fire.

This man watched the oven, added wood, scraped away ash,

moved the rolls closer to or further away from the fire, moves the fire closer to or further away from the bread. Nobody talked, their communication was silent and habitual as they worked their assembly line to produce the delicious little rolls (*paun*) for tomorrow's breakfasts. Now and then, the firewatcher shouted and a sixth man, tousled and wide-eyed, obviously shaken out of deep sleep, appeared at the door with a bundle of firewood.

The smell was extraordinary. The fresh rolls were hot and yeasty, crunchy and brown. I said, as Anton tells me I often did, that this was one gift from the Portuguese that reached everyone in Timor: fresh, oven-baked bread the like of which there is nowhere else in Indonesia.

Anton and I carried the rolls, enough for our midnight feast as well as breakfast for everyone tomorrow, still hot and smelling like heaven, back across the road. Sometimes we would sit on the rocks by the sea and munch them under the stars.

LOVE NOTES

In love with Anton, I am beautiful. I move with grace and my eyes shine. I toss my hair about. I dance. My laughter is musical, my words clever and funny. My heart is soft and open, embracing the world. When I cry my tears are hot and heartfelt, the salt of them tasting of my lover on my lips...

Anton is my workmate, my playmate, my friend and brother, my clown. He is the son I love unconditionally, my creative, joy-filled lover, my wise father, my hero. My love – for him, for the people of Ataúro, for the work we are doing here together – makes me happy, makes me beautiful, lets me dance.

BLACK PEARL

One afternoon I met Antonino, a fisherman, walking down the opposite side of the road. He beckoned me to cross over, indicating with a whisper and a glance up and down that it was a very important and possibly a secret matter. I saw he was not long out of the sea, carrying his spear, his wooden goggles hung around his neck and his hair glistened.

I love a secret, and when I was by his side, it was clear he meant to share it with me. Opening his small shoulder bag, his kohe, he took from it a bundle of seagrass, tied tightly with a grass cord. He opened the parcel slowly while I, like Alice in Wonderland, watched and became curiouser and curiouser. The cord took some time to unwind and, when it was finally loose, out of the weed and into his hand tumbled a small black stone. We both looked at it. It was a beautiful, tiny, black oval stone, sitting on his palm.

'A pearl,' he whispered. I looked closer.

'Do you think it is?' We asked each other.

The idea of a black pearl fresh from the sea was wonderful and triggered all kinds of fantasies in my heart, but I had no idea what a *real* black pearl might look like. He tipped it into my palm and I rolled it around. It was a well-balanced stone that rolled back to show its best side. Really, all its sides were good.

Then I remembered something I'd heard about testing pearls – you bite them – so I asked him if I could. He nodded and I put it between my teeth and bit gently. It was gritty and hard, but I didn't really know what a pearl between your teeth was supposed to feel like so that wasn't really any help.

Antonio suggested we take the stone to Vasco, the village head, who was a clever man. He wrapped it back in its seagrass package and tied it with the grass cord. Chuffed to be included in this adventure I turned with him towards Vasco's house, and we headed back down the road from where I'd just come.

Vasco looked at the stone as we had done.

'It might be a pearl,' he said, 'or it might not be.'

He rolled it on his palm. We all looked at the stone. I told him about the biting and he too remembered hearing about that test so put it between his teeth, as I had done. Like me, however, he didn't know what a pearl was supposed to feel like in your mouth. Vasco told us some stories about pearls he had encountered when diving but none of them threw much light on the little black stone in his hand. Finally, he shook his head and suggested we take it to Freitas.

'He'd know,' he said. 'He's a wise man and knows things we don't.' Antonio, Vasco and I walked up the hill to Freitas's house and sat on his veranda with the stone while children were sent scurrying around the village to find the wise man. When he came, Tiu Freitas was keen to examine the stone and took it, shook it, rolled it around his hand and stared at it for a long time. Neither Vasco nor I mentioned the biting test.

Freitas was clearly impressed with the stone but he too was puzzled by it, so he called his neighbour, Domingos, another Makili elder, and invited him to come and roll the little stone in his tough, wrinkled hand. The two elderly men talked together for a while in Makili language. They shook their heads, talked some more, then nodded in agreement. Finally, Freitas said, 'It's not a pearl.' We all sighed.

'What it is,' Freitas held the little stone up for us to see, 'is a stone that has been dropped into the sea by an eagle.'

I was the only one astonished by this explanation; the others just nodded.

'Sea eagles carry these stones under their wings for protection,' explained Freitas. 'And sometimes the stones fall out when the birds cross over the water. Shellfish can find them at the bottom of the sea and hide them to keep them safe. That's how you found it, Antonio,' he told him. 'You are a lucky man because this is a strong, protective stone.'

Freitas's daughters placed a small plastic table before us, covering it with a snowy white embroidered cloth and the best teacups. They brought us sweet black coffee and while we drank it, we discussed the stone and the wonders of the sky and the sea. *What will happen with the stone?* They decided to give it to me. 'You must look after it,' they said, 'and it will look after you.'

In my box of treasures, wrapped in soft cotton, is Antonio's black stone. Wherever it has come from, out of the blue sky or out of the deep, deep sea, it is a treasure that reminds me of soaring sea eagles and guardian shellfish, of faith and fantasy, of other worlds, of four men, an afternoon.

SEA NOTES

Sometimes the sea is so calm it seems to be solid. Sometimes there's not a wave, not a white cap, not a frill, nor a ripple; a deeper blue delineates the horizon, while the water is softer blue, paler even than the sky. It's perfectly still.

The world around this silent sea seems solid too. No clouds drift, no fish jumps, no dog trots, no child plays, no bird flies.

There are no footprints in the sand. No sound.

Have you ever seen a perfectly still blue sea? A solid sea?

Have you ever heard a perfectly silent sea?

I listen and hear the silence, feel the deep vacuum of it, a long and deep holding of sea breath...

GUESTS

On Ataúro, visitors are special. The visitor to your house may be the woman from down the road, the man who sells fish on a pole, a nurse, a fisherman – someone that you see regularly on the road or on the beach, someone you chat to at the market – but if they come to your house to visit and are not relatives or close friends, they are honoured as guests.

The guest ritual is this: you, the guest, are invited to sit on the veranda. Sometimes a good chair has to be found somewhere else in the house first; a child is sent on this errand while the house owner talks with you about the weather or the sea. Then, when you are seated and made to feel welcome, the host disappears. He or she has gone to organise things inside where people are whispering and have begun the bustling preparations required to look after you.

Soon someone, usually a teenager, often a girl, brings a small table and places it in front of you. Someone, another daughter or sister or cousin, brings a cloth – it is nearly always spotlessly white, hand-embroidered or edged with colourful crochet – to cover the table. In time, tea or coffee, already well sugared and in a china cup, is brought out on a tray (always carried out on a tray and never by hand) and placed on the table in front of you. Sometimes biscuits, that you know someone has just run to the kiosk to buy, are served on a plate with the coffee. You, as guest are invited to drink, but as a polite guest you don't drink immediately. Not until you are invited at least twice more do you finally pick up the cup and take a sip. It is all quite formal.

Usually, the host does not drink coffee or tea with you. You sit alone, feeling stiff and self-conscious about being so special, and finally state your reason for coming.

PART EIGHT

JOAQUIM

The Bikeli Village kindergarten teachers, the children and I were playing in the central square, exploring games we had created with materials found under the trees there. We based our games on ideas our pupils came up with. This day, some of the children had drawn shapes in the dirt with sticks and the teachers made up a mathematical activity around the shapes. The children were becoming competitive and the teachers had to move quickly to keep ahead of them; the game generated lots of squeals, laughter and dust.

Then I saw Anton.

He was not supposed to be here. Our plan was for him and Guido to bring the *Manucoco* to pick me up the day after tomorrow, not today. I saw in Anton's face that something was wrong. I left the group and went to him.

He took my hand in his and his eyes held mine.

'Rae,' he said. 'Joaquim has died.'

For a moment I couldn't breathe. I froze. My head spun.

Joaquim had died? Joaquim? Which Joaquim? There were several Joaquims in Maumeta. Some were old, crusty old men, ready-to-die old men. I looked into Anton's eyes, desperate to find there a different answer to the one I feared.

'Anton, which Joaquim?'

'Rae, *your* Joaquim is dead.'

Joaquim? My Joaquim? Joaquim, my friend? He is only nine years old. No. No. The blood rushed to my head. I was dizzy, not wanting to believe this.

The boat trip back to Vila was a haze of saltwater spray and sunlight and a normality around me that didn't make any sense; normal voices, the tossed anchor, the beach. Joaquim. Joaquim. I saw his dark eyes, his smile in the sky and in the sea. I saw him somersaulting in the water and coming up smiling. Everywhere, I saw his face and his smile. *No.*

In the small yard in front of his house people were gathering. People were wailing. They made a gap for me to enter and I went to Joaquim who was laid out on the table on a woven *tais* cloth. The little boy was dressed in his very best clothes and a candle burned at his head. Joaquim, my quiet, smiling, clever little friend was dead. His face was beautiful, serene, but no longer smiling his shy smile. I bent over him and cried. I kissed him and stroked his face and the old women sang their keening songs and his mother held my hand as we stood together beside her dead boy while the chants fed our grief.

Later, we took Joaquim to the cemetery; it was not far. We put him in his small grave and scattered flowers and lit candles all around him.

I do not know why Joaquim died. Nobody knows. He just got sick and he died. Some people said black magic, some said family problems. Some said, 'God.' We did not know. People here don't know why they lose their loved ones, their little children. They are here and then they are gone. And Joaquim, our Joaquim, had gone, buried in the soft dark earth on the hill above the sea, his many candles flickering in the breeze, the scent of his flowers carried on it.

DEATHS, AUGUST 1998-JANUARY 1999

There are too many deaths on this island. Not military murders or war deaths, not the deaths of old people whose time it is to die, but too many sudden deaths of young people, of children, of babies. Often, we are woken at night and asked if the *Manucoco* can take seriously ill people to Dili. Often, by then, it is too late and people don't want to go to Dili, don't want to risk dying away from the island. In August 1998 I started to make a list of the deaths occurring around me, deaths of people I knew.

August: Salsa's newborn twins died; one lived 3 hours, the other 24. The traditional midwife was at their home for the birth, but they were born weak, the midwife tried everything she knew to keep them alive but was unsuccessful.

Antoni, aged 38, a primary school teacher, died. He had had bad headaches but was told by the doctor in Dili, 'Nothing is wrong with you,' and was sent back to Ataúro. Three days later he died.

Fernanda, aged 37, primary school teacher and mother, died soon after. Having difficulty in childbirth with her fifth child she was taken to Dili on a fishing boat – a rough trip, and slow. Both Fernanda and her baby were dead on arrival at the hospital.

September: Our little Maumau, son of Teresa, the kindergarten teacher, died, aged 2. There were unconfirmed stories and denials that he had a fall. Maumau was sick for three days and was taken to the clinic – on the fourth day, he died there.

October: Three young children from Makili Village became sick with diarrhoea and vomiting, were brought to the clinic and died there – Augusto and Maria's daughter, aged 2, Joao and Domingas's child, aged 3, Marcus and Terzinha's child, aged 2. Vidal, aged 10, fell from a tree, was taken to Dili with injuries and died there away from home.

November: It was Joaquim, aged 9. He had diarrhoea and vomiting for several days, was brought to the clinic but "too late". Family problems were blamed for his death.

January: Two Makili children died with fever and diarrhoea. And our Alu, aged 25, with undiagnosed but suspected tuberculosis.

That was thirteen people I knew. Around the island, in the mountains, along the west coast, of course there were other deaths that I never heard about. When seven more Makili people died suddenly from eating poisonous fish people told me, 'Their faces swelled up, *Ibu*, they turned black and we didn't know what to do. They couldn't breathe and they died… one after the other.'

These were things I didn't want to hear, but heard too often. I went to funerals and heard the wailing and beating of chests that accompanied each death. I cried, held the mourners, followed the coffins to the graveyard, lit candles, placed flowers, was splashed with water to be rid of evil spirits, shared the funeral meal with the other mourners, felt the desperation of the bereaved.

I stopped keeping track of deaths. I didn't know what to do about them. There were too many. On the mainland, there were these illnesses and more deaths in the resistance war and my lists made no difference, not at all.

THE SHOUT/THE SHADOW

Anton decided to tell his parents about our relationship. It was perhaps naïve but important to him. I was nervous, but didn't try to dissuade him. They would have to know sometime. It was pre-mobile phone times, pre-telephone communication on Ataúro times and we were in Dili at what used to be the telephone exchange opposite the stadium in Audian. Big, old-fashioned telephones in booths lined the back wall. Anton invited me into the booth while he made the call to Ambon. He was as excited as a teenager, and I was wary.

I heard his mother's long, piercing, heartfelt shout as soon as he told her.

'Oh, no,' she cried. 'She's too old. Much too old for you, Ton! Ton, NO!'

And she went on shouting, high-pitched and angry. She was not shocked. I heard in her shouting that she had anticipated this and was ready with her response.

I left the booth.

My heart was stinging. Of course she is right, I thought. But she is also fierce, unfeeling, unforgiving. She took no time to try to understand. My head spun. I tried to reconcile the harsh shout with the honey-sweet woman I had spent time with in Ambon.

When Ant came out of the booth I couldn't speak to him. He was silent too. He paid for the call, took my elbow and steered me outside to our motorbike. We drove in silence to our favourite small Balinese restaurant nearby and he ordered a meal for us. I had slunk into a kind of morass, unable to think clearly. I couldn't eat. I knew she spoke the truth – from her worldview at least – and felt foolish that I had expected anything else. What could happen next? Anton is her eldest son and that meant he had to marry and have babies. That is how it went. I was too old for babies. That was the truth, and nothing would change it. Anton was part of my world, but he was also part of her world.

'Talk to me, Rae.' His face was drawn and sad. 'Say something.'

'She's right,' I said.

We were silent.

Anton picked at his food.

'Rae.' His voice was angry. 'You and I both knew it wouldn't be easy. We've talked about this. We know some people won't understand. That people might be critical. We've said all this over and over. And now when we've hit the first obstacle and you're crumbling.'

He looked at me. 'Are you serious about our relationship, or not, Rae?'

'Are you?'

'Rae, I love you.'

'But she's your mother, Ant.'

'Yes, she's my mother and you're the woman I love. Eat something.'

There was a dark shadow looming but on Ataúro we would be well out of its reach. Ataúro was another world, our world apart.

SEA NOTES: HAMETI

When the tide is very low – around the bright full moon or the "dark moon (no moon)" phases – people walk through the seagrass lagoon onto the exposed reef: hameti, the gathering of reef goodies. Carrying knives for prying under rocks and into pools, bamboo scoops for sifting out shrimp and small fishes, baskets for filling with their wet, writhing and crackling bounty of sea treats, they tread carefully in the sea. At night their lamps form a line of fairy lights along the reef, reflecting yellow in the water, the stooping silhouettes of people moving along slowly, picking their way along the dark coral ridge.

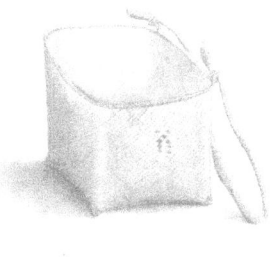

*Sometimes I go with them, stepping carefully on and over coral, eyes sharp, searching in pools and under rocks for delicate treats that writhe and crackle in our bote – our baskets – that, dripping with salt water, are taken home to boil in saucepans or directly over flames, to share with excited children and grandparents with toothless grin*s.

MAMA MARIA

If Mama Maria stood on tippy toes on her stick-thin legs and stretched her wiry little body up as high as she could, she might just reach 4 foot 6. Mama Maria was a tiny, handsome woman with fire in her eye. A healer and a midwife, as she walked through the village one of her many grandchildren held her hand, people called her to come and check… on a pregnancy, an ancient relative, a son who's had a fall.

Her voice was loud and shrill. 'Take them to the clinic. Or bring them to my house. I'm old and my eyesight is going. I can't see in your house anymore. Too dark. Take them to the clinic.'

Mama Maria believed in the clinic – for others. She would never swallow hard white pills from a glass bottle, although she had seen them ease pain. She was registered as a "traditional healer", an officially recognised and valued role in the Indonesian rural health system, and had even had some formal training; a certificate in a plastic frame grew dusty on the wall. She was called often to attend births, or deal with internal ailments or injuries.

The nurses knew things, she would admit. They'd sewn up her son after his motorbike accident, leaving him with lines of stitches on his forehead and cheek. Otherwise he might have died. There had been so much blood on him, on the road, the bed.

The nurses were not so good at turning babies though, and Maria was expert at that. Her strong hands could rotate an unborn babe so its head was facing down, ready for its journey out. She didn't need good eyesight for that. It wasn't just strength that was needed, it's the touch, she told me. Some power in the hands and not everyone has it. Maria tried to teach other people her skills, but some just didn't have the hands. She'd never found anyone with hands as good as hers, nobody else had her touch.

It was a catechist from Ainaro who first taught Maria to use her hands. She was young and he identified something in her that could be drawn out and developed, some exceptional power. She was a keen student because she herself recognised, once she tried it, that she had that power.

The catechist came to Ataúro to win souls for the Catholic Church, but he cared about their health and wellbeing too, so health care was part of his ministry. This was the start of Maria's long career as a dukun/shaman/healer.

How old is Maria? I wondered. The whole of her skin-and-bones body shook with laughter when I asked.

'How would I know?' she giggled. There was an implication in the shrug of her shoulders. 'And why would I care? I'm old, very old. I'm frail, quite frail. I can't see very well any more. But I still have strong hands and strong teeth that can chew bua malus (betel nut).' And she cackled wickedly, and popped some of the makings into her red-stained mouth.

Mama Maria had her own personal trials and tribulations. Years ago, she kicked out her husband – a man with no light in his eye or spark in his heart – and was quite content about that arrangement. But her family would not let it be and tried, unsuccessfully, again and again, to bring them back together. I was once invited to a sort of marriage guidance session where Maria's family and friends gathered in yet another attempt to resolve the old people's awkward and embarrassing marriage problems.

We sat in a semicircle that radiated from the centre in layers of importance; Maria and her estranged husband facing each other across a table at the centre and all manner of family – grownups, Maria's children and their spouses, her grandchildren, in-laws, cousins, uncles – in an ever-widening arc around them. The shaman, also a family member, and the traditional elder of the clan house, were the facilitators of the proceedings.

The old couple sat at their separate ends of the table. The husband, crestfallen, his head bowed and his hands flat on the table in front of him. Maria sat with her thin arms crossed over her chest, a shield locked hard across her heart. Her eyes stared to a distance beyond the three-person deep circle of well-wishers and accusers. Others expressed emotions – gut-wrenching sobs, fists banging on tables, harsh words and mean threats but Mama Maria's eyes showed no expression; over several hours of discussion and histrionics, her face remained a stone.

One of her sons stood by her for a while, placing his face close to hers and screaming for a response. But the old lady showed not a flicker of engagement with him. Another son, who was ill, threatened dramatically to die from the brokenness his parents' rift had caused him. At this threat, the sisters and female cousins all sobbed loudly but Mama Maria, her arms locked fast across her heart, just stared straight ahead.

Finally, the elder suggested that the estranged husband, who had sat crestfallen at his end of the table the whole time, should approach Maria and take her hand. As his gnarled fingers reached out for hers, Maria's reaction was a whiplash. Snap! Her arms unlocked into another kind of defence, a martial arts block that knocked the poor man back on his heels and left everyone else gasping. Maria pushed her chair out, rose to her full height and, eyes full of fire, stormed out of the space with no backward glance. That was the end of the session and those two never were reconciled.

MONSOON RAIN

Towards the end of the year, the days get hotter as you wait for rain. Even when you think it can't get hotter, it does. It gets much hotter and your skin is wet and clammy from dawn till dusk and into the night. You sweat in your sleep, your sarong sticks to your skin, your arms are restless, your legs heavy. In sleep, you toss and turn. Any rare breeze is a hot and lethargic one. The earth is dry, dusty; things that were once green are now pale, drooping, dying. Farmers finger their corn seed and sort through their beans, look up at the sky, waiting. They wait. You wait. Everybody waits. And the days get hotter.

Sometimes there is a dark and promising sky, then the clouds drift away to sea or over the mountain and you wait again. Day after day you look to the sky in anticipation… and then, one day it rains. It rains! Big heavy drops – you hear them, you stop what you're doing to smell the air, to look out. The sky is black, the air is cooling and big drops of rain are clattering on the tin roof. Before long, it's pounding on roofs, on tin, on thatch; on the road, the beach, the sea, everywhere.

It's raining! Bucketsful of rain pouring down! Bathtubs of rain!

Rain! Rain! Rain! Boats are bouncing, canoes filling with water. People are running and shouting, laughing as the rain catches them, waving to each other in renewed intimacy, sheltering in groups on other peoples' verandas, under tin awnings, big trees. Children have stripped off their clothes to dance in it, shouting to their friends to come out, squealing, running naked through puddles, turning their faces up to it, drinking it. Laughing, laughing, shouting and laughing; the rain has come. Joy! It's here at last, we are wet and cool, the ground is soft; corn seeds can be planted.

KINDERGARTEN

The Manutasi kindergarten program continued to flourish. Zelia, Teresa and Dulce were now running it themselves and doing it well. I spent an enjoyable morning, sometimes two, with them every week to give them support and training. The teachers and their students were fun and enthusiastic.

Then, out of the blue, as a sort of acknowledgement of our work, we were sent from the central government the *gift* of a government kindergarten teacher – an Ataúro woman who had been to college and worked in Dili and was, therefore, a *real* teacher. But after a week of her being in the kindergarten, the other teachers came to me in despair. Zelia and Teresa cried angry tears as they told me how her presence has changed the kindergarten from a happy, creative, sometimes noisy learning place into a strict and dull classroom. Some of the children had already stopped attending.

Being a government teacher, the new teacher became by default the senior teacher. The other teachers told me she had a stick that she regularly thumped on tables, chairs, the floor. She did not like the children talking while they worked. They had formal discussions, and the children must give correct answers to her questions. If she did not agree with them, she told them they were wrong and stupid. She showed them what and how they must draw. She did not read stories well. At the end of every page, she questioned the children about the content and was angry if they don't respond.

These things dismayed me but also give me heart that our teachers were seeing and recognising what was happening to the children's learning in these changed conditions. They told me the children were afraid to ask questions, afraid to be creative in their drawing or storytelling. Also, the new teacher can't do the puzzles that the children have mastered and was cross with them if they try to show her how. They laugh as they tell me this. The teachers themselves were afraid to talk with her about their discomfort because she had government status and, levels being very important here, they would not dare challenge her even gently on anything she said or did.

When she first arrived we had had three days of orientation, but now I took her aside again. I asked her how she was finding the work here and explained our approach to early education. But she was too far into the pattern I've encountered throughout Indonesia and was not going to change; she saw no need for it. When I pointed out, as gently as I could, that attendance numbers were down since she'd arrived, she said it was because the parents were ignorant and didn't make their little ones come to school. She was not open to new ideas. I felt nearly as desperate as the teachers.

Perhaps she was more sensitive than we gave her credit for, because before long she decided she'd rather work in Dili after all and requested a transfer. We four breathed a huge sigh of relief.

FISH-DRYING AND A NEW KINDERGARTEN

Bikeli Village is the most active fishing village on the island; Bikeli men are seafarers to the bone and clever fish hunters. Because they were dedicated and successful fishermen, they'd been given bigger boats by the Indonesian government. Big, wooden boats called the *Tasi Diaks* (Good Seas) with inboard diesel engines, space for ice-chests and more than ten men. In the *Tasi Diaks* the fishers could go far – out to the island of Liran, where many of them had family, and as far as the waters of Wetar and Kisah Islands. The military contracted them for fish supplies and they take their catch regularly to Hera, the port east of Dili.

But the smaller fish, those that were not part of the contract deal, were not sold in Dili. They must either be eaten immediately or dried. Of course, there was no refrigeration on Ataúro and a group of Bikeli women, wives of fishermen who had regular access to fish, asked Anton to help them develop a fish-drying business. This was right up Ant's alley. Although the women had dried fish for years, their product was for local consumption only and not of a quality they could export to other parts of Indonesia. Anton could help them produce a better-quality dried fish.

I knew nothing about drying fish, but Anton asked me to help him design a training program for the women. As long as he provided the content, I could help him with the training. As always, we worked well together and, after spending several days in Bikeli finding out what we needed to know, we had a three-day participatory and practical training program ready, several follow-up support sessions and a written proposal for some funding.

In Semarang, Central Java, a city not far from our university town of Salatiga, a women's rotary club responded to our proposal and agreed to fund the program. Anton and I spent a wonderful week doing the training with the women in Bikeli and I learned quite a lot about them, their children and drying fish. We dried a lot of fish and we laughed a lot.

On their wooden racks spread along the beach, the rows of drying reef fish were like lines of fading rainbows. The women used salting and sun-drying and we learned that the secret of high-quality product was good, fresh fish, good handling and splitting (for big fish), scrupulous cleanliness, washing and salting correctly, and protected sun-drying on the racks, i.e., protected from flies and dogs.

The military bought up all the dried fish the women could produce. Their business soon got a good name, and their fish were in demand. With some excess money from the training, some of their profits and more support from the Semarang Women's Rotary Club they built a kitchen near the beach with a bench for cleaning and splitting, tubs for washing and salting, doors to keep dogs and children out. The project went well.

We were excited to hear that the Semarang Rotary Club wanted to come and visit, and that they would bring photographers and filmmakers from Jakarta to record their philanthropy and the success of this program. Picked up in Dili and brought over by the *Manucoco*, they arrived with a big, bright "Semarang Women's Rotary Club" banner that was three times as long as the little kitchen itself. It was a challenge to arrange it for the filming, but eventually we had the banner stretched over the roof and propped up by oars or dangled over branches. The Bikeli women were given T-shirts with the rotary club's name emblazoned on the front so that when the film was shown back in Java there would be no doubt who had assisted.

I raised my eyebrows at Anton's questioning of all the rigmarole, but the fisherwomen were as pleased as could be about it all. Some of them, in their new Rotary Club of Semarang

T-shirts, were interviewed about their fledgling business and talked nervously and proudly into the camera. The three women who had raised the money with their club and come all the way out here to the backblocks to see the result were deservedly proud of their contribution to their poorer countrywomen.

The fish-drying became a good business and eventually, with continuing support from our program, this entrepreneurial group taught their methods to other women in their village and across the island. Out of this work, the second kindergarten on the island emerged. Although Bikeli was a Protestant village, which meant family planning was practised, there were still plenty of young children frolicking about, kicking up sand, splashing in the sea. The fish-drying mothers asked if I would help them start a kindergarten for these little ones. With pleasure, I would.

Juliana and Louisa became the teachers. In those days there was only boat or walking access to Pala, the centre of the village. I spent some weeks in Bikeli training them in teaching skills, discussing pedagogy, designing their program with them, helping convert the village meeting room into a temporary kindergarten. Juliana and Louisa then spent time with the Vila teachers in the Manutasi kindergarten, learning how they did things and why they did them that way.

The Bikeli Kindergarten, Lilahunal, opened in 1998.

SEA NOTES: GRANDMOTHERS

My grandmother had a hatbox, felt hats with pearl pins. She wore a cameo brooch, dresses of silk with corsets beneath and carried a purse in gloved hands that smelt faintly of camphor and lavender cream.

Your grandmother stands waist-deep in the ocean, salty sea drops glistening in her hair. Her basket drips with shellfish; crabs, urchins and shrimp, as through the lagoon she splashes, lugging shiny, crackling sea creatures home for your tea.

MUATAN LOKAL

Muatan Lokal, (local content) was part of the junior high school curriculum throughout Indonesia. The idea was good – adapting part of the curriculum to local needs. But, because it was intended to be designed locally and none of the teachers had the confidence or the know-how to do this, there was in reality no local program, just a gap in the timetable. The Ataúro high school teachers, nearly all Indonesians, asked us to help them develop a *muatan lokal* program. We met with them and talked with parents, community leaders and students, and came up with some ideas for a three-part program with practical courses in agriculture and fishing, which would be useful for the students now and in the future.

It was our challenge then to develop the content and produce teacher and student handbooks for the course. In consultation with the teachers, Baptista, Anton and I worked on lesson plans. It was a very satisfying thing to do. We worked many long days and nights to produce them, using our new photocopier – given to us by generous friends of mine in Bali – when we had electricity at night.

The fisheries course included line fishing, net fishing (with regulation nets), understanding the reef and lagoon ecosystems, swimming skills (many of the mountain kids could not swim), motor mechanics and repairs, net making and mending, and fish-drying. The agriculture course was divided into two: horticulture which was growing vegetables, experimenting with some never grown on Ataúro before and experimenting with mulches and compost; and chicken-raising as an economic enterprise – nutrition, poultry health and vaccination, general care and marketing of eggs and chickens. Apart from developing practical skills and knowledge, these courses gave a different slant to the process of education. They showed that school learning need not be dry, passive academic learning but could also be active, creative, relevant and fun.

We were a good team. Baptista and Anton had the skills and knowledge of the content areas and I had the skills to put it all together into courses and classes. We all learned heaps by doing this and at least some of the teachers were keen. It was fun for the conservative and mostly non-coastal Indonesian teachers to strip down to their singlets and shorts, and go out on the *Manucoco* with Anton and their students and learn to swim in the sea. The students loved the out-of-classroom learning and before long, some of their other subject areas were sometimes taught outside too. I was overjoyed one day to see biology lessons taking place on the beach with students exploring real life forms with their Sumatran teacher.

It got even better. Because the fairly intense *muatan lokal* sessions took place in the afternoons and school normally finished around noon, something had to be done about lunch for the students. Most of them lived too far away to go home and come back – up to 15 kilometres – and had probably not eaten breakfast either. The New Zealand aid program once again came to the rescue with funds. Mothers, sisters, aunts, cousins and grandmothers were recruited to cook; they presented rice, beans and vegetables, some eventually produced from the school garden, for the students on the three days a week the program was run. Although not sustainable in the long term unless the chickens, fishing and vegetables were sold, this became an opportunity to think and talk with the students and their parents about nutrition, as well as to give them a good basic nutritious meal.

The students built a bamboo chicken pen and run, with matching feeding and water troughs; we had a shed with a cement floor built for the fishing gear – nets, tools and motors, and with PPSDM staff and their teachers the students fenced the garden, built a small water-capturing tank and ran pipes from the spring for filling it. It was a good program that ran for a couple of years and was talked about by students for many years after.

LOVE NOTES

Sometimes I'm so happy I have to dance. Sometimes, when the moonlight shines a path across the sea and through our open window, or on moonless nights when the stars are a trillion jewels in the black sky, I have to dance. A slow dance; graceful, twirling body, arms reaching up to form circles above me, warm air kissing my skin.

Sometimes I dance to a piano sonata, a string quartet; sometimes I move to the silent music of the night, or to the sound of the incoming tide. I dance naturally, gracefully. I am beautiful. Anton, on the bed, watches me and does not laugh.

We live in a sad country but sometimes at night when everyone is sleeping, I feel so happy I have to dance.

LITERACY

Learning in the primary school here was by rote. Teachers supposedly have knowledge which they must impart to their students by lecturing them, writing copious notes on blackboards to be copied into grubby exercise books, reciting formulas and facts for the children to repeat in unison. That was the basis of learning here. If children do not pay attention, if they wriggle and squirm and whisper from boredom, they are slapped and pinched, stood in corners, ridiculed. And if their parents hear that they have been in trouble at school they are often punished again at home.

It was a tough school life but the school days were short, never more than three hours a day and often cancelled altogether if the teachers decided to have a meeting. Dressed in their colours-of-the-Indonesian-flag uniforms, the children enjoyed the breaks with their friends and the daily going to and coming from school along the beach or the village road. Their great dawdling, teasing, quarrelling, laughing, shouting, happy groups made their long walks enjoyable.

After our early education teacher training sessions, I was frequently asked to work with the primary school teachers. Once the kindergartens were established, I had time to do that. I would concentrate on literacy – especially reading and writing skills. It was not hard to see the problems: there were no books at all available to the children and they were never given an opportunity to read or write, either creatively or academically. They copied from the board. They read from the board. The teachers of grades one and two taught phonics, so we started by trying to find some engaging ways to do that.

We scrounged cardboard and made posters and games. We played sound games. We made our own books from recycled paper with staples, or pinned together with slivers of palm leaf frond. I bought coloured pencils and crayons in Dili. The children loved it. The teachers loved it too but were worried at first that the kids wouldn't learn that way. It was all very new for them.

Their relationship with the children changed when the

atmosphere was more relaxed and everyone was enjoying the class. I encouraged *Pak* Pedro to learn the names of his young pupils and use them. He had sixty year-one pupils so this was a challenge, but he agreed it was worth the effort once they started expressing ideas, questions and showing interest.

Inonesian-trained teachers were afraid of questions. 'What,' they asked me, 'will happen if we don't know the answers?' They were afraid of losing rank, losing respect if they didn't know, so it was safer not to encourage questions at all. They considered it precocious if a student dared to ask. This became a good discussion topic: what *do* you do if a pupil asks a question and you don't know the answer? What could you do? We explored possibilities. Let's pretend you have left your stick at home. *What would you do without it?*

All of this might've been treading on sensitive territory, but I had confidence because I had worked with children in many different cultural settings and knew what worked for little children everywhere. As long as order was kept, lessons are well planned and well managed, new areas of learning for teachers could be explored. It was exciting and creative.

BOOKS

In what was called the school library there were a few yellow-paged and dull reading books. They were in Bahasa Indonesia and were Javanese in all ways – names, places, activities, events – and so were quite foreign to Ataúro children. Teachers, *Pak* Pedro and *Ibu* Natalia, agreed to help me write some basic readers for young learners in Tetun, using their familiar environment, names and events. The education department said we could use the books in the schools as long as they were bilingual; Bahasa

Indonesia and Tetun. It was not so long ago that Tetun was banned in schools altogether, so things had come a long way.

Pedro and Natalia had no idea how to write a book. They had not read a book other than Mass and hymnbooks. We kept our books simple. The teachers were, of course, fluent Tetun and Indonesian speakers but had never written in Tetun so grammar and spelling – and there was no official orthography yet – were challenges.

Like the children, they were afraid to make mistakes. 'Let's just do it,' I encouraged them, 'we'll get them checked and can fix mistakes.' They also had no idea about writing fiction and allowing things to happen in books that would not necessarily happen in real life. As children, they had never read books, and as adults they did not have access to them. It was an interesting process for me, and I learned more about education in this country. We struggled on and I spent Sundays illustrating the books in my basic fashion.

LIBRARY

What we needed, of course, was a library. With books! Colourful and interesting books. Books about animals and people and planets and rivers and colours and numbers and science and art. Books about the world. Books that told stories: fantastic and amazing stories, realistic stories, scary and mysterious stories, happy and sad stories.

We were helped again by our supporters – New Zealand, Uniting Church and others through the university – and began work. One of the very few Portuguese buildings here, an unused school building known as the "red school" because of its once bright red tin roof, was vacant. It belonged to the church. We had a meeting with the local church board, and they agreed to let us use it indefinitely as a community library – as long as we repaired and maintained it. It was the perfect building – two large rooms with tiled floors, a big storeroom, some broken water closet toilets and a small veranda/entrance. All we needed were some repairs and some books.

SEA NOTES

Here come the lads walking along the beach in twos and threes as the tide comes in, and fish swarm over the reef. They walk with a swagger, these bare-chested men, spears over shoulders, hand-carved wooden goggles pushed back on their heads. Laughing, joking, they are heading for the sea, their muscles are tight, ready for the swim. Thumbs up, waving to me, goggles pulled down, then splash... one, two, three, four, five shiny bodies breast-stroking through the water, heads bobbing in the waves.

Watch out fish!

LUISA INAN

Luisa Inan had a face like a sunflower. It was a round face that beamed out to the world. The first time I saw her she had a bleeding head, cut with a stone aimed directly at her, and her shoulders drooped over her sobbing chest. I led her onto our veranda and scolded the group of children who stood at the gate taunting her.

'She's crazy,' they shouted. 'Luisa Inan is a crazy woman.' That was enough to justify stone-throwing, name-calling, jeers and injury.

I took her in and bathed her head while she cried bitterly, like a wronged child. When the bleeding had stopped, I gave her a glass of sweet tea. Luisa Inan smiled her sunflower smile at me and we were friends.

Luisa Inan – the name tells us she is the mother of Luisa – was as mad as a hatter. She also had a wicked sense of humour and a small devil somewhere not so deep inside her. She had apparently become crazy one day "just like that" and stayed crazy for several years.

Her husband and child, Luisa, lived in Makili and tied their wife and mother to a shady tree with a rope to keep her "safely" at home. But they couldn't keep her there for long, and when she could get away she wandered semi-naked in flip-flops of odd colours and size along the rocky beach to the "big smoke", the tiny administrative centre of Vila where she became famous for stealing anything she could get her hands on and had a particular penchant for keys and pens.

'She's crazy,' shouted the children. 'Crazy, crazy woman.' They jumped up and down and mimicked her actions.

'So?' I said. 'So, what does that mean to children who go to church every Sunday and learn about Jesus? What does that mean to children who pray the Rosary and carry the Virgin Mary around the village with hymns and candles and singing? What sort of Catholics are you? Do you know anything about kindness and caring for people? Even crazy people. That's what Jesus taught, didn't he?'

They hung their heads. They dropped their stones. She was safe for a while at least, until she was out of my sight again. I never saw or heard anyone else berate the children for their cruelty to her.

After that, Luisa Inan visited me often. Sometimes she came to take refuge from children, sometimes to cry, sometimes just to socialise and make me laugh, quite often to steal my bits and pieces. When I worked on the veranda at night, she often dropped in and sat at the table watching me. When she got bored with that, she'd crawl under my table and go to sleep. Sometimes I gave her a job like sorting pencils into categories of still worth using or not, or marking paper for recycling with a big slash through the printed side. She took the work very seriously and was paid with single sticks of the clove cigarettes that she loved.

Sometimes she arrived half-naked and with a glint in her eye that warned us that we were in for trouble, or a lot of laughs. She loved to sabotage our work meetings and one of her favourite tricks was her "no undies sign of the cross" caper: uninvited, and with a very serious expression on her face, she would join the group and introduce herself with a prayer. 'In the name of the Father,' touching her forehead, 'and of the Son,' brushing the right, often naked, floppy breast, 'and of the Holy Ghost,' to the left floppy breast,… and then with a swoop and a wicked laugh her hand would fly down to lift the cloth covering her genitals. 'Amen!' She would laugh and laugh at the shocked faces. If anyone scolded her, she would laugh more wickedly still. She'd laugh from the belly, would Luisa Inan, with her round, sunflower face tossed back into the air.

Her stealing was impulsive and swift. One minute she would be sitting at my table, my trustworthy, butter-wouldn't-melt-in-her-mouth friend, helping me with tasks, smiling at me sweetly… and the minute my back was turned or I popped into the other room, she was off with a handful of goodies – my pens, pencils, keys, paperclips. Out into the night she'd go, disappearing into thin air, not to be seen for a couple of days. Eventually she'd return, clutching a handful of somebody else's goodies – pens, pencils, spoons, keys; mine dropped under a tree somewhere, tucked under a rock, forgotten.

When a mental health team finally made it to Ataúro, after the referendum, Luisa Inan's family asked me to be responsible for her prescribed daily medication because she visited me frequently and trusted me. This system worked for a couple of months while she came regularly and took her tablets proudly. They seemed to calm her; she had fewer bouts of either hysterical laughter or heart-wrenching despair. Then she disappeared for a time but eventually came back half-naked, draped in rags, dirty and dragging a sack of stolen goods. Her husband came and took her back to their house in the mountains. I heard later he'd given up trying to give her medication, again tying her with a rope to a shady tree when he had to leave the house. I didn't see her for months and months. I missed her.

Then out of the blue, she was back in Vila. I saw her across the road with a group of other Makili women who had come to visit the clinic. I had to look twice to be sure it was her. Luisa Inan was clean and neatly dressed in a pretty blue and green floral cotton dress. Her hair was washed and combed; she was a different Luisa Inan altogether: calm, subdued, chatting quietly with her friends under the tree. When she saw me, she stared for a while with just a glint of recognition in her eye. She waved at me with a look of someone who remembers a dream, or a past life, and her sunflower face smiled a faint, uncertain smile.

LOVE NOTES

Anton is a string bean: he's long and thin with arms and legs that go on forever. When he's dozing on the bed, they fold around pillows and dangle over edges. I love every bit of that long, dangly man and plant kisses on his smooth brown-skin legs.

'You're a spider,' I say. 'That's what you are – a long-legged spider, Ant. A daddy-long-legs maybe.'

'I'd rather be a bear,' he mumbles, half asleep. 'Or a lion. Couldn't I be something strong and fierce?'

'How can you be a bear or a lion when you're naturally a daddy-long-legs?' I tease. 'But a nice daddy-long-legs, a really nice one.' I run my fingers down his leg. 'I love spiders, Ant. But... Ant... maybe you have the heart of a bear.'

'... a lion,' he murmurs with a sleepy roar.

THE CURE

One night when I was visiting Freitas, he received a patient. A very anxious father appeared at the shaman's house, carrying his son, a young boy about eleven years old. I was sitting on the front porch drinking sweet black coffee and listening to Freitas's stories when the little procession arrived: the father, the boy, his mother and young sister, a number of worried aunts and at least two grandmothers.

Freitas jumped to his feet, beckoned me to follow and led the group to the back of the house. I went gingerly, curious, but half-afraid of what I might witness. I still carried a bit of the cultural mindset that it was none of my business to watch other people's business. The boy was shaking violently as they lay him down on a woven mat just outside the kitchen where a fire was burning, and women were shelling beans. He was ranting and foaming in a fit. Everyone, including Freitas's family and several neighbours, had gathered to watch. The boy's father sat on the ground by his side and tried to stop his son's writhing by holding his arms down at his sides. The boy's mother moved away and sat staring at the ground, the little sister clinging to her neck.

Freitas grasped the boy's shoulders, looked into his face and forced his eyes open one at a time so he could look right into them and said some spirit words. He then started shouting orders. People moved to get him what he said he needed: a bundle of stiff twigs and a plastic bottle of warm, boiled water. Freitas took these things and blessed them with incantations, walking up and down beside the little boy. His mother was still looking at the ground, his father held the boy's arms down and his face showed no expression. The little sister, still clinging to her mother's neck, watched wide eyed as Freitas hit the boy with the twigs. All over his body and arms and legs he struck, while the father held the boy on the mat. The hitting was not hard, but sharp enough that I can still hear the thwack-thwack of it.

I caught the mother glancing at her son quickly, then slipping back into staring in the opposite direction. Freitas chewed some bark and, once masticated, placed it into the boy's foaming mouth, then takes the water bottle and forces water down the boy's throat. I was afraid he would choke, and turned my head away when he spluttered. The boy's thrashing and gurgling seemed to go on for a long time as the healer recited the incantations, and continued the hitting and forcing water into his mouth.

Finally, the fit subsided and the boy lay still. His mother's face transformed with his quieting; she held her daughter close to her breast and gazed directly at her son. The father released his grip on the boy and wiped his own forehead with a dirty cloth. On his knees again, Freitas looked closely into the boy's eyes, forcing the lids open with his fingers, and finally declared him cured. The spectators sighed with relief.

The parents, aunts and grandmothers of the patient were given cups of tea and sat around the now-sleeping boy in silence, while the household women continued shelling their beans. The neighbours were not offered tea, and gradually wandered home. Freitas invited me back to the veranda and ordered someone to bring our tea to us there. He continued his storytelling where he'd left off. I was a good audience and, as a skilled and enthusiastic storyteller, he was loath to miss such an opportunity.

Before I left, I asked him about the sick boy and the cure. 'It's bad spirits that get into this boy,' he told me. 'It has happened before. There is something wrong in the family and the spirits won't stop pestering them through this little fellow. It may be the grandparents' generation that caused the problem. It's lucky,' he said, 'that they always get to him quickly and I'm able to stop the demons before it's too late.'

THE SHOUT/THE SHADOW 2

Anton's mother's shout became a feature of our monthly visits to Dili. He rang home every month, and every month, at least part of his call was dedicated to our relationship and ended in his mother's shout. Even if he didn't raise it, and very soon he didn't, the subject would be raised and our relationship disparaged, belittled and dismissed. Anton was upset by it every time. He told me about it every time. I was upset by it every time. Sometimes we talked about it and sometimes we didn't, but the shadow was there, over us.

'She's right, you know, Ant,' I said in one of my calmer moods. 'You do need to have babies. Don't you?'

'I don't need to have babies. I don't like babies.' And he told me about his experiences with new babies: tiny, ugly, fragile things. He screwed up his face. He wanted none, he said.

'But Ant… what about your responsibility to your family?'

'There's plenty of others to have babies. The family name, Kesaulya, will go on.'

'But little Antons? Skinny little boys and girls that have your lovely Arab nose? I think the world needs some of those…'

I tempted fate, but I meant it. Impossibly, I wanted to have Anton's babies. Lots of them.

I thought he'd like them too.

We laughed and played on the edges of the shadow.

THE DEATH OF MY MOTHER

Less than two years after my father's death, my mother, Alice, also died. This time we had more time to prepare and I went back to Australia to be one of her carers in the weeks before her death. It was a wonderful, hallowed time for me.

Although she had always wanted to be a nurse, Mum didn't like hospitals and, although, as always, she didn't want to be any trouble to anyone, she did want to die at home. She had the perfect place to do it; the family house overlooked Moreton Bay, and her bedroom had a wall of glass facing out to her garden and the sea.

We, her children, were happy and honoured for her to be as much trouble as she needed. Like most adventurous daughters, I felt I had neglected her over the years of my adventures, not treating her badly, but too involved in my own affairs to give her enough time, to get to know her as the person she had become in her later years. There was not enough time to listen to her poetry, to share the music she loved. Now we had some time to do this, and I was very grateful for that. We could prepare for her death together.

I had been a part of too many deaths and funerals in Indonesia and Timor to allow strangers to come and take my mother's body from us immediately. That seemed barbaric. We needed time with our mother, even after her death. My sister and I tended her body, bathed and anointed her, dressed her in her new white Indian cotton nightdress, placed scented candles and roses from her garden around her. Her bedroom became a beautiful chapel in which we could sit with her and each other before she had to leave us.

My mother had always been my strong supporter and, although she didn't always approve of my actions, she gave me a love that nourished the very roots of my soul. Now, like my father, she was gone and I would return to Ataúro an orphan.

SILENCE

During the time I was caring for my mother in preparation for her death, I wrote to Anton's mother. It was a time in which I was very aware of mothers and mothering. I told her that my own mother was dying and, spending so much time with her, I'd time to reflect on how mothers feel about their connection with their children, even their adult children.

I told her that my mother, although she liked Anton, did not approve of my relationship with him either. Not the age difference; it was too hard for her to accept and it was something we did not talk about much. I wrote as sensitively and carefully as I could. I told her I understood her expectations and her fears and concerns, and tried to explain to her my love for Anton and how it had grown; to reassure her it was a real and a good love.

She did not reply.

A SAD WEDDING

On Ataúro, Domingas is marrying Antonio and we have been invited to the wedding party at Antonio's house. The invitation – Indonesian, pink and blue, hearts and doves and golden rings – says the event would start at eight o'clock. Aware of etiquette, we arrive just after nine; hardly anyone is there yet; young men in black trousers and white shirts are still testing microphones and sound systems, *Satu-dua-tiga, satu, dua, tiga.*

The front yard of Antonio's family home has been temporarily walled in with sheets of corrugated iron to make an extended area for the reception. It will keep out uninvited guests who are gathering on the road to watch people arriving and, if they can, get a peek at what's going on inside. A number of blue tarps form a temporary roof in case of rain, although the night is clear and moonlit.

We are welcomed, seated at the end of a row of plastic chairs that sink into the dirt with our weight, and left to watch last-minute preparations and the arrival of other guests. Everyone is dressed up – wearing short skirts and lacy blouses brought out only for church and special occasions, serious dark trousers and collared shirts, soft synthetic dresses with bright floral patterns, the best batik sarongs and traditional kebayas safety-pinned together at the front. I am wearing a mid-length floral skirt that will swing when I dance, and Anton is wearing long dark pants and one of my white cotton shirts that has an Indian collar and full sleeves and looks gorgeous on him. We are both wearing sandals and look, we think, quite spiffy.

The bride and groom are seated in their wedding throne – a two-seater lounge decked with pink tulle and surrounded by plastic flowers. The throne is in an elaborately painted pink and silver cardboard bower. Young men have spent the day making it, painting and hanging intricate palm leaf decorations. The bride is a fairy doll in layers of pink satin and tulle. Her hair has been curled and has pink ribbons and flowers entwined in it. The groom is in a navy-blue suit that is a size too big for him and is wearing white gloves several sizes too big. They have been married earlier today at the church and now both look tired, and nervous about this big event. Neither of them is smiling.

With bustle and chatter, the bride's extended family arrives in a group of forty or so people, led in by one of the groom's uncles. They are seated, with much deference, in a separate area specially prepared for them, beside the bridal bower. A large amount of toing-and-froing is still going on in the main space; consultations and shaking of heads; fiddling with electric wires and lights; moving about of tables and chairs, until finally, everything is ready to go. At ten o'clock the sound system bursts out with loud squeaks and crackles and the confident voice of the MC, Sr Fernando. In a radio announcer's patter, he welcomes us all and gives us a rundown of how the evening will proceed. Proceedings, as usual, are formal.

Protocol ('Protocol, that's what I am doing now,' says Fernando).

A speech from the groom's family.

Guests applaud.

A speech from the bride's family.

Guests will applaud.

Congratulating the bride, and groom, and their parents (shaking of hands and kissing of cheeks).

Cutting the wedding cake.

Guests applaud.

Grace.

The meal.

The bride and groom dance.

Guests applaud.

Everyone dances.

End of official part of the evening – dancing continues.

So, as announced by the MC, the party begins.

Protocol has been explained. We understand and will, of course, go along with it exactly as directed.

The first speech.

A representative of Antonio's father, an uncle, I think, a stocky, serious fellow, takes the mike and welcomes everyone to the house and to the wedding celebration. He wishes the happy couple a good life together and continues with some wise words – a few too many – about marriage and responsibility.

Everyone claps and Fernando is warming up to this and enjoying his role. He is doing it with gusto and humour, and people are starting to relax.

Bride's family's speech: there is some awkwardness while the family of Domingas decides who is going to speak for them. It is unusual for them to be so unprepared. Guests glance meaningfully at each other. Some whisper; for those in the know that is a clue, perhaps, that all is not as it should be. Eventually, after some discussion in the family group, a slight man stands up. He is uneasy and spends some time pulling up his trousers and adjusting his shirt before taking the mike into his shaking hand. He takes time to gather his thoughts together. A reluctant speaker – his speech is short and pointed – he thanks the hosts and thanks the guests.

We clap.

The queue to congratulate the bride and groom moves slowly. The couple still sitting po-faced, not exchanging a single glance. The long line of people inches towards the bridal bower… toe-toheeling along, shuffling up powdery dust, while the bride's and her mother's cheeks are kissed over and over, and the men are kissed or hand-shaken. By the time we get to her, Domingas is in a bit of a daze; she is not a girl who likes attention. Her new husband, Antonio, is stoic in his repeated response... obrigadu, terima kasih (thank you, thank you).

The cutting of the cake: It is square, three-tiered, iced pink and elaborately decorated with sugar flowers and leaves. A plastic bride and groom stand stiffly on top of it while the real bride and groom stand stiffly side by side together holding the knife and – still not looking at each other or smiling – make the first cut.

The band plays a drum-roll and everyone claps. Domingas looks relieved that she's successfully carried out this ritual in front of so many people and the rest of the cake cutting is taken over by two older women who know what they're doing. The bride sits down without a glance at her new husband.

The meal; it is after 11:30 when the bowls of food are carried out to the tables by women in matching apricot blouses and dark skirts, uniforms sewn on treadle machines in various houses for the occasion. The women have the bustling air of self-righteous authority common to women's organisations everywhere. As the younger women pile the buffet table with rice, vegetables, beans, chicken, pork and goat dishes, the more assured or senior women take it on themselves to rearrange dishes until they get the placement of them just right. There are three tables: one for the ordinary wedding guests, one for the Muslim guests (Indonesians) and a separate one, nearer the bridal bower, for the bride's family. The food is placed on this table first as a token of respect. On an occasion like this, the groom's family must show the great respect they have for the family from which their new family member (feto-foun) has come. Everyone expects this, in particular the family members of the bride who are watching keenly for any lapse of protocol or slackening of good practice.

The food is plentiful and smells delicious. Anton digs me in the ribs and widens his eyes with gleeful anticipation. We don't see a spread like this every day on Ataúro.

Everybody stands while grace is said.

Then Sr Fernando, who, despite the crackling sound system, has so far competently steered the evening through one or two moments of discomfort, does an extraordinary thing and makes a fatal mistake. Ignoring traditional etiquette, he invites *everyone* to approach the tables to partake of food.

He invites everybody. Together. Some guests, including us, start to move towards the table… then stop in our tracks… aware of an awkward silence and an awkward stillness in the area. People are not moving. They are whispering, some are looking at their shoes. There is a disturbance in the bride's family area, people there are muttering amongst themselves. We step back to our places, sit back on our chairs. We wait but there is no help from the MC, no announcements or directions. Just silence.

Then, as if by some secret signal, the bride's entire family stands up and walks out; out of the area, out of the party, out of the yard. Passing the elaborate table of food laid out for them, they ignore the shocked expressions of their fellow guests, cross the floor and leave. I watch my best running shoes – the ones Ameo borrowed from me to wear to the wedding – leave with them. Everyone is stunned. Members of the groom's family run into the house. Whispering and shuffling breaks the silence in the yard. Domingas, the bride, bursts into tears. She crumples and sobs into her pink satin skirt. Antonio places his still-gloved hand awkwardly on her arm, but she is not to be comforted. My heart goes out to her; this is big, it is awful.

We stand waiting for instruction, then sit and continue to wait. Explanations are whispered along the line: "they" have been offended. They are offended because they were not invited to their table before the other guests were invited to theirs. As umane (family of the bride) they should be treated as honoured guests, not as ordinary guests. This is wrong, and exacerbates whatever was already "wrong" prior to this breach. It's seriously wrong. Domingas sobs; Antonio's gloved hand sits on her wrist.

Anton tells me he is faint with hunger and if he doesn't eat soon, he will drop off the chair. More whispers; we are told the bride's family have taken their gifts of rice, chickens, woven cloth, corn, etc. with them as they left. Whispers: there is no blessing, the couple will be doomed, their marriage fraught with problems. Their babies will die.

I watch Domingas's heaving shoulders and listen to her sobs. Her pretty face is swollen, her ribbons undone. Antonio has given up trying to comfort her and sits staring straight ahead. The rest of the bridal party are whispering together and don't know what to do.

Something is happening. A plan is being hatched. Someone is taking control. Fernando takes up the mike at last and, as if nothing at all has happened, invites guests to the table to eat.

There is a rush and Anton does not hang back. The women in matching apricot blouses hand out plates, spoons and forks, paper napkins. The food is delicious and plentiful and there is palm wine, Coca-Cola, Sprite, beer or water to drink. Nobody goes near the abandoned table, except the two women who are shaking cloths over the food to keep flies away.

Anton is revived by food, but not Domingas. She is offered food but refuses to eat. She has stopped crying, is looking down into her lap and her face is puffy. It is tragic for her.

Someone tells us the groom's family is out the back, trying to work out what to do. Word has come that the bride's family, and all the gifts taken with them when they left, are down the end of the village waiting for some kind of apology, which will involve compensatory gifts of pigs and goats and chickens. The groom's family are trying to reach an agreement about what they can offer. We are invited for second helpings… and couldn't resist, although I am acutely aware of Domingas sitting hungry and heartbroken in the bower.

Before any resolution is reached, someone tells us that it is too late now because the offended family have gone back to Makili. They will not come back to the wedding party. Domingas begins crying again. Tables are removed and Fernando picks up the mike.

The bride and groom will dance: Oh no. But they do. Moving to the dance floor, Domingas a crumpled rag doll, in drooping satin and tulle. The band start to play and they dance, stumbling across the dirt floor following protocol, but dazed.

Everybody claps but the applause is lukewarm.

Fernando is not giving up. He has a party to finish.

Guests are invited to join the bridal couple on the dance floor. People stand half-heartedly. When Anton and I walk to the dance area there is cheering and clapping as usual, but tonight it is subdued. Although the little band keeps thumping and singing away and Fernando continues encouraging people through the crackling mike, there is little gaiety; things are not right. Antonio and Domingas leave the dance floor and finally also leave their bridal bower. They disappear. The musicians bow and pluck and thump but find it hard to keep the spirit in their music. The dancers are half-hearted.

Instead of dancing, people start to leave. The wedding celebration is over. We listen to the music fade as we walk down the hill towards the beach. Ataúro can be a harsh place, tradition can be excruciating.

THE SHOUT/THE SHADOW 3

Ant's mother brought in reinforcements. Uncles, aunts, cousins were there to talk with Ant on the phone when he called. They all told him his mother is right and he must do the right thing by her. His quiet, gentle father never comes to the phone, but other male relatives talk in loud voices: some sympathetic, some sleazy, some authoritative. In accusatory or cajoling tones, female relatives begged him to see sense. I never went into the phone booth but sat out on a bench under a tree, swinging my legs and biding my time until he came out and either laughed and mimicked them, or was tearful. An Australian man might've stopped calling, stopped letting them lecture him, stopped listening. But Anton is an Ambonese man and that is not at all the same thing.

TWO MEN (WHO'VE BEEN DRINKING IT) TALK ABOUT PALM WINE

Man 1: 'It's like this. We pluck our wine from palm trees, harvesting the juice in bamboo tubes or plastic bottles.'

Man 2: 'We don't "pluck" it exactly… what we do is milk it, we squeeze the white juice from the palm fronds.'

Man 1: 'This is what we do: we slit the flesh of a thick, ripe frond with our knives, then insert a bamboo tube. And then juice oozes out slowly like milk from a mother's breasts – drip by sweet, white drip into our bamboo tubes.'

Man 2: 'And, like a new mother only has a little milk at first, there is only a little wine at the start of a new tree… so we have to coax it and squeeze it till there is more and more.'

Man 1: 'The tubes are like babies tied to the mother's breast with hungry mouths, sucking, sucking at the milk.'

Man 2: 'To get that milk we first have to climb up into the branches and cut the frond so we can insert the tube. We climb with a katana and a knife, and our bamboo tubes tied to our hips. We use our hands and feet to slide up the trunk and when we reach the top we hang there and do our work of slitting, inserting, coaxing the milk out.'

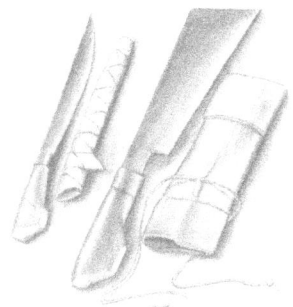

Man 1: 'We do it slowly and carefully.'

Man 2: 'We do it respectfully.'

Man 1: 'We sing in the palm tree while we work. Singing keeps us happy and helps us do our work well; with songs we express our thanks to the spirits for the wine we are taking.'

Man 2: 'When a tree is ripe and productive, we have to go up every morning and every evening; harvesting as the sun comes up and again as the sun goes down. Singing as the sun comes up, singing as the sun goes down.'

Man 1: 'This keeps the juice flowing, keeps our bamboo tubes full, not for a day, a week or a month but for a long time, for three or four months maybe.'

Man 2: 'We like to drink our wine when it's fresh from the tree. Fresh palm wine is so sweet and white, it is like drinking mother's milk. Like mother's milk we need it to live…'

Man 1: 'We can't sing without our wine…'

Man 2: 'We can't work or play, dance or love without it.'

And the wine harvesters – men who love palm wine – take up their coconut shell cups and drink the soft, milky fluid.

VIOLENCE

From the mainland, we begin to hear things we don't want to hear. We can't close our ears to the stories of violence, stories of suffering. There are stories about the military and their cruelty: rape, enforced prostitution, torture, cold-blooded murder. And there are stories about cruelty within and by the resistance movement: intimidation, rape and murder of Timorese by Timorese. There are stories of Timorese using the Indonesian military to get reprisals against neighbours with whom they have had conflict. These things are heartbreaking and ugly. We don't want to hear them. They make us wonder about humanity, about who we are, and if we can be any different.

It is said that Timorese are gentle people, the innocent victims of their fierce Indonesian neighbour, and there is a bitter truth in this – but of course, it is not all true. In 1996 it is heresy to say so, but not all Timorese are soft and gentle and probably, like the rest of us, not many Timorese are soft and gentle all the time.

Ataúro people are clever and opportunistic and know when gentleness works for them. Some are bullies; domestic violence is common, it is considered normal to hit women and small children. Teachers have open slather, both the freedom and the power, to bully and intimidate with their desk-banging, through-the-air-whistling wooden weapons. And this bigger war, this battle against Indonesian oppression is not, I see, fuelled only by love of country and of countrymen but also by ambition, frustration, lust for power.

SEA NOTES: OCTOPUS

March and April are the best times. When the nights are dark, when the quarter moon is rising late, that's the time for going after octopus.

If the moon is already up, it's too late. You need a bright lamp – a hissing Petromax is best – a spear, and a friend. Some people "have the eyes" for them – like Armindo, he's one who "sees" them so you try to go with him. You can find big ones out on the reef and smaller ones in the lagoon.

In the lagoon you wade slowly in the shallows where the octopus have gathered to find their food, and, holding the lamp low so that it reflects in the water, you drag your spear to draw them to you as you go. When you see one clutching at the spear with some or all of its legs, you know you have him and you lift him carefully into your basket. Octopus are not graceful. Ungainly creatures they are, and their many legs make escape easy; you have to kill them to prevent them getting out of your basket and back into the sea.

Unfortunately for the octopus, they are delicious fried or stewed or wound around a stick and grilled over a flame. In the right months, when the moon is "dark", Anton and Juliao, Guido's brother, often go with lamp and spears into the lagoon and, although not as skilled as the famed Armindo, they usually bring home a bucketful of octopus for a midnight feast around our fire.

ELECTIONS

What turned out to be the last general elections in Suharto's New Order regime were held in 1997. It was interesting to watch the campaigns and hear different discussions on Ataúro as the election drew closer. As in other parts of Indonesia, what many people thought and whispered to each other was quite different to what they said out loud. None of the three parties contesting the election ever clarified policies or explained how they would achieve their goals to reduce poverty and corruption, so people really had nothing to evaluate or compare between them. But it was made clear that GOLKAR (Partai Golongan Karya /Party of Functional Groups), the conservative party of the long-term government, the party of Suharto, was the party to vote for. Strong pressure was put on people to do so. Public servants who wanted to retain jobs and get promotions were told directly which party they should support and village and community leaders were also left in no doubt.

On the wall of the Vila military office was a hand-drawn map of Ataúro that supposedly showed the political persuasions of each village and hamlet. I was invited in to admire it. Yellow buttons (yellow for GOLKAR) were scattered across the map.

People would joke with us – everyone knew Anton was anti-GOLKAR – and among themselves about how they fooled the authorities into thinking they were all supporters of the Suharto regime, ha-ha. But according to official results, 84.7% of the East Timorese who voted, and according to official records nearly 335,000 did vote, had, in fact, voted for GOLKAR. Intimidation, fear and bribery, of and by both Indonesian and Timorese, probably played a large part in achieving that result.

On the day of the election, May 29, I was called to Dili urgently – I forget why – and the *Manucoco*, being repaired, was out of action. Anton approached the election officials and, surprisingly, the government team that was carrying the Ataúro ballot boxes to the mainland agreed to give me a lift on their small, open boat. It was an odd but quite merry trip with two heavily armed Indonesian policeman, the locked ballot boxes, the electoral team and me bouncing about on the waves. It was only when we got close to Dili that the seriousness of the excursion became clear – the electoral leader received urgent messages on his walkie-talkie; everyone jumped to attention and all light-heartedness disappeared. They told me that as soon as we hit the beach, I must get off the boat as quickly as possible, and run well away from them and the ballot boxes.

I did as directed, splashing into the dirty Dili Harbour water and lugging my bag up the beach, hailing a taxi and getting myself away. Later we heard that there had been trouble at several of the polling booths and an ambulance used to carry ballot boxes down from the mountains had been blown up.

East Timor was not the only province troubling the national government at this time, Indonesia had a lot on its increasingly cracking plate. But of course, no one was surprised when, regardless of all the undercover anti-GOLKAR, anti-Suharto sentiments, GOLKAR won the election by a mile and Suharto was back in power.

UNEXPECTED EVENT, 1998

Indonesia was in crisis. The economy was spiralling downhill, poor people were even poorer and confidence in the government was at a lower than ever ebb. It made little difference to people on Ataúro really; they were subsistence farmers who relied on their store of corn and beans and the odd fish or chicken to live, and in some ways were therefore immune to the effects of the economy. But drought that year made things worse, and people were hungry and worse off than usual. Everyone on Ataúro received food aid of rice – they complained because it was brown rice – and cooking oil from an American aid organisation.

Like everybody else on the island, I was allocated a sack of rice and five litres of oil. The leaders insisted I take it because if I gave my share to anybody else it would cause problems of envy. To avoid such problems and to alleviate my feelings of guilt (because, although I didn't have a real salary, I did have a monthly cash subsidy) we incorporated my aid packet into our household and school programs. Although people were struggling with survival, their support of our programs continued, the kindergarten and the high school lunch programs were even more important at that time.

Not many Timorese had confidence in the Suharto regime to resolve the economic and political problems that plagued Timor and most of the rest of Indonesia; they maintained hope for change only through the determination of the resistance movement on the mainland. It was a great surprise to everyone when it was announced suddenly that, after thirty-one years as president of an oppressive regime, Suharto was stepping down and his vice-president Habibi was stepping into his place.

On the night of the announcement, Baptista was watching television in the office with some of his friends and shouted out the news. We all ran to the little screen and Anton turned the volume up. People passing by on the road or the beach heard, and ran in to listen with us. Both Indonesians and Timorese, cheered and hugged each other. So much for the overwhelming free choice of the elections less than a year ago when Suharto was reinstated as ruler of the country.

It was an even bigger surprise when a few months later, Habibi announced that he would support a referendum for East Timor to choose its own future: to remain as an autonomous region within the Indonesian Republic or to become an independent nation. Although the resistance movement had fought for years both in and outside the country and, especially since the Santa Cruz massacre in 1991, foreign activists had run campaigns for the freedom of the little country, this news came out of the blue and everyone was stunned by it, could talk about nothing else, could hardly believe it was true.

Excitement and anticipation grew. But so did suspicion and fear.

PART NINE

CHANGES

After the announcement that the people of Timor Timur would be given the opportunity to choose their own future in a referendum, things began to change quickly. Under President Habibi, the provincial government of East Timor started to become more open. Foreigners began to visit the country, activists and journalists, supporters of activist movements posing as tourists, coming in. We even got the occasional visitor to Ataúro.

An activist from Darwin arrived one day, fired up with his mission to tell the world how badly the Indonesians have treated the Timorese. He was noticeably indifferent towards Anton although readily expecting his hospitality. We told him that on Ataúro things have not been bad, but he didn't want to hear that and asked us to organise a guide to take him, discreetly, to the mountains where he would make a video of living conditions there. We have doubts but ask our friend, Domingos, who was quite happy to make a few dollars by taking this man up the mountain track to Macadade. As as I am still the only western foreigner on Ataúro it would be difficult for him to be discreet. Another foreign person would hardly go unnoticed, his actions would be observed by everybody.

When he came back down the mountain, the young man was

keen to show us his film. It was of a Macadade woman cooking for her family in her kitchen. She squatted on the dirt floor, chopping vegetables and feeding the fire with sticks to keep it alight. She cooked the meal in a battered aluminium saucepan and a large wok. A dog slept beside her, and a chicken wandered into the open kitchen. It could be our kitchen. Anton, Baptista and I do not react.

'Well,' says the man. 'What do you think?'

We don't think anything. We are waiting for the punch line, unsure what point he was trying to make with this film.

'To show people what terrible poor conditions the Indonesians have forced the Timorese to live in,' he explained.

We three exchanged a glance and I told him this was the way people had lived here for generations. This was the way people all over rural Indonesia lived. All over most of rural south-east Asia, in fact. There were points to be made, but we didn't think he was making the right ones. Indonesia is a poor country, and the film did not show that the woman had been deprived of anything. This is the way people live here.

But the man was not interested. He was proud of his film and planned to take it to the world of tiled kitchens, electric stoves and dishwashers, where people would gasp in dismay. His film, no matter how inaccurate, would win sympathy for the cause.

THE LIBRARY

With the help of a little Oxfam-produced book called How to Make and Run a library, we started to develop one. NZAid and the United Church agreed to fund it. There was no potential for raising funds on the island; people on Ataúro were as poor as ever they had been. Besides that, it was a challenge to convince an illiterate community that they and their children would benefit from having access to books. Even teachers and those who could read had never had books and had not considered them necessary.

The difference between the ability to read words – and most Ataúro readers still read aloud from the only books they had: the Bible, Catholic Mass, and hymn books – and being literate in a deeper sense, was not understood. We mostly developed projects that had full community understanding and support before we started, but I was willing to go out on a limb with this one. How could people know the value of a library if they had never experienced one? Our funders agreed and several of my friends and family also contributed.

In those times of uncertainty, developing a community library was a positive and satisfying project. As with all our programs we applied a "learning as we go" approach and it was fun.

The unused "red school" building was painted, and the ceiling and toilets fixed. A local carpenter began building shelves and storage cupboards. Julieta, who was to be our new librarian, and I spent a couple of days sitting on the floor in the primary school "library" surrounded by unopened boxes of education department books. We sifted through them to choose the ones we thought suitable for our library. Although the books were made of poor-quality materials, some of the content was okay. We discarded the many that were blatantly moralizing or spouting Indonesian propaganda.

Teachers wandered in and told us we were wasting our time with the library. They claimed their students didn't like reading books. I didn't believe that and at recess when the children swarmed in wanting to see and read the books, I smiled at Julieta and suggested that the reason the kids haven't been interested in books was because they'd never been given access to them.

In a predominantly illiterate society, reading was sounding out words from the Bible and/or studying a dull school text. It wasn't reading for pleasure or for useful information. Nobody, including Julieta, had ever had that experience. The library was an exciting challenge for us.

A JAVANESE TEACHER

'Selamat pagi, Bu Guru.'

'Selamat pagi, Pak Guru.'

Most mornings we passed on the road and greeted each other in the usual Indonesian way: 'Good morning, Mr Teacher,' 'Good morning, Mrs Teacher'. At 7 am, six days a week, *Pak* Dahlan started out from his tiny government house in the centre of Vila to walk to the junior high school up on the edge of town. He was either a little ahead or a little behind groups of his students. On the road, he kept himself apart.

Dahlan was Javanese. Of slight build and fair skin, he was a quiet man with a certain presence that everyone respected; he was a diligent and caring teacher who had been posted to this remote island of Ataúro; far, far away from his kampung, his home in Java.

No matter how stiflingly hot the day was Pak Dahlan wore his government teachers' uniform – a synthetic grey safari suit, black leather shoes and white socks. He was a formal man, softly spoken, private. His pupils told me they love him because he cared, knew their names, prepared interesting lessons and gave them extra time and attention if they needed it.

Pak Dahlan was a Muslim, a long way from any mosque or imam. A small room on the side of his house served as his prayer room. When invited to village parties – weddings, anniversaries, funerals – he attended, eating from the specially prepared halal table with the handful of other Muslims on the island. He mixed with everyone but did not join in the drinking, leaving soon after the loosening-up stage – the stage that can sometimes drift into riotousness – begins.

Dahlan came to our evening English classes and was an earnest student. It was a lively class with lots of discussion, singing and laughter and he joined in, but hesitantly, shyly. When Anton, Baptista and I were preparing the local content curriculum for the school, he was our local education department contact and supporter. The school principal, an *unprincipled* man from Flores, was hardly ever on the island, hardly ever at the school. Anton joked that his contract must have stipulated that as long as he accepted the hardship posting to remote Ataúro, his reward was that he never actually had to be here for any longer than a couple of days a month.

So, Pak Dahlan was principal by default – although he couldn't make decisions without consulting with his absent superior who is several hours boat trip away across the strait and appears quite indifferent to most things. The absence of the real principal makes the process tediously slow, but Dahlan, who was as keen as we were for the program to begin didn't, apart from an occasional shake of his head, show his frustration about the delays. He never criticised his boss and stayed loyal to him like the diligent and loyal public servant he was.

I was impressed by the man's equanimity, his dedication, his goodness. So were Anton and others. Dahlan is one of the many good Indonesians who have been posted to this distant part of their island nation, who live away from family, religion and other supports, among people who could hate them. People like Dahlan accepted their remote posting, adapted to it, accepted their responsibility as teachers, nurses, doctors, and regarded Timorese as their countrymen. They cared about them. Many ordinary Indonesians worked hard here to develop health facilities, education, agriculture. Of course, not all Indonesians in East Timor, or in other parts of their country, were good, but I knew a lot who were.

In my second year on Ataúro, Dahlan, perhaps feeling more secure, brought his wife, a young mother in a hijab, and their two young daughters to live on the island. Like him, they fitted in and were respected by the community. Years later I was told by ex-students, then adults in an independent nation, that Pak Dahlan was the best teacher they had ever had.

We had some good discussions about education, Pak Dahlan and I. He often asked for my thoughts on education problems specific to East Timor. We spoke of education and community development, but we never talked politics. We never mentioned the military. That would've been too hard, too dangerous. I expected Dahlan heard the government propaganda and chose not to question it, at least publicly. He was an intelligent and sensitive man who lived in East Timor so was informed, but as a junior high school teacher away from home, a simple family man, he gave all his attention to his teaching – and that's all he could do, really.

HIGH SCHOOL MUATAN LOKAL

The high school program continued to go well. The teachers and students learned about chicken immunisation and how to vaccinate their fowls. Steve, an Australian vet and AusAID agriculture advisor based in Dili, came out to the island with his team to teach the women, teachers and students about poultry health. They supported Baptista's small livestock program and taught them about nutrition using local grains and greens. The horticulture group planted vegetables and learned about mulching and seed saving – of course already a traditional practice with corn and bean seeds.

The fishing group loved going out on the Manucoco, swimming, fishing, and pulling motors to bits. Pak Dahlan and the other teachers were enthusiastic about learning along with their students and the parents continued to volunteer to cook lunches. Once the curriculum was written up and the students' and teachers' books were printed, I didn't have a lot to do with the program but I'd wander up to the school now and then or join the students on the boat. It was always fun and satisfying to share their enjoyment of it.

SEA NOTES

Things that here you might regularly check for in the sea:
fish traps
lobsters under rocks
tiny shrimps
shellfish big and small
seaweeds and grasses
sea cucumbers
urchins
nets
ropes
anchors
barnacles on boats.

KINDERGARTENS

Our kindergartens, now in Vila, Bikeli and Makili, were going well. I visited each of them regularly for a few days at a time, Through the university we were still being helped to do the work with funding from NZAid and the Uniting Church. The teachers from the three kindergartens (Makili now had one too) and I met once a month, usually in Vila, for training, discussion and mutual support. They shared ideas and made teaching and learning materials like puzzles and books. They received a small, monthly stipend, certainly not enough to be called a living wage, but enough to contribute to their subsistence household economy.

In Vila, at the Manutasi kindergarten, we were trialling a food supplementary program. We had built a small kitchen and fireplace and were giving the children lunch three days a week. We (PPSDM) provided rice and a protein – dried or fresh fish or beans – the parents provide greens – local leafy vegetables, cassava or papaya leaves – and firewood for cooking. Under the supervision of the teachers, parents, grandparents and older siblings, the children took turns to cook and serve the meal.

We started a vegetable garden at Manutasi kindergarten and, with Baptista's supervision, the children and their parents dug and prepared the soil. The garden required water, of course, and we did some basic engineering to make sure we had enough available for the plants and to wash dishes after the meal. The problem was that, being a scarce commodity, water was taken by neighbours as soon as there was water in the tank. In Vila, people were not good at resolving water problems, not good at organising around water use, not good at sharing or conserving. It is an ongoing problem the community faces. We tried through education to assist people to find and implement solutions, but in this, we were not very successful.

INDONESIAN NURSES AND TRADITIONAL MIDWIVES

Quite often we were woken at night for emergency evacuations. The Manucoco was the most reliable and fastest boat on the island and the clinic called on us if a patient needed to be taken to Dili. A knock on the door after midnight meant a clinic call, and if the nurses advised that to go to Dili was the best option for a seriously ill or injured person, and their family agreed, Anton always made the boat available. Our donors agreed to cover the cost of emergency trips.

Guido, a skilled boatman, often had to be persuaded into taking the boat out into the sea at night with a patient who might live or die on the voyage. Each time our boat was called upon he explained to us the difficulties, and the repercussions if the patient died on board. The family of the patient could blame him and the crew. If death occurred on the boat, then ceremonies would have to be performed to cleanse it of bad spirits before it could go to sea again. We listened every time. We knew this was true. It was difficult to make a decision that would affect our crew but not directly affect us. But we always decided to send the patient and persuaded Guido into making the voyage, stipulating that at least one nurse must go to care for the patient and be a witness to any event that occurred on the way.

One night around midnight, we woke with a sharp rapping on the door. We knew it would be a nurse or a family member of someone who needed to go to Dili, so we leapt to our feet, scrambled into clothes. Anton sent for Guido and the boat crew. I accompanied the nurse back up to the clinic. Outside, two young Indonesian nurses greeted me. They were distressed.

'It's a mother giving birth, Ibu.' The girl took my hand as she spoke, 'And the baby is dead and won't come out.'

'We're afraid she'll die on the trip to Dili,' said the other nurse. 'We don't think she can survive much longer. We can't get the dead baby out.'

They took me into the little birthing room and there was a young woman with the tiny dead baby that tried to be born and was not. I could see the small head and face – quite blue, quite still. Contractions had stopped. The woman was in great pain. The nurses told me again that they had tried to deliver the baby and couldn't, and soon the woman would die. I felt helpless, as I frequently did here.

Outside I saw Mama Maria, the traditional healer and midwife. She had been called by the family of the young mother to come and assist. She pulled me aside and said she could get the baby out and probably save the mother, but she needed the nurses' permission to go to the patient. I talked to the nurses. They agreed that this seemed the only chance the woman had but explained that, although for normal births they use the traditional midwives, they are not supposed to turn an emergency patient over to them. I imagined the long trip across the sea with the boat bouncing over waves and knew the woman would surely die in great agony.

'Can't you turn away and not see Mama Maria go in?' I suggested. They agreed to do that, and literally turned away from the clinic, looking towards the sea while Maria slipped in. Not long afterwards she came out again, a smile on her face. She had taken the dead baby and the mother was alive. The nurses thanked her and went to their patient.

To the relief of the crew, boat preparations were cancelled and we all went back to bed for the few hours left before sunrise. The mother survived.

BROKEN WINDOWS AND POLICE

The police on the island were a mix of Indonesian and Timorese men, several of them Ataúro men. Once again, I had to decipher and appreciate the layers of complicated relationships – the Timorese men, proud to wear their brown police uniforms, pleased to have jobs that supported their families, working well as a team with Indonesian colleagues to maintain order on the island, were probably all resistance supporters. Behind the scenes, they were probably working to remove the Indonesian police – including their friends and workmates – from the country.

The police sergeant, Pak Gil was a kind man from Flores who was liked by people here. He liked life here too. I often saw him fishing on the beach or mending nets and we'd have a chat. He watched football on the television outside the police station with the local boys and girls, and came to watch their inter-village soccer and volleyball games. He had a positive attitude and led a good police team.

Once, in a moment of despair, Anton called on him. The crew of the *Manucoco* had a worse than usual argument, to do with roles and opportunities; as we usually only needed three crew for a trip, the five members of the team took turns when the boat went to Dili or to other villages and were paid accordingly. Jeremias was angry because he believed others were not giving him his fair share of work. He was a sensitive young man and believed the others laughed at him behind his back. Anton tried to help them sort it. As usual, he listened to everyone's point of view and encouraged them to find a solution.

But after their meeting Jeremias was still not satisfied. Angry and seeking revenge, he swam out to the *Manucoco* and smashed all the small glass windows on both sides. When witnesses ran to tell Anton this, he was angry; he had just spent so much time with the crew patiently trying to resolve the problem. He was responsible for the boat and always made sure it was regularly serviced, cleaned and in good condition. We loved that boat and relied on it. Ant decided to go and report this vandalism to the police.

Pak Gil listened to Anton and understood his anger, but persuaded him not to press charges or ask him to take police action. He was a wise man. He knew Jeremias well – everyone knew everybody else in that small community – and said he would have a quiet word with Jeremais to suggest that he help repair the windows when Anton got some glass cut.

Anton came back calmer. He told me what the police chief had advised and it had impressed him. It was a wise decision to avoid a stir about this small event; if families get involved, simple incidents become bigger and more difficult.

Pak Gil had his chat with Jeremias, who agreed to help repair the windows. As Anton and he worked together, the problem between them was resolved and they explored ways of resolving it with the rest of the group. Sometimes Ataúro people find it difficult to consider the perspectives of others and to compromise – especially with non-family members – and we found helping them resolve work conflicts took a great deal of time and understanding.

We were constantly learning about this and, in this instance, learned the way from the Indonesian police sergeant.

PERSISTENCE

Anton's mother didn't give up. Although there was serious trouble in Ambon, worsening conflict between Muslims and Christian that was said to be provoked by the military, Anton's mother was intent on getting her son back. She enlisted even more family members – cousins, uncles, aunts – to present her case to Anton. They put enormous pressure on him and more than once he came away from the telephone with tears in his eyes. I suggested that he go back to Ambon to talk with his parents, and he considered it. But it was a time of great change and activity in East Timor and we were preoccupied with our work.

SEA NOTES: OUTRIGGER

We skim along close to the surface of the sea, saltwater on my lips and tongue, tingling on my lashes, in my eyes. The small outboard motor putts away and the bamboo outriggers dip, slap-slap on one side and then dip, slap-slap on the other. I run my fingers through the water, peer down into the clear depths, watch rippling shadows of fish and swaying soft corals, lick salt from my lips. The sun is hot; I wrap my sarong over my shoulders and around my head. Anton, his hand on the throttle, gazes ahead, squinting into the sun; sometimes he looks at me with smiling eyes and begins to sing.

DEMONSTRATIONS

Anton and I were in Dili in June/July 1999, when the first big anti-Indonesian demonstration took place. We watched from the post office corner in Audian as hundreds of trucks, filled with flag and banner-waving Timorese came down from Balide through the streets of the town. It was the first time I had heard the chant, *Viva Timor Loro sa'e! Viva!* (Long Live East Timor!) pounding the air. Everyone in the street was excited. We were excited. You had to be. But it was excitement with an undercurrent of fear. It was hard to believe this was really being allowed to happen. We were alert, watching for military, waiting for sirens or military vehicles and loud hailers. But no – the long procession wound around the city and the cry for freedom echoed everywhere. It was extraordinary.

After this momentous occasion there were other demonstrations, other processions expressing the determination of the people to be free of Indonesia. *Viva Timor Loro sa'e! Viva!* And the military continued to hang back.

THE GATHERING OF GUNS

Coming back from Dili on a calm sea with a group of Ataúro men, we talk about the demonstrations: how amazing they were, how extraordinary that they could happen at all, how it seems now like the referendum might really happen, that Timor could be free. One of the men, Daniel, shakes his head knowingly.

'But they are gathering guns,' he says. 'My cousin told me that there are warehouses full of guns ready for war if we choose independence. They aren't really letting us get away with this. It won't be that easy.'

The others nod. They too have heard this story.

'Could it be true?' I ask. 'Would they really give Timor the chance to choose and then use weapons against them if they choose the wrong way?'

The Ataúro men smile at my naïvety. Someone pats my arm.

'Wait and see, Mama,' he says. 'We'll all have to wait and see.'

UKSW

The university sends us a message; they want us to return to Java as soon as we can. Anton and I resist. We delay. We turn a deaf ear. We don't want to go, don't want to leave Ataúro. In these times of growing uncertainty, we want to be there, we want to be working with the community, we want to be with them. We hear that all Indonesian public servants will soon be encouraged and supported to leave East Timor and return home.

The suddenness of the referendum created a sort of dizzy excitement, but with it came continuous rumour and fear. The local Consuelho National de Resistance de Timor/National Council of Timorese Resistance (CNRT) became more active, more organised. PPSDM now had a photocopy machine that could be used at night when we had power. It was a gift from friends of mine and was the first on the island, the first one many people had seen. It was a godsend to the education program. CNRT organisers trusted us enough to ask us to photocopy their documents and, of course, we learned a lot about what was going on behind the scenes this way.

We knew it was only a matter of time before we'd have to go back to Java; we would soon run out of excuses to delay the inevitable. Our fear was that, for political reasons, the university would abandon Ataúro, and all the work the community and PPSDM have done. We knew the kindergartens and school and Baptista's agriculture work might not be able to continue without support. We prepared our petition to the university.

PREPARATIONS

Lansell, an Australian friend who ran the AusAID water project in East Timor, was asked by the Australian government to prepare an escape route for the Australians and other foreigners working on the mainland. There were only eighteen foreigners living in Dili – aid workers, Red Cross, coffee industry people – and there was speculation about what they'd be able to do if things turn bad.

Escape to Ataúro and then fleeing by boat to somewhere else was the best option. Lansell asked me to help him prepare a food kit in case this eventuated. Anton and I shopped in Dili and brought back boxes of noodles, cans of fish and beans, a bag of rice, drinking water, biscuits and snacks to store on the island. It was an odd time – so much positive hope and yet a persistant current of fear and uncertainty in the air.

SMALL INJUSTICES

In Dili there was now a different atmosphere and it wasn't a good one. With the promise of independence and the world at last taking an interest in their plight, Timorese youths were becoming confident and bold, retaliatory.

STONES THROUGH A WINDOW

I was in the Dili salon having my hair cut by an Indonesian hairdresser when there was a loud banging on her door. The hairdresser, a middle-aged widow who came to Timor under the transmigration scheme, had lived in Dili for twenty years and established her business to provide for her family. She worked hard to support six or seven people. She put down her scissors and went to the door. I heard shouts and then children's laughter as the door closed again.

As she took up the scissors, she told me that the callers were Timorese teenagers with rocks in their hands demanding money from her. She said they came regularly now and threatened to smash her windows and destroy her salon if she didn't pay up. They'd threatened to kill her, so she paid up. And next month or next week or tomorrow they would come to demand more.

A TEACHER'S FEAR

Anton's cousin's wife had been a high school teacher in Dili for many years, but now she was afraid to go to her school. For weeks her East Timorese students had threatened her. They demanded that she give them high marks although they didn't attend lessons. She is torn between not wanting to falsify their results, and fear of being hurt by them. The school administration was lying low and didn't give her the support she needed to stand in front of hostile classes. She was stressed, a nervous wreck, and wanted to leave the country. She was now an absent teacher.

CHICKEN RESTAURANT

Ant and I often ate at a small daytime warung in Dili, a streetside café that opened during the day to sell tasty chicken curries and vegetables. An elderly West Timorese man and his daughter ran the café. They told us they came over the border to set up this little business five years ago. It was a chance to improve their lives from the abject poverty they lived in, in Kupang. They were not rich people, they worked hard and, because their food is good and cheap, many Indonesian and Timorese people ate there. This meant the daughter's children could attend school and there was enough money for their uniforms and textbooks.

One day the café was filled with Timorese students who had ordered up big and had plates of curry and fried chicken, cans of Bintang beer and Sprite on the table. They made room for us, and we ordered our favourite coconut chicken and joined them. They were a merry and friendly group.

Finishing their meal, the boys politely excused themselves, stood and started to walk out. When the proprietor reminded them that they hadn't yet paid for their meal they turned back and laughed. One of them threw a couple of small coins on the floor at her feet.

'*Terima kasih!*' they shouted as they went into the street.

The woman looked over at us, shrugged her shoulders and picked up the coins.

I was angered by the small injustices I saw in Dili. It hurt that I didn't know where to place my anger, where to lay blame. Anton was calmer and understood the attitude of the East Timorese, their need for retaliation, even their targeting of the wrong people. We knew that ordinary people, Indonesians and Timorese, were victims of power, of poverty and ignorance, of ambition. Unrealistically, I wanted poor people to be sympathetic towards each other, to care and work together to change things, to understand what's been going on. But that, of course, could not be part of the picture here. Those who had been subdued were beginning now to show their power in small ways – even against others who were powerless.

Right now, the truly powerful Indonesians and the truly powerful Timorese were preparing for a future that would likely not make any difference at all to the lives of the poor and powerless. I wanted the world to be a better place. But it wasn't. That was hard and it hurt.

A TRUCKLOAD OF STUDENTS

One day a stranger, an Australian woman, rushed up to me on the street in Dili. Upset, she grabbed my arm, needing desperately to tell me something.

'I've just seen a military truck go by,' she gasped. 'It was full of school students, packed tight with them. I think they're taking them away and might kill them all… the children were singing.

They don't know what could happen. What can we do?'

I patted her arm. In this instance, at least, I could reassure her.

'There's a big inter-school sports carnival down on the Scout oval,' I explained. 'I've heard the army is helping out with transport of participants from the districts. The kids are all going to the competition, that's all. Perhaps they're singing because they're excited and happy.'

She burst into tears. In the shades of grey, you could easily get it wrong.

LIQUICA MASSACRE

The injustices grew bigger, and much, much uglier; blood flowed and seemed to feed a terrible anger, a terrible thirst for more. One day in April, pro-independence supporters – reportedly over sixty and up to two hundred – were massacred, hacked to death in the church at Liquica. That was when it was confirmed for us that Indonesian military and police were supporting Timorese pro-Indonesia militias. In this instance, Besi Merah Putih (Red and White Steel) was being used to terrify citizens into voting to stay with Indonesia. They would stop at nothing.

It was still four months away from the referendum and ordinary citizens were being slaughtered for their political opinions. The military had tried unsuccessfully for twenty-five years to bully the Timorese into acceptance of Indonesian integration and now Timorese militia groups, backed by the army, were trying the same tactics. It would not work, but it spread terror throughout the country and awakened the terrible need for retaliation.

Timorese murdered Timorese. They were forced to do it, we heard. They were given drugs, we heard. They were being paid to do it, we heard. Poor people are so vulnerable, we heard, they cannot refuse. I was sick with the horrible reality of it. Perhaps there was some truth in each of these excuses, but the bigger, uglier truth was that Timorese were killing their own countrymen because of a difference of political opinion. That was happening. On Ataúro, people began to worry about their children at school in Dili and their relatives working on the mainland, and once again we all blessed the sea for keeping the island safe.

VISITORS

We received more visitors: Indonesian and Timorese strangers came from Dili in speedboats to sit on our veranda and, disguising their interest as polite conversation, plied us with questions about our work and political viewpoints. The first time this happened I was fooled. The three well-dressed Indonesian men, too well-dressed for a boat trip, hung back, allowing the two younger Timorese to do the talking. The Timorese were jovial and appeared sincere in their interest in our work, and in me. One of them was a linguist, a graduate from a Yogyakarta university and knew our university well. He offered to bring his thesis out for me to read next time he came, and I was interested. We appeared to have a lot in common.

They came again and I was given the thesis, as promised. This time I talked more freely. We drank coffee together. Anton refused coffee and called me aside.

'For God's sake, be careful,' he said. 'Rae, you are still too trusting. Who are these people? We have no idea. Don't talk so freely with them.'

We learned later that my young graduate friend was one of the senior government supporters of Aitarik, the fierce militia group that by the end of that year would be responsible for hundreds of murders, burnings and torture on the mainland.

THE ROCK, FEBRUARY 1999

I am sitting on a rock. In flip-flops, my feet dangle into the warm, glassy sea that is pink and blue, reflecting the evening sky. There's no wind and no sound but the waves crashing gently on the reef. The cliff behind me is ochre and orange volcanic rock; pale, wiry trees, their roots grasping at crevices, cling to it.

I am sitting here by the sea experiencing some kind of mystical moment, some kind of enlightenment. My eyes are suddenly wide open and my heart wide open too. I am filled to the brim with something… a kind of overpowering wonder… an intense universal love. And, for the first time perhaps, in a deep, spiritual way, I feel truly at home here, as if I belong.

I am sitting on a rock on the eastern side of Ataúro Island. I am sitting on a rock with my flip-flops and my feet in the sea and my heart soft and open and full of wonder, like a child's. It is evening and getting dark. A canoe slides into the sea, its bamboo outrigger wings bobbing on the water; heading to Makili, it moves along just outside the reef. As they pass, the boatmen wave to me, they are singing and the language of their ancestors drifts over the water. I don't understand the words, but I feel them on my skin, the sounds of them reverberate in my heart.

Some Makili people walking home along the beach stop to ask

me why I am sitting on a rock, alone. They tell me it is getting late and I should go home before dark. Spirits are abroad in the night, and they are not all good. They themselves have two kilometres to walk around the rocky coast and there is no moon, but they are with friends, not alone like me, they say. They are carrying baskets and boxes and tell me they have just arrived back from Dili in Nicalau's fishing boat, the *Tasi Diak, Number 81*.

Earlier this evening, I watched Nicalau bring his boat in over the reef, then walked north up the wide low tide beach. I walked as far as the mangroves, cut across a corn garden, doubled back down onto the dunes, passing Mama Luciana's house. I stopped to admire her chickens, then turned south, passed Vasco's crumbling mansion and the rusted Portuguese shipwreck, and headed on towards Lampia. I still have a lot of energy, a heart tingling with it.

This evening, sitting on the rock by the sea with my back to the cliffs of Ataúro, I feel the sharp, sharp sting of beauty and of mortality. I am reeling with the power of it in my heart which is momentarily strong and brave. And there is another dimension to what I am feeling… time. Just now I feel that I am history and history is me and tonight that excites me. I am here and I will never be here; I will be gone and I will always be here. It is a calm and persistent, pretty sea that curls towards me and I am exhilarated by the obvious: that whether I am here perched upon this ancient rock or whether I am not, the waves will continue to curl around its barnacled curves and sharp edges, will slap and foam against it till the moon sucks them back out to sea.

Whether I am here in ten minutes, whether I am here tomorrow, whether I am ever here again – like Portuguese and Japanese soldiers, Angolan rebels, exiled families of Fretilin guerrillas, thieves, misfits, and the original people of the Macadade, Makili, and Manroni clans – all here one moment gone the next, the waves will continue to wear away at these rocks, rolling pebbles from one place to another, depositing weed and shells and dead crabs on ever-changing grey sand beaches.

The reality of it prickles in my blood and I want to press myself back into the sharp, orange cliffs and feel their hardness against my bones. I want to lie on the seabed clutching seagrass. I want to be with the spirits on the peak of the great mountain Manucoco, hidden in dark, soft swirling clouds. I want to be this place. My soul is now entangled with its soul. I feel the spirits of the island, feel them watching me, feel their breath in the air around me – in the sea and rock, salt and dust. More Makili people pass by, remind me with gentle practicality that it's getting dark. They say to go back because you're alone and the night is full of mystery and danger. 'We are not safe here.' And so, I walk back, my rubber flip-flops, like theirs, slapping through water and over smooth and rough stones. They walk in the opposite direction, past the cliff face and out of sight.

Later in the night, in our small house by the huge sea, I begin to cry. My chest heaves, opening up and up; tears well up, flow and soak my pillow. The pillow is wet, the sheet is wet and I cry with such vibrant energy I don't ever want to stop. Anton cradles me in his arms and doesn't speak. I cry because I understand at last that we are not safe. None of us. I cry for those who have been brutally murdered in this country. They were not safe. I cry for the little boys, Joaquin and Maumau, who were not safe. I cry for Lu who was not safe. Those spirits who were with me on the beach, who are in the rocks and in the sea, and linger in the forests here, are with me now and both foment and succour my tears. They know.

I cry for all those who were here and are now not here. For my mother, it's the first time I have courage enough to cry with a full heart, to moan and weep and grieve for her. For my father, I cry for him with all the tears still stored away in my soul. And still I cry; tears of a little girl, tears of an adolescent, tears of a middle-aged woman who has had some kind of epiphany on a rock by the sea. I cry because my mother is dead. I cry because my father is dead. I cry because I will never see their faces again, never touch their soft, thin skin, never hear their stories or their songs… and because there is nobody now, nobody at all between eternity and me. Even little children have gone before me and, facing death, we are all little children; powerless, tumbling towards it. My heart is full of wonder, my pillow wet with tears. I am overwhelmed by the mystery and strength of this place, of life and of death and spirits in the rock, on mountaintops. I fear the near future and what is in store for us. I cry for the evil in people's hearts, and for the good.

Anton, silent, cradles me in his arms while I cry.

ATAÚRO GHOSTS

The ghosts of old men and women don't leave Ataúro but hover around keeping sharp eyes on the comings and goings, the various doings of the living. They rest near freshwater springs these invisible spirits; in forests, in caves and on mountaintops, watching and listening, demanding, through mediums that speak their tongue, consultation and animal sacrifice. The building of a fence across a path, a new house, the launching of a boat, the cultivation of a new garden – all such change must be sanctioned by them.

Priests want to chase these ghosts away; with prayers, candles, incense, plaster-of-Paris Virgins strewn with flowers; with sweet voices and the singing of hymns, they try to undermine the reigning ghostly power. But they are strong, and determined, the ghosts of Ataúro, ignoring candles and incense and the chanting of prayers, they cling tenaciously to misty mountains, hide in the dry crevices of gullies and cliffs and deep, deep in the uncertain hearts of men and women. They have not gone yet and probably never will.

AN OPINION

Suspecting that the university intended to close the Ataúro program around the time of the referendum, Anton and I explored possibilities for handing the work of PPSDM over to a mainland Timorese non-government organisation before going back to Java. There were only two local NGOs in Timor – one with an agriculture focus, and Bia Hula that works with the AusAID Project Water on rural water accessibility.

We talked with one of the more radical Timorese graduates and one of the founders of the first Timorese NGO. We had heard that in recent months he had changed his position on the independence issue and now believed that choosing autonomy within Indonesia rather than independence would be a better option for the East Timorese people. It was not long after the Liquica tragedy and everyone was still recoiling from the horror of that. In the shadow of that military-backed massacre, we asked this respected man why he now favoured autonomy. He was direct in his response: he did not believe that an independent Timorese government would benefit the poor of Timor, that rural village people would be any better off than they were now. He thought they would probably be worse off. Still forward-thinking, he believed that it would be more beneficial for Timor to remain a part of a changing Indonesia and, as an autonomous province, support those who are working towards social and economic justice in that country.

It was a radical view for those times. He knew his view was very unpopular – especially with foreign journalists and activists – and he had made a decision not to be interviewed by them again. Even the Vatican press, he complained, berate him for his view and secular journalists lectured him about the way he thinks. He was an intelligent, thoughtful Timorese man who had come to his opinion out of personal experience. How could foreign journalists criticize this, try to carry him on their wave of certainty about what is best for his country? We appreciated his sincerity and left with much to think about, although without an answer to our dilemma. We were starting to understand that even amongst UKSW graduates and non-government community workers there was so much political diversity that it would not be possible for them to work together and take over our program.

PART TEN

SALATIGA

Aleixio, Director of Bia Hula, a Timorese NGO, is a graduate of Satya Wacana, our university. He agreed to come back to Java with us to ask the university to officially hand over the Ataúro program to Bia Hula. Bia Hula already had a program on the island, working on provision of potable water and could perhaps take the education, agriculture, livestock and fish-drying work under their wing, or at least be a conduit for support and funding from our loyal donors.

In a meeting with the rectors at the university, we were told that the Ataúro program would be closed. They expected us to go back to implement that closure and then return to Java. We objected and presented our case for the continuation of the kindergartens and the work in the schools. The leadership of the university had changed since Willi Toisuta started the Timor programs and the current leaders, in the current political climate, were not willing to listen or negotiate. Aleixio presented his case. They were sympathetic but adamant. We were told we should all get out of Timor as soon as possible because there would be trouble there. When I continued to point out that doing so would abandon the work that was now well established, abandoning the people that we have worked with so long, I was told by our bosses that, 'Indonesia has many hundreds of islands, Ibu Gabrielle, and the university will find you another one to work on.' Although they have supported my work, they don't understand the depth of my love and commitment to Ataúro.

Aleixio, who had been anxious about his family while he was away from them, returned home to Dili. Anton and I together made the decision to resign from the university and return to Ataúro to continue our work. We were not sure how we would do this, but we'd find a way.

AUSTRALIA

Without the university's sponsorship I no longer had a visa to work in Indonesia and had to return to Australia to try to organise one. Brother Dan, a friend from the Edmund Rice Foundation, had begun working in Dili and agreed to help me through his Catholic Church channels. The visa would take a month or more to come through, so I visited my family in Brisbane. Anton went to visit his family in conflict-torn Ambon and then on to Jakarta. The visa took longer than expected.

It was the longest time Ant and I had been apart in nearly four years but we were both clear about returning to Ataúro, continuing our work and being there for the referendum.

After a couple of weeks in Brisbane I took a month-long consultancy in the community of Noonkanbah in Western Australia. I needed some income and welcomed the chance to visit and work in a community school. My contract was to assess three children with special needs, one in the kindergarten and two in the primary school, and then assist their teachers to design appropriate learning programs for them. I was an experienced special education teacher and my community development experience in Papua New Guinea, Indonesia and East Timor was valuable, but I had much to learn about this desert community; I found it challenging.

I loved the edge of the desert and the river and the stories the students told me. If I had another lifetime, perhaps that's where I'd be… but I was preoccupied with what was going on in Indonesia and Timor and wanted to get back there.

In June 1999 there were elections in Indonesia. Anton was either in Jakarta where there were huge processions and fierce riots, or in Moluku, where his family home in Ambon had been destroyed in the ongoing conflict between Christians and Muslims. In East Timor, anticipation of the referendum and its result stirred up violence in the military-backed militias. It was a worrying time.

Friends and family asked why I was returning to Timor at this time but there was no doubt in my mind that this was what I wanted to do. In the media there was nothing but stories of violence and danger, but I knew in reality there were other things too – markets and fishing boats and kids going to kindergarten, church services and fish-drying and songs and singing. I wanted to be on Ataúro with Anton, Baptista, Guido, the teachers, the parents and children for this momentous and extraordinary time.

SEA NOTES: AUSTRALIA

Living for a time at the edge of the desert in WA, I have been involved with rivers and dust – a long way from the sea. I've almost forgotten how seawater mingles with sand from faraway places, forgotten how it's never still, how it carries music from islands, carries stories and songs, coconut shells and twists of rope crusty with barnacles and weed.

Now back on the east coast of Australia, the sea is clear and empty; no wooden canoes, no voices singing across the water. Apart from its own music – the music of foaming and crashing waves – this sea is silent. But the music of Ataúro is in my soul and the songs that swirl even in these distant waters, call me back.

A seabird that's flown across vast skies and vast seas lands beside me. This bird has flown through storms – wild winds, stinging rain – over high, angry waves. It has flown through icy clouds and cold currents into hot, bright sunlight dancing on deep tropical waters. This journeyed bird has landed on the sand close to me, and stares at me with one knowing black eye. And there, at home and far from home: the sea, the seabird and me.

THE SPY

Wayan was at the Dili airport those days, his job to monitor the comings and goings of journalists and other potentially dangerous visitors. When I arrived, he was immediately at my side to accompany me through the terminal and fend off any questions or delays from the military. Anton and I always brought him a gift to show we appreciated his assistance. He appreciated any token of our friendship, no matter how small a trinket it was. Coming back from Australia I brought him a kangaroo pen and an Australian flag key ring, and he was delighted.

BACK TO ATAÚRO

Anton arrived back in East Timor before I did, and he, Guido and Jeremais brought the Manucoco to pick me up in Dili. Ant had heard many stories. Everyone had stories to tell. They told me about the strengthening of the militia groups on the mainland, about the new Indonesian military commandant now based on Ataúro and how he had been threatening people with a gun.

All but six of the Indonesians on the island have left. The only ones still here are: the police chief, one other policeman who is married to an Ataúro woman, a primary school teacher in Bikeli, our new gun-toting commandant, his Javanese lieutenant, and Anton. All other teachers, nurses and administrative personnel had been sent home. I was sad not to have said goodbye to Pak Dahlan and the others.

The place was full of whispers. Several men including Vasco, Janario and Eduardo told me that the new military man held his revolver to their temples and threatened to kill them if the referendum results were not to his satisfaction. The men are scared but are absolutely committed to their cause.

We continued our work and I never saw this commandant. I looked out for him as I passed the military compound, expected to see him on the road as I cycled to the kindergarten. I thought I might perhaps meet him on my evening stroll along the beach, but I never did. I only heard about the man and his threats and his tough demeanour and, though curious, of course I don't seek him out.

Prior to the referendum, it was an even more than usual double-layered world; everything was normal and yet nothing was normal. There was school every day and the market on Fridays. Children played by the road and on the beach. Men fished from boats, throwing nets, diving with spears. Women carried firewood, drying fish, washing clothes at village taps, cooking over fires. And there were secret meetings at night, people coming to photocopy documents, whispering. There were what-ifs, hows and whens. There were plans. There were rumours and fears. There was a military man holding guns to people's heads. There were certainties and uncertainties.

We painted the library. We sorted and catalogued the library books.

UNITED NATIONS MISSION IN EAST TIMOR (UNAMET)

11 June 1999, Press Release SC/6689:

Security Council Establishes Mission in East Timor to Conduct 8 August 'Popular Consultation' on Territory's Status

19990611

Adopts Resolution 1246 (1999) Unanimously; Ballot to Decide on Special Autonomy or Separation from Indonesia

The Security Council this afternoon decided to establish the UNAMET to organise and conduct a popular consultation, scheduled for 8 August, to determine the Territory's future status, in keeping with the agreement between Indonesia and Portugal of May 5, and the Agreements between the United Nations and the two governments.

Adopting resolution 1246 (1999) unanimously, the Council established UNAMET until 31 August and approved the modalities for the consultation, which will ascertain, on the basis of a direct, secret and universal ballot, whether the East Timorese people accept the proposed constitutional framework providing for a special autonomy for East Timor within the unitary Republic of Indonesia, or reject the proposed special autonomy, leading to East Timor's separation from Indonesia.

The UN Security Council and the Indonesian government agreed that UNAMET would consist of political, electoral and information components and that up to 280 UNAMET civilian police would be deployed to work with the Indonesian police, and fifty military liaison officers to work with the Indonesian Armed Forces. The Government of Indonesia was to be responsible for peace and security in the lead up to, and the conducting of the referendum. Many people had serious doubts about the wisdom of this.

The UNAMET team on Ataúro stayed in the Beloi Beach Hotel, an Indonesian "tourist hotel" which until this time had never been used due, among other things, to lack of basic facilities. Jerry cans and drums of water had to be carried up the steep path for the UNAMET team's ablutions. I was to be an official observer on referendum day and spent some time with the team prior to it. A group of six men of mixed nationalities, they seemed to find living in such close quarters in the isolation of Ataúro a challenge even for such a short time. Surprised to find me there, they invited me for a meal a few times – I think I was both a diversion and a source of information.

Anton was not invited and chose not to come when I suggested it. It was very strange for us to have a group of white foreigners living on the island. I pestered them until they agreed that, when the day came, as well as officially observing I could film at the voting posts of Vila and Beloi.

AUGUST 17 1999: INDEPENDENCE DAY

This would be the last celebration of Indonesian Independence Day in East Timor. We knew that. Everybody knew that. But officials were pretending, hoping, still trying to hold back the tide. By chance, Anton and I were in Dili on the Independence Day holiday. Because of the growing tensions in the city, an AusAID car picked us up from the beach. It felt strange; it was not normal for us to travel in cars other than the old taxis in Dili.

People gathered in front of the Palacio, truckloads of dancers from the districts had been brought in to celebrate. There was an odd atmosphere in the city because most of those celebrating Indonesia today would, in less than two weeks, be voting to separate from that nation and send it on its way. But for the time being, the charade continued and we were part of it.

A block down from the beach our vehicle was stopped by a group of young Timorese men. Enrico Guterres, the leader of the militia gang Aitarak (Thorn) was on the side of the road directing them. He was on a huge motorbike and looked tough. His men slapped stickers all over our car. 'Vote for Otonomi!' said our car, ten, fifteen, then twenty times. We decided to leave the car and wandered over to where the festivities would take place in front of the Palacio. Anton had the video camera and wanted to catch it all on film. As we walked along the footpath, a stranger tailed us, walking frighteningly close behind. As we reached the gate of the Palacio, he grabbed Ant by the shoulders and whispered to him. Ant turned to me. 'I have to go with them,' he said. 'They want to talk with me. You keep walking, pretend you haven't noticed.'

An Aitarak gang member took him by the elbow and led him up the side street. I didn't know what to do. Ant looks Timorese, like a very tall Timorese, so perhaps they thought he needed "educating" about the referendum, or at least wanted to question him about it. Although I knew that these people would spill blood in a flash, I also knew that Ant was clever and would not make mistakes. He is Indonesian and that, of course, will work in his favour. Remembering the way he handled the military interview in Tutuala the previous year, I was confident he'd be okay.

He was gone for about twenty minutes, and I distracted myself by watching the dancers and musicians arriving: young girls from each district in tais sarongs, men in tais cloth and feathered headgear, musical instruments – bells, drums and gongs. It was as

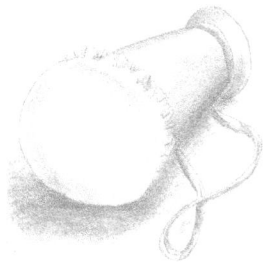

beautiful as usual, but this year there was palpable confusion, hesitation. With less than two weeks before the referendum, there was anguish in the faces of those who'd been brought into town to perform in the celebration of a country they are about to reject.

Ant finally came back, unscathed, but a little shaken. The Aitarak militia that had just released him was one of the most brutal Timorese militia groups and would soon wreak bloody havoc on the city.

EDUCATION FOR A REFERENDUM

UNAMET had the task of ensuring the referendum was successful. This meant educating an illiterate population so that everyone was clear about its purpose, their right to vote and the form that voting would take. Teams went out to all districts, local people were trained to supervise the voting and all the processes leading up to it – registering, setting up the posts, organising voters on the day, inking fingers.

They produced a fantastic television program that was broadcast every evening all over the country. It was fifteen minutes of local actors playing recognisable characters in different scenarios, having different conversations, asking different questions, in preparation for the referendum. Each segment was repeated in four languages: Tetum, Indonesian, English and Portuguese. It ran for several weeks and became an evening ritual. It was simple, funny, and informative. Friends and neighbours came to watch in our office, sitting on the floor, on chairs, on tables to watch all four segments one after the other. Every house that had a television set was filled; it was the first time anyone had seen a Timorese drama with Timorese actors and people loved it.

The program had a beautiful theme song: Oras To'o Ona Mai Ita Hili (The time has come… come let us choose). The lyrics were beautiful, the melody haunting. That song captured the long wait, the struggle, the anticipation… but I heard in it an element of unreality, something ethereal in its tone, something cautionary.

At the end of every segment, every day, there was a statement designed to reassure. Loud and clear and in four languages, the people of East Timor were told they had nothing to fear. Every night we heard that 'UNAMET would be here before, during and after the referendum and so there was absolutely nothing to fear'. Although in parts of the country there had already been fearmongering, murders and destruction, people clung to that reassurance – people needed to believe that there was something big and strong overseeing all this, something that would keep them safe.

DILI WEDDING

The son of a well-to-do Timorese family, a graduate from our university, was to be married and Anton and I were invited to his wedding party in Dili. It was to be a big wedding, with many guests. Besides relatives and friends of the couple, there were three or four AusAID foreigners who worked in Dili, Timorese intellectuals and activists, senior Timorese public servants, senior Indonesian military personnel and public servants, and Anton and me.

It was a strange mix of people in a strange atmosphere. In two weeks' time there would be a referendum to decide the fate of this country and its people. Everyone there was aware of shadows, no one knew who of their fellow wedding guests was involved in what, or with whom. There were those who pretended the outcome would be a good one for Indonesia, there were those who spoke out for rejection of autonomy. In the shadows there were militia groups and weapons, just in case. But at the wedding and dressed in our best, we shared good food, enjoyed live music, mingled and danced. I watched closely and wondered who of these powerful guests was who… behind the scenes whose hands were these people holding? Who were they listening to? What did they know and what did they want? What plans were afoot and how were they involved?

This was not an Ataúro village wedding; it was much more sophisticated and something of a charade. Educated and influential Timorese and Indonesians socialised in an undercurrent of uncertainty. Like the other guests, we pretended to ignore that and laughed and danced into the night.

SOLDIERS AND NURSERY RHYMES

We saw neither hide nor hair of a soldier when the huge pro-independence demonstrations wound their way through Dili. We never heard a peep from them when the chant of 'Viva Timor

Loro sa'e' was in the air. But daily, in the early mornings, they jogged through the streets; a fit and disciplined block of young men in tracksuit pants and khaki T-shirts that fit snugly over their chests and clung to their well-muscled shoulders, their bulging upper arms. As they ran, they sang, these men; they sing the words of Indonesian children's songs and nursery rhymes. The rhythms of these little songs kept their powerful legs moving in unison, pounding the roads and down the lanes of the city, echoing through the compounds and into the houses. They sang songs about flowers and stars, ducks and little geckoes creeping up on mosquitoes; snap! The soldiers' voices were hard and clipped, and just a little bit mocking. They made the hairs on my arms stand.

Anton and I watched from the upstairs window of Steve and Julie's house in Ballide. Steve and Julie were AusAID agriculture workers, and we stayed with them when we were in Dili. From our vantage, we heard the thudding of soldiers boots on bitumen and the sweet words of nursery songs as they passed. Although we knew all the words by heart, we didn't sing along with them.

CAMPAIGNS

At times the people of Ataúro can work together seamlessly; recent squabbles, entrenched and bitter differences, long-standing grudges can be forgotten for a greater cause. August 1999, the time of organising and running the campaigns prior to the referendum, was one of these times. The island CNRT leaders devised a strategy, a clever plan and on both campaign days, when pro-independence and then pro-autonomy campaigners came out from Dili, it went like clockwork.

To keep their real political inclinations hidden from authorities, it was agreed that everyone would wholeheartedly support both campaigns. First, everyone would show support for the "no" to autonomy, within Indonesia, and then they would show support for the "yes" to autonomy, within Indonesia. In Vila, the campaigns were held under the big trees next to the community library. Many people took part in them. Anton and I went up to watch. The events on both days were extraordinary.

The first gathering was the "No to Autonomy" campaign. Under the terms of the referendum this, of course, meant "Yes to Independence" and was what people wanted. Mothers, fathers, grandparents, children with their aunts, uncles and cousins all turned up to the campaign event, bursting with enthusiasm, waving flags and shouting 'Viva Timor Loro sa'e'. A sound system had been set up on a stage. One after the other, community leaders presented their case for the no-vote. People cheered wildly. A campaigner or two from Dili presented the "no" case. People cheered support. A string band played stirring music. People danced and cheered. At the end of the speeches the whole crowd became a shouting, happy mob. The dust rose around the dancers, the singers. 'Viva Timor Loro sa'e! Viva Timor Loro sa'e! Viva Timor Loro sa'e! Viva! Viva! Viva!' A stirring afternoon.

There was no sign of the commandant, no sign of military or police – not even the local Ataúro soldiers or police who might have been there to, secretly, support the campaign. There was no militia.

Two days later the "Yes to Autonomy" campaign was held; same place under the same trees, same time of day, attended by the same people. They were all there again to cheer and sing and dance for autonomy. This campaign had more funds, of course, so gifts were distributed to the crowd – scarves and T-shirts with Ya Otonomi! (red on white) blazoned across them. Ya! Free T-shirts! One after the other, community leaders presented their case for the yes-vote. People cheered. Several campaigners from Dili in their Otonomi Now T-shirts presented their "yes" case. People cheered. A string band played stirring music. People danced and cheered. 'Viva Timor Loro sa'e! Viva Timor Loro sa'e!'

It was all the same; carbon copy. Except that during the second event, the shouting was less spontaneous, the dancing less feverish, the music more subdued, and the dust hardly rising. This second campaign needed organisers to whip up enthusiasm, conductors to stir people up, promises and gifts to keep shouts and smiles coming. Again, there was no sign of the commandant, no sign of military, militia or police that afternoon. The sea protected Ataúro and the clever Ataúro tricksters pulled it off. I have proof of the ingenuity and audacity of those days on film, and smile remembering.

REFERENDUM DAY, 30 AUGUST 1999

'Oras to'o ona

Mai ita hili…'

(The time has come, come let us choose…)

The day had come. The day that still seemed like a miracle, the day that brought the chance to vote for independence, the chance offered out of the blue by President Habibie one year ago. People thought it would never happen. After resisting Indonesian occupation for nearly twenty-five years, such an opportunity was a dream. And now it was real and it was here. The Indonesian government was true to its word. The UN and international observers were here. It was referendum day.

In Vila, the voting would take place at the primary school next to our PPSDM office. I was up at daybreak to see people arriving. They were coming in droves by boat and on foot; old people with sticks, young people just old enough to vote, children and their parents. One elderly man was wheeled up in a wooden cart from the beach to the school. I saw several very old women carried from outriggers. Everyone wanted to vote, and nothing was going to stop them. There was a festive crowd gathering in front of our place long before the booths open.

Police were helping the UNAMET team prepare, but there was no sign of the military. That was good, very good.

I went inside for coffee. I poured two cups and looked for Anton.

'Ant?' I found him in his small study curled up on the mattress on the floor. The curtains were still drawn and it was dark in the room.

'Anton, what's wrong?' No response.

'Ant, there are so many people here already. It's amazing. Come outside and see.' I was buzzing with the excitement of this moment.

Anton was silent and I saw at last that something was wrong. Anton was crying. I was astonished.

'Ant, what is it? What's the matter?'

He shook his head but didn't say anything. I knelt beside him.

He cried silently and my heart reached out to him, but my brain was unable to grasp what this was about. Finally, he sat up. Crumpled and embarrassed, he took time to sort his thoughts.

'I know it's stupid,' he said, 'but I feel sad.'

He looked at me, embarrassed and desperate for me to understand. Both he and I were hesitant, afraid that I wouldn't.

'It's my country they hate. It's what we've done to them. They want to be rid of us... all of us.' He took a deep breath. 'They hate Indonesia and I am ashamed.'

And I was perplexed.

'But Ant, you've known this all along. It's not new. You know why, you hate it too, you hate what your country's military have done here.'

He stared at the floor and I began to see, began to see what was momentarily breaking his heart. I am Australian and sometimes, away from home, I still get goosebumps when I hear the music of Waltzing Matilda and even Advance Australia Fair... but, unlike Anton, I have not been raised from birth on nationalistic propaganda, mantras and songs. I have not sucked in deep national pride with my mother's milk, have not, from the age of six, worn a uniform the colours of the national flag and daily repeated passages extolling the greatness and goodness of my country.

I am mostly proud to be an Australian, but I cannot imagine what it feels like to grow up patriotically Indonesian, to have cut my teeth on the Pancasila and, somewhere deep down inside, have a partial belief that all that propaganda about my country is true. Anton is smart and educated, he is discerning and critical, but he is Indonesian. At that moment, as an Indonesian, he felt great shame and great pain.

We sat in silence, each trying to unravel something that had penetrated so deep into our separate psyches we couldn't find it, something that marks a difference between us, and something that is so deep it is us. It was a moment of illumination because we both knew there was nothing else to do just now but accept this moment, this difference, this painful acknowledgement that the world is full of tricks and, to some extent, we too are victims of its deception.

We drank the coffee that had grown cold and went out to watch the voting begin. I was an official observer and would also film the day's events. When Ant met the crowd gathered next door on the road, they greeted him enthusiastically and at last he too felt the excitement and was swept along by it. Taller than everyone in the crowd, he looked across the tops of voters' heads, grinned at me and gave me the thumbs up.

'Oras to'o ona

Mai ita hili…'

A PARTY

The day after the referendum, when the ballot boxes had been flown out on a UN helicopter to Dili and people from all over the island had rowed, sailed, hobbled, been carried or skipped back to their villages, we were invited to the commandant's house. The young Javanese soldier who was his right-hand man came to our house to deliver the unexpected invitation.

So now, at last, we would meet the elusive commandant. We were uneasy. Anton asks the soldier to explain.

'It's a party,' said the young lieutenant. 'A party to celebrate the success of the referendum!'

Success? What was success? This explanation raised huge questions and did nothing to alleviate our unease, but Anton had the composure to ask who else was invited to attend. The young soldier ticked off on his fingers a list of leaders, significant people in the community. Hesitantly we accepted, we had no choice really, and it would be better for us to be at the party than not. We sent word around the village suggesting that we, the invitees, should meet at the corner first and all go to the military compound together. Truly, we had no idea why this man was having a party to celebrate what was surely going to be a defeat for his country; it was worrying.

This was the first time we'd laid eyes on the commandant about whom we'd heard so much. He was a thickset man and taller than most Javanese men. His shoulders and arms may have lifted weights, his chest and neck were rigid barrels connecting his large head and stocky limbs. He sat well back and deep into an armchair, heavy thighed, his feet in scuffed army boots firmly planted on the crumbling cement floor. His arms stretched out along the armrests of the chair, his plump hands hanging over the edge.

The commandant remained seated when we arrived and smiled widely as he watched us being ushered to our places. A Cheshire cat, his smile was enigmatic, discomforting. It hung in the air and we didn't know what to do with it. When we were all seated, shuffling along the bench to make room for each other, when our nervous coughs and throat clearings were over, he made a short speech.

'Welcome to my house,' he said. 'Welcome to this small party. You've been invited here to celebrate with me… to celebrate the success of our referendum.'

We looked at our feet, our hands twisting in our laps; the commandant allowed a minute or two of silence before he continued, 'The referendum on Ataúro has gone smoothly and without mishap. The votes have been taken safely back to Dili to be counted. Now we must just wait to hear the results.'

He smiled, raising his eyebrows questioning, menacingly. Of course, we all already know the results. We don't need counting to confirm the outcome. The smiling cat had become a tormentor now that we, the mice, are sitting obediently in silent rows in allocated places on his wooden benches. He allowed another silence – perhaps half a minute that felt like an hour – before he continued.

'Please relax now and enjoy our celebration.'

He gestured towards the table laid out with plates and cutlery for a meal; bowls of chilli and cucumbers, cans of soft drink, bottles of beer and cheap brown whiskey, sealed plastic cups of water. He gave a sign, and a line of women appeared, bustling obediently from the kitchen with bowls of rice and vegetables, beans and meat. The women were dressed in their Sunday best and were unsmiling. Their faces did not hide their fear but, as always on special occasions, they fidgeted and fussed until the spread on the table looked just  right and then, in a line, they bustled out again. They made no eye contact with the guests – some their own husbands, sons and brothers – or with each other. The poignancy of this ritual, the uncertainty, was palpable. It hurt.

This party was like a play in which we'd all been given roles but had been offered no chance to rehearse. We wanted to get it right but were unsure what "right" was in this context. Each moment was a try-out to see what would happen next. Several of the guests here had, not long ago, had a gun – the very one that even now sat in its holster on the commandant's hip – held to their temples by this, our gracious host. The commandant, who remained seated well away from the table, invited us to eat and we rose, gingerly, one by one, to approach the food. It occurred to me that it might be poisoned but I dismissed the idea as a nervous whimsy; it had been prepared and cooked by watchful Ataúro women. We eat. Silently. The commandant watched and urged us to take more, drink more, enjoy ourselves and relax. 'This is a celebration,' he reminded us magnanimously. Nobody spoke. Nobody had an appetite for words or for food.

After we had forced spoonsful of rice and overcooked goat meat into our dry mouths and wet them with warm beer or warm

Sprite, we put down our spoons and glasses with relief. On cue, the women in their sombre line came in to clear the tables.

'And now,' said our host. 'I have surprises for all of you.'

I glanced at Anton who stared straight ahead. I noticed a few others exchange glances. Surprises?

On cue, a uniformed Ataúro soldier brought out a large cardboard box and placed it beside his commander on a side table. The soldier did not look at us. Our host dipped into the box and took out a radio, a small, black plastic, portable thing that he turned over in his large hands. He whispered a name to the soldier, who took the radio and presented it to one of the guests.

The big military man was playing Santa Claus and seemed very excited about that. He sat in his chair, beaming as Sr Antonio, with some embarrassment, accepted his gift. I squirmed, watching our friends, one by one, nod an awkward thank you for an unwanted trinket.

Nobody understood the purpose of this gift-giving, so it was awkward. There were radios and bottles of whiskey and yellow T-shirts and pen sets. I glanced at Anton who frowned as the gift-giver called my name.

'Now, Ibu Gabrielle,' he said with just a hint of teasing in his voice. 'Will you also accept a gift from me?'

I remembered Anton's reminder to be very, very careful and felt his body tense beside me.

'Certainly.' I felt a false smile on my face.

'It's a T-shirt,' he said, 'a pro-autonomy T-shirt.' He held it up. 'Would you accept it as a gift from me?'

A simple trap?

'I will,' I said. 'If there's one big enough for me, I'll accept it.' I meant it to be funny – my size can always be made a joke – but he did not smile.

Instead, 'Then you will wear a pro-Indonesian shirt, Ibu?'

He held out the white shirt with the red letters so we could see the size and read the message Ya Otonomi. Hundreds of these T-shirts had been given out over the last few weeks so they are very familiar to us all. Now was my time for careful words. And suddenly from somewhere they came to me.

'Oh no. I wouldn't wear it, Pak.' I managed to sound quite shocked at the suggestion and then smiled at him with a warm, false, apologetic smile. 'Everybody knows, Pak, that I'm not involved in politics so, of course, I would never wear a shirt with a political message. Never.' I watched his face as he took this in and then, as a consolation, added, 'But I'll accept your gift as a souvenir and keep it as a memory of today. Terima kasih.'

He smiled his cat smile, a satisfied-enough smile that might've even had a touch of humour in it, and passed over the T-shirt which I immediately folded and stuffed into my bag and out of sight. Anton's body beside me softened.

At the commandant's exaggerated insistence, we drank a little more whiskey, beer or Sprite and then someone took the initiative and stood up; the party was over. He let us go. Still wondering, confused, we walked home along the deserted road in silence. No breath of air, leaf or animal stirred.

THE ANNOUNCEMENT, SEPTEMBER 4

It had been announced that the results would be broadcast on September 6th, a week after the referendum. But suddenly on Friday the 3rd, we heard that the results would be broadcast on Saturday instead, two days earlier than expected. The commandant who, since the party, had begun making frequent visits to our house, did not know this. He had not been told of the date change and at first did not believe us when we told him. He was not happy that we all knew before he did, obviously his headquarters in Dili were not keeping him up to date and I could see he was feeling isolated and unsure of himself. He roared off on his motorbike.

On Saturday morning anyone associated with PPSDM came down to the office, creeping through the back of houses, down narrow paths, keeping off the road to get there. We turned on the television to hear the announcement and stifled shouts of joy when it was announced that over seventy-five percent of the people had voted to reject autonomy, which meant independence! But our smiles faded when, minutes after the announcement was made, the television went off air. The screen went blank, ominously dead. There was silence and what began as an ecstatic, joyous moment was suddenly tinged with fear. Everyone hugged, everyone whispered. Anton wrote the results on slips of paper and each person copied them on the hems of their T-shirts or skirts.

When we heard the roar of the motorbike outside there was panic, a scurry as everyone left by the back door, disappearing before the commandant stomped up the gravel path and straight inside.

'Assalem waleikum!' he shouted, without the slightest trace of humour in his voice. We did not respond with words but went to greet him.

'UNAMET has done this!' he shouted as he paced our veranda and scratched his head. 'They've rigged the results. They've changed votes. They've interfered.' He was beside himself with rage. Pacing. He was furious. We were puzzled. Did he really believe what he was saying? He seemed to. He seemed to find it incredible that the people had said "no" to autonomy. We found it incredible that he hadn't predicted the outcome. He paced up and down, shaking his head.

'I'll make some tea,' I said and darted back inside while he continued to harangue Anton about the treachery of the UN. Anton said nothing and let the man rave.

The commandant took his revolver from its holster before he sat down to tea. He slammed it on the table. He asked me what I thought of the results. I said I thought they were predictable. He shook his head and went back into his rant about UNAMET and how it had not been predictable at all. We didn't argue with him.

He did not drink the tea. He stood up again and paced. He put the revolver back in its case and left suddenly, crunching heavy boots back up the path and roaring away on his motorbike, without a word.

Anton and I had not had a chance to talk about the result. We were worried about what would happen next, what this man might do and what we could do to calm him down. The tea went cold in our cups.

Twenty minutes later he was back again, stomping angrily up the path.

'You've got to tell them not to run away,' he said. 'They're running away. They're going up the mountain. They're mad, crazy. They're taking things… television sets and chairs. Food. They can't run away. That's going to cause more trouble.'

Anton took the man's elbow and guided him to a chair. He sat down with a thud.

'Can you explain what you mean?' Ant asked, stalling. 'Who's running? What for?'

'These Ataúro people. They think I'm going to do something bad.

But I won't unless they run away. They're going up the mountain. I have to keep control... if they run, I'll have to send soldiers after them. They don't understand that. They have to keep calm. They have to stay here.' He dropped his head to his chest. 'They hate me.'

This surprised me. It was almost like he cared what they thought of him. He sat there like a disappointed little boy; a dejected and dangerous small boy with a dangerous toy at arm's reach.

'If you want us to tell people anything,' said Anton, 'We'll have to move around the village and visit them. You'll have to let us do that.'

It wasn't that he'd ever banned movement around the village, it was just that since the referendum, people were afraid and stayed indoors.

'Yes, yes,' he said. 'Do that. Stop them from going.'

He sat looking down at his hands, open on his lap in what could have been a gesture of defeat. I wondered which soldiers he thought he would send up the mountain. If he sent the Timorese soldiers away, would any of them come back? Not likely. He was more or less on his own here. We were all silent.

'What do you think, Ton?' he asked Anton sadly. 'About this result?'

Anton leaned in closer to him, the way he did when something important was being discussed, empathically.

'I think they don't want to be Indonesian any longer,' he said. 'I've known that for a long time. It's no surprise to me.'

I thought about his early morning sadness on referendum day.

The commandant didn't speak. For some time, nobody did. The whole village was silent. It was as if it had stopped breathing. I was aware of the waves lapping the shore as the tide came in. Even the air was still. After a time, he stood up.

'You must come to my house tonight,' he said. 'Both of you. I don't want to be alone. Come to my house and we can talk more about all this.'

The last thing I wanted this day was to talk with him about anything at all but Anton was saying yes, yes, of course, we would come up to the military headquarters in the evening… and then the military man left. Anton was right. We had no choice really. We thought it might even help to calm him, or at least bide his time, if we were there with him tonight. We had no idea what was going on inside that man's head. And we were not at all sure he had a heart.

NIGHT SEA

Sometimes, at night, the sea roars. In cycles that start outside the lagoon, it crashes on the reef and then rolls in over the seagrasses with a dreadful moan. It's on full moon nights, the nights when the creamy boiling foam is lit with silver and the tide comes in high; right up the beach to the dune grass, it dances wild and ragged. I cannot sleep for the constant roar of it and the bright night calling my soul to be awake to watch and listen. I stay awake and alert with salt on my skin and the smell of ocean sharp in my nostrils.

THE COMMANDANT

His house was a low bungalow, a green corrugated iron rectangle on a slab of concrete under a mango tree that dropped leaves and fruit on its rusting roof. The rooms and the windows were small. It was poky, but because there was hardly any furniture it didn't feel cramped. In the sitting room there was one small wooden coffee table and three rattan easy chairs, in a corner a number of open cardboard cartons were stacked – beer cartons and a carton of leftover Ya Otonomi Now T-shirts.

He welcomed us warmly with handshakes, the second wife bulging close to his thigh. We were seated around the coffee table before the weapon was brought out without ritual and placed on the table beside a plate of banana fritters and several cans of warm beer. A plate of fried cassava was also squeezed onto the table, and we were invited to eat and drink – only when we are pressed to drink a couple of times, with perfect Indonesian manners, do we reach out for our cans.

Our host was stressed. Our host was depressed. He told us again that people have headed up to the hills. They've taken furniture and clothing with them so they must intend to stay there. They must be frightened. They must be running away. He told them not to go. He told them if they stayed, they'd be safe and he would not do anything but keep everything in order. That's what he's here for. Only that. But if they went, he'd have to react, he'd have to send soldiers to bring them back. That would be dangerous. Why were they doing this? Why were they afraid of him? He didn't understand. Why did they want to make this trouble for him?

We listened and tried to show empathy with nods. Anton had reminded me to say as little as possible tonight and I do not feel comfortable there sipping my beer with this man who emits disease and anxiety, this man who, since we arrived, has knocked back two cans already and petulantly flung the empties into the corner. This man whose pistol sits within arm's reach of us.

'Why are they afraid? What are they afraid of?' he asked forlornly. Under the circumstances, it seemed an absurd bewilderment. We were silent for a while then Anton spoke.

'It may be because of your appearance,' he said, taking me by surprise. 'It may be the tough image you project. It scares people.'

The commandant, also a little shocked by Anton's bold words, asked him to explain.

'The cloth band around your head, for example,' Anton continued. 'They don't know if you have head pain, or you are trying to be a Rambo warrior.'

I took a deep breath. Anton was talking tongue-in-cheek, with humour, but I worried he might be going too far. I stayed silent and reassured myself that Ant was good at assessing situations and probably sensed that the big man in the warrior band was truly desperate for a friend tonight, perhaps open to listening, does want to hear the words of another human being.

'Your sleeves rolled up high like that. That makes you look tough… maybe threatening even.'

Will he mention the gun that has been held to the heads of our friends? That cold steely wife that has touched their temples, has flirted with their lives and left them hanging uncertainly, hanging nervously on the edge of fear? I frowned at Anton to convey caution, hoping it looks like confusion. He paused.

'Then you must tell them not to be afraid!' the commandant burst out. 'They listen to you two. You must tell them not to be afraid and not to run away. They must not.'

Anton reminded him again. 'We'll have to move around the village and talk with people. You'll have to understand and allow us to do that.'

I thought of the lifeless village, the silent, empty streets without children or dogs and people hiding behind doors, waiting for the worst.

'Of course,' he said. 'Of course, you can do that. I never told people to stay off the streets and in their houses. Everybody is free. There is no curfew. Of course, you are free. Free to visit anyone. Please do, please tell them from me that they must not be afraid, they must not run away. They must just be normal. Relaxed.'

It was clear the man was delusional. I thought of the whispered voices, the fear-filled eyes, the secret meetings, people slipping through back doors, moving stealthily in shadows, the terrified silence of a village in anticipation of something very bad. At night, the black ute moving through the village without lights; the night of his bashing of the policeman, Saturnino, our neighbour, because a poster of Gusmao, the Timorese resistance hero, had been seen in his house.

The commandant helped himself to beers, knocking them back one after the other while Anton and I sipped hesitantly at our first cans, looking at each other above their rims. We reminded each other of our need to be calm, that we were in this unpredictable situation together and together, we could manage it.

The commandant turned the conversation back to his image problem and became sentimental and misunderstood. He brought out the photos of his wife and daughters and fingered them till his eyes were tearful and his voice unsteady. I came up with some comforting words to say about separation from loved ones, about human need and the sacrifice he had made. He liked all that, as I knew he would, and his face melted into a look of maudlin self-love. Anton, surprised at my sudden skilful hypocrisy, looked at me with smiling eyes and became bold again, raising the subject of relationships between people and how important it was to feel loved wherever you were. This muddied the waters but appealed to the commandant's sentimentality.

And so, the night went on and we nibbled at fried bananas and clutched our cans and listened to the man sometimes ranting angrily, sometimes dissolving into sentimentality. It was a long, hard night.

Twisting and fiddling nervously with my everlasting can of beer, I accidentally cut my finger on it and the crimson blood that appeared brought the commandant to his feet. Taking my finger in his big, meaty hands he examined the tiny cut with exaggerated concern.

'It has to be bandaged,' he said and reached into the pile of discarded Ya Otonomi Now T-shirts, grabbed one and began wrapping it tightly around my finger, creating a red and white bandage which he fastened tightly.

It was overkill. Anton and I said nothing while our host, satisfied with his display of tenderness, helped himself to another beer and sat down with a sigh. I pressed the shirt around my finger expecting to see more red on white as my blood seeped through it.

When our cans were finally empty and Ant and I were giving each other time-to-go-home signals, the commandant suddenly had an idea. Ignoring Anton, he addressed me in a polite, beseeching way, apologising and then asking my permission to indulge in what he called his "nightly habit". Aware of being scrutinised by both Anton and the drunken officer I assured him a little apprehensively that, as this was his house, he was free to do what he normally did. He stared at me for an intense thirty seconds then left the room.

He came back with a box of paraphernalia that he began setting up on the table between us. There were transparent tubes and a candle and a tiny spoon. His big hands shook as he arranged it all. I looked at Anton hoping for some explanation but there was none. We were both mystified. It was not until the white powder came out and was heated in a little bowl and then sucked through the tube that I had any idea of what was going on; our seven/eight cans down, gun-toting host was now indulging in his daily ritual of amphetamine taking and he did it with a deep sigh of satisfaction. It was time for us to leave. Happily engrossed in his activity, the commandant, after shaking our hands, checking my finger, thanking us effusively for our visit and our company, and unsteadily seeing us to the door, let us go.

Outside the night was dark and silent and the smell of the sea strong. We walked quickly, not speaking till we got to our house and closed the door behind us.

'Jee-sus!' I collapsed into Ant's arms. 'That man is crazy. A mad man with a gun. Probably with lots of them.'

Ant stroked my hair, saying nothing for a while, then, 'But we did it, Rae. We pulled it off. And after tonight we are his best friends. And while we are being his friends, he doesn't go out to threaten or hurt anyone.'

We laughed half-heartedly and I threw the blood-spotted Otonomi Now T-shirt onto the floor: another souvenir.

SIXTEEN

Indeed, the commandant now regarded us as his friends, his only friends, and he visited us often. One day sitting with me on the veranda, he told me about some of his military history. He told me that in Timor he had personally killed only sixteen people.

'I've been here for sixteen years,' he said. 'And have killed just sixteen Timorese. One for each year.'

He seemed to think this evidence of his restraint would impress me.

'And,' he added, 'I never looked any one of them in the eye when I shot them…' This, I think, was said to show his sensitivity. 'I always made them turn away from me before I did it. I could not look them in the eye.'

What could I say? I cleared away the teacups in an impolite

gesture to show our conversation was over, but he remained there reminiscing, nodding his head, deep in his own thoughts for some time. I, of course, had no idea what those thoughts might be.

ORAS TO'O ONA; AN UNFULFILLED PROMISE

By the next day we knew that the frequently televised promise of UNAMET, to be here with the people before, during, and after the referendum, would not be fulfilled. The nightly assurance that people had nothing to fear, that they could and must vote freely and fearlessly for the future of their country and their children, turned out to be meaningless. Like others, I'd heard those words over and over: be confident, there is nothing to fear. But there was plenty to fear; the country was aflame with fire and emotion. Buildings were being torched, people murdered. Thousands were forced to flee to the mountains or over the border into West Timor.

And such was the fury, the need for retribution, for retaliation; such was the hatred of the pro-Indonesia militias towards their countrymen who had chosen to break away, that UNAMET could do nothing. Such was the preparation – those warehouses filled with weapons we'd heard about – that UNAMET was powerless. Most UNAMET staff and election volunteers were evacuated, those few brave people that did stay, unarmed, were forced to barricade themselves in a compound surrounded by mayhem.

A nightmare was unfolding on the mainland but on Ataúro, although we heard the news, saw the smoke and flames leaping high in the distance, and felt the fear, all was calm. The sea kept us safe.

THE NIGHTS

The days were long and silent. People did not stir out of their houses. The roads and lanes were deserted, empty, without even a single hungry dog or a bony, runaway goat. The beach was deserted – long and grey and still. The silence was deafening… it hung around the village obtrusively, thick like cotton wool. Sometimes the cry of a bird would make you jump and even the sea only whispered as it came and went.

The nights were silent too, but for the odd thump of a branch falling, a door closing, a cough. Those nights were full of secrets, things moving in the dark, things that you sensed or heard but did not see.

'Tonight, the militia will come.' The words were whispered and spread from house to house, with eyes growing wider and more fearful. 'Tonight they will come in boats,' it was said. 'They will bring guns and machetes.' 'Perhaps they will kill us.' 'For sure they will kill us.' 'For sure they will come.'

At night we waited, looking from the window over smooth, dark sea.

'Don't wait at the window,' said Anton. 'Don't stand there waiting, making yourself more afraid. They won't come. Why would they come?'

He had a point. Why would they come? Why would they waste their time and resources coming out across the sea to us? They would gain nothing. Yet people said they would come. People believed they would come. And when we heard the faint chug of an engine over the sea, the tiny rumble of a distant motor, we were silent and scared, breathing deeply, listening, saying nothing, looking out to sea, waiting for the dark silhouette of the boat to slide into view. Night after night we waited.

The militia didn't come across the sea. Night after long night they didn't come. Occasionally, a boat would come bringing refugees from Dili, chugging out of the darkness of the sea onto our beach; the hushed buzz of voices rushing up the road, disappearing into houses, to family, to the relative safety of Ataúro where there were no militia, no screaming, no killing, no burning. They were getting away from Dili where hell was breaking loose.

We sighed and tried to sleep through those silent, secretive nights, not knowing what the dawn would bring, not sure if there would be one.

We talked each other out of fear. We reassured and stroked each other's faces, we made jokes and hot chocolate while we still had the powder, we sang songs very, very quietly, pretending we weren't listening for boat sounds on the sea.

No militia came to Ataúro. No reinforcements came to strengthen our Koramil, the commandant who slept restlessly in his camp bed with one eye on the guns wedged upright in the corner, an ear to the door and the window, one hand ready to reach out and grab. Dawns came quietly and everyone, including those who had escaped from Dili hiding low, low in wooden boats and dragging them silently up the beach, breathed a sigh of relief.

SEA NOTES

The sea was sometimes silent and sometimes not. When the tide was going out, the moon tugging at it, pulling at its sandy bowels and through its vast, grey body, it sometimes roared. It was the roar of everything in the universe then, the moan of pain and fear and despair. If you listened to that roar – and you could hear it with your ears and feel it in your bones – it called you away, away to far-off places you didn't want to go to and from which you might never want to return. And then when the moon sent its waters back, tossing and leaping and creeping up the beach, the sea roared again – but a softer but more determined rumble that you wanted to be a roar of hope.

THE KNIFE EDGE

We were living on a knife edge. I felt we might, at any moment, slip onto the blade. The commandant insisted that we were his friends and under the circumstances, we were obliged to be. We didn't like the man. We didn't trust him, but we had no choice but to listen to him moaning about the UN, and groaning about the referendum. We nodded at his crazy, egocentric stories and illogical hopes of "saving" Ataúro. Although it was far too late, we learned he was trying to talk the island leaders into signing an agreement for Ataúro to stay with Indonesia – that Ataúro leaders want autonomy.

We sat with him and served him tea in a make-believe civilised fashion. We filled in his time. We gave him human contact. We stopped him, perhaps, from going off the deep end. But whenever we heard the roar of his motorbike cut the silence of the village we shuddered and waited for him to come swaggering up our path onto our veranda. When we heard the first sounds of the motorbike, we turned off our hidden CB radio, given to us by UNAMET at the time of the referendum, in case it suddenly spluttered, announcing its illegal existence.

Our radio connection to Brother Dan in Dili worked until Dan and his household have to leave. On his last call, I heard panic in Dan's voice and constant gunfire all around him. 'We're leaving,' he told me. 'We're going to try to get across the border and drive to Kupang. We have to get out. We can't stay. Sorry, but we have to leave without you.'

Of course, they had to get out and, unlike them, we had no gunfire or burning city to flee from. Their situation was desperate. The day before, Dan had told me that the embassy had asked him to tell me I must come to Dili because the last plane out of Timor was leaving and I should be on it.

'Will they meet me at the beach and get me to the airport?' I asked.

'No,' he said. 'It's far too dangerous for that.'

This was protocol. They had to offer me a way out, they had to try… but we all knew there was no way I could get to the mainland and onto that last plane, and it would be madness to try.

We were nervous talking on the radio. The commandant didn't know we had a link to the outside world and he, himself, by that time was quite cut off. We knew he would feel deceived by us and we didn't want to risk his suspicion. As hard as it was to be his friend, it would have been far, far worse to become his enemy. During Dan's last radio call to us, the big man arrived sneakily, silently. Ant cleverly distracted him while I yanked the antenna connection out of the wall and threw it and the receiver under the bed. That was the end of our contact with Dili, but there was no longer anyone there to talk with anyway.

The village remained silent and the sea was mostly calm. The days were long. To keep ourselves occupied we continued to sort, cover and catalogue books for the community library. My short-wave radio brought us news from Radio Australia and the BBC. We knew Dili was in chaos; we knew people were being murdered, buildings burned and scores of people fleeing into the hills. A few refugees from the mainland arrived with more news, horror stories that we knew to be true. Ataúro people with children or other relatives in Dili shook their heads and cried for them. People came to our back door, sneaking between the houses and down behind the school. We spoke in whispers and always had one ear alert for the sound of the motorbike or the crunching of boots on the gravel path.

We heard that the Australian Prime Minister, John Howard, had given the Indonesian government twelve hours to stop the ransacking of Dili. This was extended by a further twenty-four hours. Vilanova, whose children had been at school in Dili and had not come home for the referendum, shook his head slowly, disbelievingly. 'They'll all be dead by then,' he said.

Indonesia now regarded Australia as its enemy and Australians in Indonesia were warned of danger. We didn't know if the commandant was aware of this, but it made us anxious. Anton was particularly concerned and reminded me the military man was capable of madness.

'Gabrielle, you know you could become his enemy just as easily as you've become his friend, and that could mean anything, to his mind it would justify anything.'

Rightly or wrongly, I half-believed that my "respectful pandering" to the man's ego – a skill I'd picked up in Java and knew he was responding to as Javanese "big" men often do – would work in my favour for a while at least. As one who was generally honest, my hypocritical behaviour towards the man surprised and amused Anton and comforted, though did not delight, me.

At night small boats continued to sneak into shore bringing groups of frightened refugees from Dili. We watched their silhouettes in the moonlight, relieved they were not militia. Traumatised and weary people scuttled nervously up the beach and were taken in by Ataúro people. The commandant never appeared on the beach; he either didn't know or turned a blind eye to the refugees. He was virtually alone now anyway and could do nothing about it. His power was in his one shiny pistol and in keeping the military weapons out of the hands of islanders.

He was afraid. He and I knew that his soldiers – only Ataúro men left now – would, if given half the chance, get rid of him. If they could get hold of a gun, they would kill him. It would have been easy, were it not for the commandant's lack of trust of the group. But he had confiscated the weapons and now slept in his office on a camp stretcher placed diagonally across the corner of the room with the weapons jammed between the walls and his bed. He showed me this sleeping place. He told me he didn't trust the soldiers; he hardly slept at all. I imagined the creaking of the small bed all night under his heavy, tossing body and his eyes staring out into the darkness. He was terrified and so was becoming more terrifying. He seemed to be cut off from contact with the mainland, and quite alone.

A small boat secretly brought Max Stahle, his son and two journalists from Alor to Ataúro. They were coming to Timor the back way. It was the first time I met Max, a hero of Timor, and the group stayed with us for a couple of days while they organised a boat to get them to the mainland. Max's son, who was fourteen, confided to me that one of the journalists had taken and finished his last bottle of Sprite on the way over. He was angry and, given the dangerous circumstances of their sea trip, their hiding with us on Ataúro and the enormous risks they would take going to Dili, I found it endearing that the boy shared this small, private grievance with me.

EVACUATION

On Monday, Anton was called to the police station. Domingos, one of our team, had come across the mountain from Makili to check on us and kept me company while Ant was gone. Mingos and I sat on a mat, sorting books for the library, both of us nervous and fearful that Anton would not be allowed back. We sat on the floor and said prayers, which was a strangely intimate but comforting thing to do together. Anton wasn't away long, he'd been told about government orders: all the police – mostly Timorese left now – were to leave the island on a boat early next morning and Anton must go with them. 'It's getting too dangerous for Indonesians to stay here,' he was told. 'The boat will leave at dawn and you have to be on it.'

They did not invite me, now the enemy, to go with them. Ant told them he'd leave with them in the morning but, 'Of course I'm not going,' he told me. 'I'm not leaving you here with that madman.'

But he started to become more worried as growing numbers of traumatised mainland refugees arrived. Apart from our military man, a teacher and the police chief, who was leaving at dawn, he was the only Indonesian left on the island now and Indonesians, if they hadn't been before, were hated now. People from the mainland did not know what kind of an Indonesian Anton was.

I was getting worried too – about Anton's safety here and about my family. My daughter had not heard from me since the referendum. She had no idea about me; whether I was safe, detained or dead. Thinking of her anxiety and not being able to contact her was breaking my heart. That, and our knife-edge relationship with the commandant, made us both uneasy.

For the first time, we talked that afternoon about leaving the island. That night we snuck around the village, asking the opinion of friends. If we stayed, we might be a deterrent. As witnesses to the commandant's actions, we thought our presence might serve to contain his madness. Our Ataúro friends all agreed: although befriending the big, crazy man played a role now, no one really knew what he might do next. At any time, the militia could arrive and everyone would have to evacuate the village. They might have to clear out and find hiding places in the mountains to get away. They were worried about whether I could run with them into the mountains. No, it would be better for me to leave, they said, to go somewhere safe. Everyone had given up the idea of a UN rescue by then, everyone was thinking of saving their own and their loved ones' lives. They gave permission for us to go.

Later that night at Antonio Freitas's house, out the back by the kitchen where a dull lamp and a smoky fire burned and women were heating water in a big, battered cooking pot, a number of Timorese policemen had gathered. Some were leaving on the boat at dawn as they'd been ordered – into whatever unknown future was out there for them – others were shedding their police garb and heading for the mountains that night. Everyone knew the order to leave was hollow; nobody would delay the boat to come looking for them if they weren't on it.

We squatted on the dirt floor drinking steaming glasses of black coffee and whispering goodbyes. The uncertainty of everybody's future made the moment sweet and unbearably heavy. Brought out from deep in our souls was a love for our fellows… I could feel it burning like a flame between us, a sharing of helplessness, of vulnerability, of chance, under a determined veneer of hope.

The sea was dark and calm as we walked home along the beach, avoiding the main road. Stars reflected in ripples. The sound was gentle. We could see the hellfires of Dili burning red across the calm water. If we could find a boat to take us, we would go somewhere safer.

PART ELEVEN

A HARD DECISION

I heard the boat taking the police away leave before dawn. Nobody came looking for Anton who had gone up the mountain to hide, just in case. Guido went to Bikeli to try to find someone who would be willing to take us to Alor, the Indonesian island to the west of Ataúro. We'd decided it was the only place to go to – Liran, the Maluku Island to the east was closer, but once there we would be stuck; it was very isolated and there would be no way to go from there to anywhere else. With Indonesian naval boats and other marine traffic in the strait, it was a big ask for anyone to take us to Alor and it was uncertain if we'd find someone willing to take the risk.

A Bikeli fisherman agreed to take us. He said he would bring his boat to Vila during the night and we could leave the next morning at sunrise. We had the supplies the Australian government had stored with us in case of an emergency evacuation – rice, noodles, coffee, tins of fruit and fish – so we packed those and a few clothes for the voyage.

I went to tell the commandant we were leaving and asked him for a *surat jalan*, the letter of authority you need to travel around Indonesia. As a foreigner, official permission would make my journey less difficult. He wasn't happy about us leaving and tried to talk me out of it, saying he'd get military friends to contact my family in Australia and assure them I was safe. I didn't think a phone call from the Indonesian military at that time would be of great comfort to my daughter. Eventually, he wrote the travel letter I needed, endorsed it with his rubber stamp and reminded me it was dangerous to leave the island.

Holding his pudgy hand in a goodbye handshake, I asked him to promise me he would not harm anyone on Ataúro after we left. Was he aware that I knew about his many threats and intimidations? Did he think I believed him as he pressed my hand and assured me he would not harm a single soul? He murmured something about not knowing what he would do next and muttered something like an invitation for me to come and meet his wife and family in Surabaya. He wished me luck. It was weird, like a separation of friends.

The boat didn't turn up. At dawn a group of women – Mama Luisa, Sara, Maria, Tia Domingas, other women and their children – were on our veranda, keening, weeping, singing for us, afraid for us, afraid that we were risking the sea and all that was happening out there, afraid that we would die and never meet with them again. But the boat didn't come. The boatman's family had forbidden him to leave the island. It was too dangerous to go out into Indonesian waters, they said.

Guido took the *Manucoco* and went back up to Bikeli. At 9 o'clock, a fibreglass fishing boat, the *Loro sa'e No 18,* sailed into the lagoon. It was Tiu Jakob and his nephew, Cedes. And, if we could find another crewman willing to help them on the boat – no one else from Bikeli was willing to go – they agreed to take us to Alor. Ilario, one of our *Manucoco* crew, said he'd come with us. We threw our gear on board.

The women began to cry and keen again. A group of them

stood on the beach with their children, singing parting songs and weeping. As I kissed the wet cheeks of each one, I began to cry too. I could feel the sobs rising from a terrible pain in my chest, a fear that they might be killed, that we might be killed, that we all might die and never again meet here on this beach.

The boat's diesel engine throbbed as we pulled out of the lagoon. I sat on the roof with Anton and my tears were unstoppable as we passed the headland of Lampia and lost sight of the women. I could still hear their voices in my head. The tears did not stop as we put-putted slowly along the rocky Ataúro coast then headed out across the strait, not taking the usual turn south towards Dili where we could still see smoke rising as the city burned, but heading west towards the island of Alor.

LEAVING ATAÚRO

We left Ataúro, with me sobbing and the others silent, uncertain for the safety of those we were leaving behind and for ourselves. Sailing away from our friends, we watched the fires of Dili spread their smoke across the sea.

We sailed for two days and a night on Indonesian seas in a Timorese boat called *Loro sa'e* (Sunrise/Dawn), passing large Indonesian naval ships on their way to Timor and small Indonesian fishing boats. When Cedes forgot to leave the charger on as we hid in mangroves overnight, we had no engine and sailed for a day using a tattered piece of tarpaulin on the mast. Fishermen from a tiny village along the coast, seeing us hugging the shore and moving slowly, lent us their battery charger and finally, on the evening of the second day, we sailed into Kalabahi on the western end of Alor.

It was a peaceful little harbour some twenty kilometres to

the northeast of the town. We reached it just on dusk and all breathed a sigh of relief. We decided to spend the night on the boat and in the morning at first light, hire a *bemo* (van/bus) and go into the town. I would first ring my daughter in Australia, then we would all go to a café and have a good feed. After that, we'd go to the market to buy goods to send back to Ataúro. We'd fill the boat with rice, beans, oil, sugar, tea, soap, cigarettes; in these circumstances NZAid wouldn't object to us using the last of their cash. Before we'd left the island, food supplies were running low and there was no way of getting supplies from Dili.

The five of us lay on the deck under the stars and talked that night about many things. Not the sort of things you usually talk about with Ataúro fishermen: life and death and love and families. These things were sung about on the island, stories were told about them, but talk of personal relationships, feelings and fears was not common. That night we were still on the edge of danger – what would happen next was uncertain. Yakob, Cedes and Ilario still had to get back across the sea to Ataúro and we didn't know what they might find there. The night was poignant with uncertainty, with relief, with love and appreciation of each other. The boat rocked beneath us, and the stars shone above.

KALABAHI

The deliberate and deadly chaos in Dili had spread to Alor. Indonesian and Timorese refugees, military, militia, intelligence forces were all here – all reactionary, all emotional, all seemingly either vengeful or terrified. The East Timorese, for better or worse, had chosen independence and here in Kalabahi any person or any nation identified as having assisted them to oust Indonesia was hated. Rumours were spread to fan the flames of hatred and fear.

Outside the door of our hotel room, intelligence officers gathered; men in running shoes followed us down the street. In the café, people spoke pointedly and in loud voices about the stupidity and ungratefulness of the Timorese and the treachery of Australians who were preparing to lead the United Nations military peacekeeping forces, INTERFET, into East Timor.

It was frightening. The lack of empathy or concern about was happening just across the sea in East Timor – the murders, the terror, the burning of houses – tore us apart. The threatening presence of our surly "watchers" made us reluctant to stay at the hotel. For the first time in my life I was, through no fault of my own, a hated enemy and that did not feel good.

RESTAURANT

After phoning my daughter, we found a room in a cheap hotel. But by nightfall Anton and I were hungry and had to go and find something to eat. We slipped out of the room and across the lounge where men in groups sat, watching us. The way they stared was unnerving. Two of them followed us out. The street was dimly lit, and we walked down the block to a Sumatran restaurant we had seen at the bottom of the hill. We found a table and an empty bench and selected our food at the glass cabinet. We were hungry but had no appetite. Around us, people were talking loudly, there was a terrible excitement in the air. We picked at our food in silence.

Then we heard someone say, 'They're dumping them in the sea over there.' They pointed south, to East Timor. 'Bodies. Scores of them,' he laughed. 'They are killing them and dumping them in the sea. The bodies are piling up this high in the harbour.'

My stomach turned. My weary body recoiled.

'They are dumping them in the sea, the bodies

Dumping them in the sea

They're piling them up, the bodies.

Piling them up… this high.'

He said it twice. He said it like poetry. He was excited, he was laughing and he showed just how high with his hands. It was a victory. And the others, all excited, gathered round, listening and asking, 'How many? How high?'

Anton and I pushed our meals away. We left the restaurant. We were sick, stomach-sick, head-sick, heartsick. Filled with horror, we crept back to our small room through the foyer, through the groups of staring men. We bolted our door, sat on the bed, held each other and cried.

The next day we sought refuge with the local priests, Indonesian men from Flores and Java. Even they were not comfortable with an Australian at their presbytery, but they were hospitable enough. They were kind, fed us, and let us use their phone to contact my family again. I rang Father Peter, an Indian friend from Dili whom we'd heard was in Kupang. I suggested Anton and I might go there – we knew the language, the culture and the situation – maybe we could help.

'No,' he said. 'No, Gabrielle don't come here.' He was adamant. 'It's dreadful here, there's fighting and mayhem in the streets of Kupang. Don't come. As an Australian, you'd be of no help; you'd be in danger. Go west. Keep going west. And be careful.'

The priests wanted us out of Alor. They said they'd assist us to get away as soon as possible. 'You, an Australian, shouldn't stay here nor should you travel in Indonesia without a priest or some other official with you. It's not safe,' they said. Their plan was that one of them would accompany us by ferry to Flores. It might not be safe even there, but at least we could make our way further west, away from trouble.

Then the priests heard that the government line Pelni ship, the AWU, was calling into Kalabahi that evening and heading west to Bali. They would get us onto that instead.

THE AWU

So there we were on an overcrowded ship, thinking we were heading away from trouble but soon learning that we were taking trouble with us. The ship, the AWU, had, like us, come from East Timor. Out of the terrible mayhem of Dili it was carrying thousands of terrified, fleeing Timorese, hundreds of terrified, fleeing Indonesians, dozens of Indonesian and Timorese military and pro-Indonesian militia, and now, one Australian.

The priests advised me to say I was an English traveller and student of Indonesian language. 'Do not say you are Australian. Do not say you have been in East Timor,' they said. I am not a good liar and found it hard to accept that Indonesians now, suddenly, hated Australians. We had always been friends – *tetangga* (neighbours). *I* had not changed. *They* had not changed. But the situation had changed dramatically and I, like them, was a helpless victim of its politics and power. I was the subject of untruths and rumour, the cause of fear and mistrust. As advised, I lied about my nationality and denied my Australian identity.

The ship's horn was already blaring as we pushed our way up the stairs and through the crowds onto the first deck. Boarding time on the government-owned Pelni Line ferries that served the islands of the Indonesian archipelago was always hectic, but this night in Kalabahi it was worse than usual. There was panic, pushing and shoving, and shouting out above the rumbling engines and the persistently screaming horn.

On board, we wedged ourselves onto a wooden ledge in the ship's main foyer and watched a stream of anxious people still pushing up the narrow stairway. I glanced at the slips of torn paper that were thrust into my hand by the ticket collector. There was one word scrawled on each of them: *Pengungsi* (Refugee).

We were leaving Kalabahi, Alor, because the city was in chaos and because I am Australian and in Kalabahi, for the moment, Australians are hated. It was September 1999 and East Timor, just across the sea, was exploding in a rage that reached out to the nearby Indonesian islands. But only on reading the scraps of paper that substituted for tickets were we aware that, like many others at this moment, we were officially refugees. It slowly dawned on us that this ship was filled with traumatised people who were, like us, escaping. The AWU was a refugee ship and nearly all its passengers are escaping something dreadful, sailing into a terrible unknown. We had come out of a small frying pan and into a raging fire.

Trouble was everywhere on the ship. It was in the conditions of overcrowding, tension and fear. After several hours on our narrow ledge we needed to move our legs – that meant climbing over people, squeezing through corridors jam-packed with families, finding the toilet already awash with water and urine and faeces, picking our way through the noise of too many people crammed into small spaces.

Trouble was in the fear and suspicion of everyone on the AWU. For me it was hearing young men snarling 'UNAMET' as I passed them, and seeing that some of those angry young men were holding guns. In the meal queue, I was verbally accosted several times by youths with weapons and I was still naïve enough to be shocked and hurt by the threats and slurs.

I speak Indonesian, but trying to explain that I had been a

community worker volunteer in Indonesia and Timor for many years, that I have many friends in both places, that I am a *good* person would be of no use. I was typecast. Nobody would listen. As a westerner I was "The Enemy" and, for the time being, there was no way around that.

Anton, who was still relatively calm and clear thinking, left me sitting on the ledge while he scouted around to find us a better spot. He found it in the corridor of the ship's clinic, up on the top deck. Although it was crowded there – five decks up – the space felt safer and was big enough for us both to either sit down with stretched legs or for one at a time to lie down with bent knees.

A badly injured man lay groaning on a bare and dirty mattress beside us. He was from Sulawesi and told us he had jumped from his burning apartment above a store in Dili when militia in the street were firing weapons and torching houses and shops.

He was very probably not a bad man. He told me he had lived in Dili for nearly twenty-five years and made a modest living repairing radios and cassette players. He had no family and was carried to the ship by other Sulawesi people who had found a space for him in the clinic, on the floor. Like me, he had not asked to be anyone's enemy and probably did not deserve to be forced out of his home onto hard backbreaking concrete by hatred and flames.

He was in great pain and receiving no attention, so I rubbed his damp forehead with salve and rubbed his shoulders and back as gently as I could. He blessed me for it. Anton brought him food, biscuits and coffee, from the kiosk. He told us his story and called me a foreign, English, angel. But at night when everyone is asleep, he lay awake in his pain and listened to the news on a little radio with some of the ship's crew. When East

Timor was mentioned and Australia's role in the INTERFET mission announced, he cursed with them. Australians were devils and turncoats and treacherous villains. I listened, lying in my narrow space under the glare of the corridor fluorescents. Anton took my hand.

On the other side of us, wedged into their own small space, was a Javanese mother and her daughter fleeing from East Timor to Jakarta. They didn't know where their father and husband was, or if he was alive. The little girl, Yanti, and I filled time by singing nursery rhymes I knew from my work in Indonesian kindergartens. We sang about stars, and animals, colours, the sea, about families and flowers. We sang *Lihat Kebunku* (Look at My Garden), full of flowers, red ones and white ones that I water every day, roses and jasmine; they are all so beautiful. Our songs and laughter went out into the cramped corridor that smelt of sweat and urine and pain and fear.

Trouble was all over the ship – in the lounge areas, on the decks and up and down the stairs. Timorese kept to certain areas, lying low, those of them who had been active in the resistance, hiding. Indonesians, also refugees, fleeing from the only home they have known for the past twenty-five years, crowded into other areas. I ventured out of our corridor again and sat on the floor with a group of Sulawesi people: men, women, children, huddling together, each with sadness and uncertainty written on their faces. Their leader told me their story: they had been chased from their homes in Dili by guns or by burning, and herded onto the ship, terrified children clinging to confused and frightened parents.

Most were small traders – fishermen, or market and street vendors – and had completely lost contact with their families back in Sulawesi. They were poor migrants who had gone to

Dili as part of the government transmigration scheme that relocated people from the crowded islands of Indonesia to the less-populated eastern islands. It was a scheme that offered an opportunity for a new life to poor people who barely survived in their homelands. These people, refugees now, had nothing to return to and their lives in Dili had literally gone up in smoke.

Their leader told me that two days ago when the ship docked in Kupang, West Timor, the military had tried to force them off the AWU, but he and his group had made the bold decision to stay on board until they were delivered back to Sulawesi. Although it was now bound for Bali via Flores and Sumba and going nowhere near Sulawesi, which was much further to the north, his people were adamant that they were not going to leave the AWU until they were "home". They do not actually have homes to go to anymore, but at least they have language and culture and history there. He told me that if they had disembarked in West Timor as ordered, they would probably have been left there forever.

At gunpoint, he had stood firm and finally, because the ship was filling with other refugees who had fled overland to Kupang and Kupang was in a chaotic, crowded, treacherous state, the soldiers had let them stay on board. The Sulawesi group did not know what would happen next, but they would stick together and not leave the ship in some "foreign" port. They would disembark only when the boat took them to Makassar.

The hours were long, and I wandered about a little, but not far. I made friends with a small group of Indonesian academics who camped in the foyer of the hospital corridor where we had our safe spot. A Sumatran man somehow guessed my true story and asked me in a whisper about our journey, where we had come from, what was happening in Timor. He was clearly aware of the situation and sympathetic. We talked a lot in low tones while

Anton stayed back and watched from the corridor, concerned again by my trust of strangers.

After many hours the little girl, Yanti, tired of sitting in a crowded passageway told me she wanted to see the sea. She wanted to see dolphins and flying fish and blue water. Here we were on a boat, but we couldn't even see the sky – only people cramped and hot in a smelly, narrow corridor. I too needed fresh air. Her mother agreed for me to take her on deck, to try and find a place where we could at least glimpse the sea. Anton didn't like the idea but agreed to stay and guard our piece of floor. The little girl and I pushed through tight groups of people, stepped over them, held tightly to each other, and went down the stairs to the open deck.

But of course, it was very crowded, people two or three deep along every inch of rail. Because I was taller than most, I could actually see the sea and I hoisted Yanti onto my shoulders so that she might see it too. Between peoples' heads and hats, she glimpsed a tiny patch of water.

'But there's no dolphins,' she said, disappointed. We stood there for a while but there were no flying fish either and most of the time no sea visible at all because of the swell of people surging in front of us.

Turning to go back, I noticed a young man staring at me across the heads of the crowd. Because I was a foreigner everyone was looking at me, but this man's stare I will never forget. His face, framed by wild and wiry hair, was hard and hateful. Although he wore a non-military tracksuit, I knew immediately he was a Timorese militiaman. That steely, wild-eyed drug-stare that I'd seen in Alor bored into me as he pushed people aside to get to where we were standing.

I tried to push our way out but he reached us. He stood in

front of me, his face thrust within an inch of mine, his breath on my skin and his eyes drilling into me. Yanti gripped tighter around my neck. I glanced down to see if the man had a weapon and saw only tightly clenched fists against the soft blue of pants. I shoved him away and pushed through the crowd, to the stairway, up the stairs. I knew he was following close behind and felt rising panic. I put the little girl down and pulled her along close by my side.

We finally reached the fifth deck foyer, and there, sitting cross-legged, amongst all the others was my new Sumatran university friend and his group. I slid down to the floor into the space they made for me, and pulled Yanti into my lap. The militiaman was right behind me and stood with his legs pressed against my back. I could see his sandals on either side of my thighs and feel the pressure of his legs on my ribs. I froze. The Sumatran man sized up the situation in a flash and, staring coolly up at the man, said in firm but polite Indonesian, 'Would you stand back from my friend, please. Why are you bothering her like this?'

Out of the corner of my eye I saw Anton coming down the corridor. He stood beside the man in the aqua tracksuit and from his height leaned over him and asks what he thinks he is doing... then the Sulawesi man, the leader of the Indonesian refugee group who were refusing to leave the boat, called out and asked him too... and the man in the tracksuit, the man with the wild, crazy eyes slunk away, stepping over people and back down the stairway.

We heard that twelve people disappeared off the AWU on that voyage – twelve Timorese were killed and thrown overboard by militia or soldiers. I don't know if it was confirmed but it was believable; that boat was so full of the hatred of angry, patriotic madmen of two nations.

After that episode, I no longer had any desire to see the sea and did not venture further than the corridor or the foyer where my friends sat. We were afraid to line up for food on the long, disgruntled queues waiting to be served, so Anton went alone down to the kiosk a couple of times a day and came back with biscuits and cold, condensed milk sweet coffee to keep us going.

Once the ship's crew asked me for my passport, demanding to see it, "For security reasons" and I had no choice but to show it. 'Australian!' one of the younger ones shouted when I handed it over.

'Then we are not responsible for your safety or your life on this ship.'

His older colleague nodded to me with a gentle smile and whispered, 'Don't worry, *Ibu*, just stay up here with me and you'll be safe.'

A wealthy Balinese businessman, *Please do come to my restaurant as my guests when we're back in Bali*, had "bought" himself a cabin in the ship's clinic, (while my friend with the injured back slept on his hard mattress in the corridor with us). This cabin not only had a bed, but a toilet and a washbasin. He invited Anton and me to use it when we needed to. This meant we did not have to go down to the public lavatories that were awash with stinking waste but also, for me, means not walking through hostile people with guns. Of course, we disapproved of such injustice – the rich ousting the poor and sick from the clinic facility, of course we despised such corruption – but of course we accepted this rich man's generosity towards us.

Three nights and three days is an awfully long time in such a cramped space. The AWU called at Ende in Flores but we saw nothing but the inside of the ship. Foreigners were not allowed to get on or off, the crew told us. We go south and called at

Waingapu in Sumba but saw nothing but the cramped and dirty insides of the AWU. I told Anton, little Yanti, her mother, and the man on the mattress – none of whom had been there – some stories of Sumba and my work there: a wonderful, rich and dramatic island with horses; extraordinary *ikat* weaving; and houses built on rocky crests around graveyards with huge stone tombs; the Pasola event – combat on horseback, men and ponies decorated with ribbons and streamers and bells; our teacher trainings with wonderful, vibrant women who came together for the first time from tiny isolated kindergartens with broken bamboo walls.

We talked about the wonderful, diverse cultures of Indonesia as we heard the blasts of the ship's horn and felt the jolt of the wharf. But we sat in our places and saw only the writhing innards of the dilapidated AWU as it plotted its way west, south and then turned at last northwest, towards Bali.

BALI AND SEPARATION

There were no luxury liners at the Port of Benoa in Bali the day we arrived, only a line of military vehicles, ambulances and many soldiers. We took the phone numbers of some of the Timorese refugees, saw them into taxis as they left. Our heads were spinning. The wharf was chaotic with the unloading: crowds of soldiers and civilians, crates and boxes and cages of chickens, vehicles backing up and pulling out. We found a taxi, checked that nobody was following us and asked the driver to take us to a cheap tourist hotel near the beach. Any hotel, any beach.

Quite suddenly we were free.

Anton and I paced around our hotel room; we tried to stretch into its space. We were alone for the first time in days but carried the weight of past weeks with us. Our heads were heavy, we still felt uncertainty and fear in our cramped limbs and knotted-up stomachs. We paced about, not knowing what to do with ourselves. We tried to be happy. We hugged each other. And then we sat together on the hard bed and once again cried our hearts out.

It was partly relief that made us cry – we were safe. It was partly fear, partly confusion, partly remorse. We allowed ourselves, for the first time since leaving Alor, to think back to Ataúro and our friends there, to think of Yakob, Cedes and Ilario crossing back over the sea in the *Loro sa'e 18*. We had no idea what had happened to them on that voyage, had no idea if, back on Ataúro, the commandant had gone berserk with his revolver and his rifles. No idea if people there were alive or dead. And now we felt the guilt of our abandonment and, in our filthy, hungry, exhausted but finally safe, condition, that guilt was hard to bear.

Bali is a tourist destination and, regardless of the nearby reign of terror where fellow countrymen and neighbours were fleeing in fear of their lives, regardless of mayhem, death and destruction in parts of this country, the claptrap of tourism, the sand and surf, cheap bars, thieving monkeys, temple ceremonies, dance, pretty trinkets, gamelan, river rafting, continued to entertain and beguile its visitors. We could hardly believe the contrast of it. Streets and lanes filled with happy foreigners on tropical holidays, hawkers touting, massages on the beach in the blazing sun, beer and surf and loud music. Everything was Bali-normal; ignorant of Timor and what was happening not so far across the sea. Our heads spun. We were isolated and could talk with no one. We had just arrived from another planet.

We learned that Timorese refugees were being hounded and hunted by the Balinese police. They were not allowed to live in the community with relatives or friends but were being rounded up into refugee camps. There were numerous Timorese students studying in Denpasar and some long-settled Timorese families living there, but those who had been forced to flee on the AWU or other boats were afraid, and were moving from house to house each night to avoid being caught.

We visited the Balinese Catholic Bishop who was courageously defying the central and provincial governments and providing refuge for Timorese who have arrived in Bali. The Catholics agreed to look after our fellow travellers and keep them out of police hands.

We met with Chris Dureau and Christine Perkins, Australian activists, who were coordinating and providing information for Timorese and helping to arrange flights and escape for intellectuals and activists who are on a wanted list. Bali was not just now the pretty holiday destination it pretended to be: it was a two-faced monster with a dark underbelly. Ant and I slipped out of one of its worlds, the one of our hotel: smoothies and fresh juice, morning smiles, flowers in the hair, offerings and incense; and into the other: police hunts, insecurity, suspicion, and fear. The contrast was dizzying.

We were both offered jobs when in Bali: Ant to work with fishing communities for an environmental NGO in Labuahan Bajo, Flores, and me to work with Oxfam GB back in East Timor. I'd been invited to apply for this job before the referendum and had thought it would be a challenge and a privilege to work as education coordinator for Oxfam in a new country with new aspirations and a strong emphasis on education. Goodness only knew what would be needed before education could get off the ground in that devastated country now, but whatever it was, I was confident that I had something to contribute and would be useful. Anton was not sure what to do – his heart was still on Ataúro but he did not feel it was the time for him, an Indonesian, to go back there. He had the skills and experience for the job in Flores and, in Indonesia where jobs are hard to come by, it offered a good opportunity.

We talked about our choices and it was remarkably easy for us to make them. We were still not clear-headed but knew we would have to go in different directions for a while and we both accepted the offers. Such was our bond then, our love, our certainty that these decisions did not augur a warning of any kind. We parted.

THE MONASTERY

We went our separate ways. Before going to Flores, Anton went home to visit his family in troubled Ambon; I went back to Salatiga in Central Java. We didn't think about when we would meet again, our hearts and minds are still so unsettled that we step into our immediate future without each other and without too much thought about how we will resolve that.

My friend and LPM colleague, Jenny Toisuta, who knew East Timor and Indonesia and their politics well, knew Ataúro and Anton and me and had been one of the strongest supporters of our work, knew exactly what I needed now. She arranged for me to spend some days in retreat in a closed Carmelite monastery in the hills above the town. I was in tatters and, without Anton, my mate, to share the emotional strain of the past weeks, I was falling apart.

At the monastery I had a small white room with a bed, a table and a porch. It overlooked a valley of alpine green forest and was silent. I was alone. I wrote in a new notebook. I sketched. The silence melted into me and quietened the blood that raced in my veins, throbbed in my head. I went to chapel in the morning when the nuns sang, and I went in the evening when they sang again. Their singing was beautiful. For days I'd felt my head was floating somewhere above me, a distant, disconnected part of me but with the pure, holy singing of the nuns and the silence of the hills I feel it gradually sink back down to settle on my shoulders and connect to my heart. There in the convent, the bits of me gradually come back together again.

Sister Martha, the American abbess, asked me to go into the closed part to speak with the nuns and novitiates about what was happening in East Timor. She wanted them to know the real story behind the outrageous propaganda that was being broadcast throughout Indonesia. In Salatiga, I saw television news footage of Australian INTERFET soldiers in Timor manhandling women and beating up old Timorese men. I believed most soldiers were capable of cruelty towards enemies, but I did not believe what I saw with my own eyes on Indonesian television – these old people were not enemies of Australia, it did not make any sense. But the millions of Indonesians watching it, the millions who didn't know what was going on, who could not see beyond this misinformation, would watch and believe what they saw.

I told the cloistered sisters, some of them from the eastern islands of Indonesia, everything I knew: what I'd seen, heard, and experienced. It was good for me to talk about it, to try to put it into some order and make some sense of it. The sisters, some of them Timorese, were dismayed.

An open day for families to visit the novitiates fell on the Sunday and Sister Martha asked me to keep a low profile. Such was the growing hatred of Indonesians for Australians that she does not want it known the convent is sheltering an Australian. She suggested I pretend I am on silent retreat and have no contact with visitors and certainly not let them know that I speak Indonesian. It was still incredible to me that I was now an enemy of Indonesia, but it was not difficult to lie low at the monastery; I have my porch, notebook, box of pencils, the silent forest.

SULAWESI GROUP

While in Java, I somehow heard news that the group of misplaced Sulawesi people who had befriended me were successful in forcing the government Pelni ferry AWU to take them all the way back to Makassar. This cheered me. Although they would now be lost souls in their own land, at least they were not languishing for years, as many were doomed to do, in some camp in another part of the country.

OXFAM AND OXFORD

I had never been to Europe and would not have chosen to go at that time. Oxfam Great Britain employed me as national education coordinator in the new Timor but because of the continuing chaos there, it was not time for that yet. In the meantime, it was suggested that I work on the emergency team with Oxfam Australia (then, Community Aid Abroad). I could do that immediately; I knew East Timor. But because of some need to prove their independence and capability, a power game played between Oxfam Australia and its Great Britain counterpart, this offer was rejected by Oxfam Australia.

So, although I knew the language, the geography and the culture well and would have been a useful emergency team member, I was instead flown across the world to Oxford, for an orientation. This was disorientating. I'd tried to find out what had happened on Ataúro but nobody I contacted in Australia, even the military, knew anything about the island, or had ever heard of it. In England, the Ladbroke Grove train crash happened just after I arrived and that understandably dominated the news. East Timor was never mentioned. It was weird.

On my way through Jakarta, the ABC television program Four Corners interviewed me about the last weeks in East Timor and the trip on the AWU but I said little, unwilling to take any risks in case the madman commandant was still in control on Ataúro. Now that I was far away from him, I saw even more clearly that he was a mad and dangerous man.

TIMOR, OCTOBER 1999

I returned to Dili.

The city was devastated: burnt buildings, burnt houses, burnt offices and shops, traumatised, homeless people. A poor city cannot take this. People had run away, fled to the hills or found shelter in makeshift camps; many have been forced into West Timor. The atmosphere of Dili was sad and the air was heavy, smelling of smoke and fear. Foreigners were everywhere. On every corner was a sandbag fortress/citadel, a soldier with a weapon, INTERFET.

Oh Timor, oh Indonesia, what have you done?

An Oxfam vehicle picked me up at the airport and I directed the driver first to the beach, to Dili Harbour where the Ataúro boats come in. I still hadn't been able to get any information about the island and was desperate to meet Ataúro people and hear their news.

And the first people I met at the beach were Yakob and Cedes! I was overjoyed and hugged them and cried just a little with relief.

They were pleased to see me, a bit embarrassed by my show of emotion but I didn't care. They told me nobody on Ataúro was harmed and the mad commandant left the same way as we had done, via Alor, about a week after us and just before INTERFET came to the island. They told me they'd made their way back safely from Kalabahi with the food and essentials for Ataúro. Then they'd decided to do a couple more trips and make it a commercial enterprise. By chance, they'd met with their cousins who live in Kalabahi and they helped… so in the end they had done well bringing goods to the island from Alor. Happy ending.

Talking with Yakob and Cedes and other Ataúro people who gathered around me, I had an overwhelming urge to jump on a boat and go to the island. The sea was calm and the sky was blue and, apart from several huge foreign naval ships in the way, looking away from Dili and out to Ataúro, it seemed as if nothing had changed.

But of course it had.

Oxfam said I could not go to the island. I could hardly believe it and didn't like it. They said it was too dangerous. I don't believe that. My island friends told me everything was fine there. Because I now work for Oxfam, I don't go, but my heart was full of longing, and I find it hard to settle in Dili. I was now a foreigner among many foreigners. I lived in a safe, fenced compound, shut away from the street, the community, the Timorese. Soldiers guarded the street corner outside. I understand the reason for this, but I don't like the reality of it.

BACK TO ATAÚRO 2

After several weeks and much pestering, I was finally permitted by Oxfam to return to Ataúro. Because of the dark, uncertain atmosphere in Dili, not many Ataúro friends had visited me there and I was very excited about going home for a few days. I think somewhere in my subconscious, I believed that back on Ataúro my life would be just as it had been, that back there I'd just take up where we'd left off, and all would be well.

The boat trip seemed longer than usual and the closer we got, the more wildly excited I become. And finally, there we were; that island, that mountain, those people. It was wonderful to jump from the boat into the warm water, wonderful to feel the coarse sand between my toes, the pebbly beach under my feet. It was wonderful to be greeted by people, to hug and kiss and laugh, swap stories.

Everything felt the same… but of course it wasn't. There was no Anton. Our house was empty. The terrible, cavernous space of Anton's absence almost bowls me over. He was not there, of course, and he wouldn't be again. But his books were there stacked in a neat pile by his computer, his clothes were there, folded on the shelf, a pair of his sandals hung on a hook and the echo of his laughter was everywhere. On that first visit and for a long time after, I felt his absence as acute pain, felt his presence where he no longer was, heard his voice, and waited for him to appear. In Dili I was involved with other work that kept me occupied and preoccupied but on Ataúro there was this gaping chasm, this terrible emptiness. There was no Anton.

That night I slept on the floor in the manleka – our thatched raised platform overlooking the beach – and that became my permanent bedroom when I returned to

Atauro to live. I never slept back in our shared room again: a place of music and dancing, laughter, tears and love was now my storeroom.

CONUNDRUM

There were many stories to hear on that first visit back. It seemed as if years had passed when it was less than two months since we'd left on the *Loro sa'e 18*. I heard many stories about the crazy commandant – Fernando's was vivid and heart-wrenching, Guido's macabrely funny, Jesuina told me that the people had decided to kill him but couldn't work out how.

'It turned out okay in the end, though,' I said. 'It was good nobody got hurt and he didn't have to be killed.'

'No,' she was adamant. 'We should have killed him. He was a very bad man.'

He had flown the coop and was now presumably back in Java or on some other military mission, fingering his revolver, thumbing through his photos, sucking in his amphetamines.

No damage had occurred on Atauro except what the community had themselves looted and destroyed. This included destruction at the high school – including our Muatan Lokal resources; the chickens were gone, their pen dismantled and stolen, the fisheries shed, tools, motors all gone, the garden destroyed and pipes to the water tank taken. I was disappointed and perplexed. Why had people stolen and destroyed resources that were established for their own children's education? Why had they stolen and destroyed resources that had been part of a program they themselves had developed and supported?

The books from the main school library were also stolen, burned, ripped up; several classrooms significantly damaged.

When I asked about it, I was told, 'Those things belonged to Indonesian times,' that was the main motivation for the destruction. I partly understand – people wanted a new start, a clean slate – but I was concerned about the naïvety of believing that, with their new status as an independent nation, everything would be renewed, replaced, upgraded, everything would be better, all problems solved. That people seemed to think that stealing community property was okay under the circumstances also puzzled me and, I feared, was not a good sign.

EDUARDO'S STORY

Sr Eduardo told me what happened after we'd left the island. On the 14th, the commandant called CNRT leaders to come to the military post in Vila – the youth leaders from Bikeli, Beloi and Macadade – and Sr Eduardo, Januario and Bosco, the three main Ataúro resistance leaders.

In Eduardo's words, 'Januario and me and the boys were ordered to go to the army post. We were afraid not to. The Indonesian flag was still flying there, and he made us all stand in a line and salute it. We had to stand up straight and perfectly still, not moving at all. The boys were standing in a line to one side, but Januario and I had to stand up close, right under the red and white flag. We had to stand for a long time like that, we weren't allowed to move and had to keep saluting the flag to "show respect".'

'The commandant was drunk and after a while he started to scream and hit the boys. We had to watch that too. Then he took out his pistol and started shooting. At first he was shooting bullets in the air to frighten us. Luckily, we were standing very still. The big man was drinking beer and tossing empty cans on the ground near our feet then shooting at the cans; he told us if we moved the bullets would hit us. The cans were very close to our feet… we could hear bullets hit the cans or the ground right next to us. Then he hit the boys with his hands again and hit me a few times too. He was drunk and angry, so we did what he said.

'There was no one else around. His Indonesian soldiers had all gone and no Timorese soldiers were there. The only witnesses were Carlos, Adriano and Agustino. They were standing nearby and saw it all – the boys from Macadade, Beloi and Bikeli all forced to stand in a line saluting; Januario and I forced to be still and salute the flag. When they saw the commandant hitting us and shooting at the cans they were scared and ran away.'

'Bosco was the second in command of CNRT on Ataúro and, even though the commandant had called him, he hadn't come, so the commandant forced me to go and get him. He told me to tell Bosco that if he didn't come his house would be burned down and his wife and children would be targets. When I told Bosco that, he did go to the commandant the next day and was beaten up by him. Bosco had to be treated at the clinic because of that beating. It was very severe, and he was quite ill. Bastard.'

OECUSSE

During the emergency period, October to December 1999, Oxfam assigned me to work in Oecusse, the enclave separated from the rest of East Timor, surrounded on three sides by Indonesian West Timor. Most of the population of Oecusse had been either killed or forced over the border at gunpoint during the September devastation, and it was only in October that INTERFET troops finally got there to chase away the last of the militias and ensure that the region was safe for people to return.

Matt, an Oxfam GB water engineer, and I were assigned as a team to work in Oecusse. Initially, our task was to assist returning refugees to establish and maintain safe water and sanitation systems in the camp in Pante Makasar, which before its destruction, was the main town and administration centre. We flew by UN helicopter to a largely deserted district where this town had been devastated. It was a smaller version of Dili: burnt-out buildings and no people. A handful of UN and Medicine San Frontiers people camped in the remnants of a beachside hotel; we found an empty, crumbling room with no roof and set up our mosquito domes there. The INTERFET troops were using the other end of the hotel and there were four or five large, armoured vehicles parked in front.

It was a challenging assignment. Many of the returning refugees were still in a state of shock and fear; having been reassured that all would be well "before, during and after the referendum", they had experienced all hell breaking loose upon them when they chose independence. Many of them didn't yet know if their family members were dead or, if alive, or where they were. A camp had been set up near the cathedral and that's where we started work. Matt was the technical water expert and my job was community consultation and sanitation education. We worked well as a team and learned from each other. I learned about pit toilets and groundwater, about rain catchment into "bladders" and sourcing spring water.

Our living conditions were rough and there was absolutely no privacy so I was very appreciative of Matt as a teammate, not only for his skills and knowledge but also for his sensitivity. We had no camp stove on that first visit – we heated our tins of beans or stew at the edge of the soldiers' beach bonfire and sat on the sand in front of the tanks, eating from the cans. I remember the wonder and mystery of those nights, sitting on the beach under the extraordinarily beautiful sky, the immensity and endless possibilities of the universe stretching away from us, while behind us a burnt-out town that had recently experienced the depths of human evil.

The soldiers laughed and joked around their fire, while Matt and I sat under the stars and talked. He told me stories of his wife and baby daughter, and I talked about my daughter and about Anton. Each day we faced sad and traumatised people who had lost homes, family, and the familiar, and at night we talked about things that mattered in our own lives.

Because the UN interpreter was a Timorese Australian who spoke Tetun and not Indonesian, I was often called to interpret. Oecusse people speak their own language, Baikeno, and Indonesian; few of them know Tetun. I sometimes disagreed with the approach of the UN team that was working there, and said so. Even Medicine San Frontiers (MSF) seems to sometimes make decisions that don't make sense to me, Matt, or to the returning refugees. The foreign teams had knowledge and experience that could be helpful in the situation, but I strongly believed that the people of the area had knowledge and experience that we needed to listen to. This sometimes put me on the wrong side of the foreign aid team.

I refused to be just a representative of the UN, and openly used my unofficial interpreter role to put forward not only theirs but several other points of view. In my role as interpreter, I saw how local leaders sometimes appeared to agree with the confident and bustling foreigners when in fact they really didn't. Often, when the foreign team thought it had reached an agreement that would solve a problem, it was clear to me that they hadn't. It was a difficult time and although the foreign emergency workers were well-intentioned and it was, after all, an emergency situation, I thought they were sometimes too pushy, too much in a rush, and that this created unnecessary (sometimes hidden) discord. Over the next several years of working with international organisations, I confirmed this opinion.

BORDER PREPARATION

Matt and I did not stay permanently in Oecusse but flew by helicopter from Dili every couple of weeks to stay there a week or two, checking on the water supply, sanitation and general wellbeing of the camps. On one of our visits, we went up to the border to help with preparations in setting up a new camp for returning refugees who were expected to soon come back from West Timor. We are taken in a UN 4WD accompanied by soldiers in two armoured military tanks – one in front and one behind. It was still considered dangerous up near the border; no one had been able to ensure there were no militia gangs still operating there. It was an amazing journey along deserted mountain roads, past the remains of deserted, burned-out villages. Five armed soldiers formed a walking circle around us as we surveyed the area for the establishment of a campsite and looked for a level, high spot for a large water bladder. I wasn't sure whether this circle of armed men made me feel more, or less, secure.

As we tentatively explored the area, there was a sudden sound in the forest, the sound of breaking twigs. The soldiers, telling us to be still, lifted their weapons. We waited, peering anxiously into the trees from where the sound had come. We waited, the guns lifted and ready. And along a bush path came a very old man and his dog. He was startled to see us and stopped dead in his tracks. He told me he'd come across the border looking for his two cows.

He'd taken them with him into West Timor when he fled but they keep wandering back home… The old man in his ragged sarong and dirty woven bandana squatted by the side of the track with his dog at his feet, and looked bewildered at what he'd come across in his forest: a group of foreign soldiers, Matt and me.

In this context of helicopters, armoured tanks, soldiers with guns, night vision goggles, all the hullaballoo and razzamatazz of politics, war, militias and terror there was this simplicity: an old man and his dog looking for his two lost cows in the forest. He was no more real than the soldiers, the guns and the tanks, but he touched something that was far more real in me.

HOMECOMING

There was an official return of refugees from West Timor into Oecusse. They came in a convoy of trucks that the Indonesian police turned over to INTERFET at the border near Oisila. Matt and I were there a few days before the handover and spent time with some of the local men who, for whatever reason, had not fled from the militia. One man, a village head, told me his wife and small daughter had been forced onto a truck and taken away. He'd not seen or heard from them for weeks and didn't know if they'd been killed or not. Hundreds of people were killed. Nobody knew who would be returning on these trucks and who would not.

When he spoke of his little daughter this man's eyes shone as fathers' eyes do, with love and then with tears. She was four years old and his only child.

On the day of the handover, I filmed the trucks coming up the Indonesian road to the border. It was a joyous occasion. I asked the Indonesian police if I could film it and they were happy for me to do so, 'We've nothing to hide,' they told me, curtly. Maybe,

maybe not… so I filmed the whole return, which was fantastic.

Up the mountain came the overloaded trucks with people hanging over the sides, standing on tiptoe, holding each other for support, wanting to see the border, the INTERFET troops who were there to protect them, their homeland. They'd not been gone long but it was too long, and the circumstances of their going had been horrific. They hadn't known if they'd ever return.

There were six or seven truckloads of people and each one had to be searched by INTERFET soldiers. There was still fear that militia might be amongst them, that weapons might be hidden, that strife could seep back in with them. The trucks were stopped on the edge of the soccer field where people disembarked with their goods and uniformed UN soldiers waited.

After filming some of the returnees being searched, I decided to wait on the other side of the field with the few people who had not gone away, the anxious ones who waited for their families or, at least for some word of their families. I waited with the father of the little girl as he looked and looked across the field at the returnees. His eyes searched through the lines of foreign soldiers, among the growing crowd of people. He looked and looked as people climbed down from the trucks. Each truck he examined from his distance, each person, one by one. He shook his head, giving up hope.

And then we saw a tiny figure slip through the lines of soldiers and sprint across the field towards us. It was a little girl; she had seen her father and came running into his arms. They held each other tight and laughed and cried and kissed each other's cheeks.

Through my own tears, I saw the soldiers on the other side from where she'd broken free look at each other, look over the field at the little girl in the arms of her father, shrug their shoulders, and turn back to their work.

FOREIGN INVASION

There'd been eighteen non-Indonesian foreigners living in Dili before 1999. If you saw a white face in the street, you knew it. The few foreigners working there kept a low profile, fitted in. The streets were filled with Timorese and Indonesians, and it was clearly an Asian/Indonesian culture in the 90s. Despite the underlying tensions and resistance, despite the statements by Timorese living overseas that there was no commonality between the occupiers and the occupied, it was clear to me that Indonesians and Timorese were culturally similar, that their values and interests were similar, their tastes in music and entertainment similar, their sense of humour, their personal aspirations more alike than not.

Now there was a new invasion and it was truly foreign; the streets were filled with thousands of foreign faces, thousands of new cars, big white UN cars, military vehicles. Manye Timorese wondered what was going on. Not everyone was aware of the agreement that United Nations Transitional Administration in East Timor (UNTAET) was to administer the country until it was ready for true independence. With all the UN agencies and international NGOs starting up and their staff pouring into the country, it felt like another invasion.

Restaurants that few Timorese could afford to eat in, sprang up. Foreigners had money; Timorese beggars appeared. Two luxury ships were brought into the harbour, providing accommodation, restaurants and entertainment for foreigners. Most Timorese could only watch from the roadsides and marvel or despair at all this. Foreigners with money soon had Timorese girlfriends and this angered many young Timorese men. Foreigners had money; prostitution grew. I found the change difficult to accept, so I could imagine what Timorese felt, being powerless in the face of all the foreign wealth and control. I didn't want to be seen as one of these new invaders but, of course, Dili people don't know my history and so to most of them, I was. For the first time ever, I walked past a group of teenagers sitting on the side of the road and heard them make sexist and sexual jokes about me; a sign of new times.

I did not feel comfortable in Dili. Timor obviously needed assistance from other nations, other organisations, but what came with that was disturbing. Overwhelming. When I learned that the UN did not HIV test its personnel (and many of their personnel come from countries where HIV is rife) I feared for the vulnerable Timorese. The UN and many big International Non-Government Organisations (INGOs) had to be there to help Timor-Leste get on its feet, perhaps, but I feared what came with their sudden presence in that poverty-stricken and traumatised little country.

ATAÚRO CHIEFS MEET UN NEW YORK

A UN delegation from New York came to East Timor and visited Ataúro. I was asked to accompany them by helicopter from Dili to the soccer field in Vila, raising dust that covered the entire village, to meet with the five village heads and their assistants. Thinking along the lines of health, education and economic development, the UN people wanted to hear what the village chiefs considered priority needs for the island.

The UN brought their own interpreter. My role was to give the delegation a brief overview of the island, to observe the discussion and add to it if I thought clarification to either group was needed.

The chiefs came dressed in their best clothes and ready to pour out their aspirations, but the UN interpreter was not skilled and had trouble interpreting in both directions. I bit my tongue on several occasions and sometimes intruded to clarify, not just a concept, but a question, a sentence. We stumbled along, but it was not a good meeting. I could see the chiefs had not been well prepared and misunderstood the purpose of it; they saw this predominantly as an opportunity to "get things".

They had wish lists as long as your arm: balls, bicycles, boats, fabric, generators, motors, radios, sewing machines, soap, soccer balls, television sets, tools, toothbrushes, tractors, typewriters, volleyballs and water tanks. I was astonished to hear these leaders whom I thought I knew well, present their demands like children on Santa Claus's knee. It had not taken long for word to get out that the new foreign invasion meant the possibility of "goodies".

The UN men were rather stuffy and impatient. They hadn't been well prepared either and had no sense of humour or time for it. They kept trying to explain that what they were after was a broad overview of the island's needs. But the interpreter, an Australian Timorese, didn't seem to understand that concept and I felt reluctant, and not encouraged by anyone, to help her. Everyone was clinging to his (they were all men) own view of what the meeting was about, and not listening to each other or me. In the end, as frustrated as I am, I had to resign myself to its cross-purposes. It was the first of many discussions I would observe over the next couple of UNTAET years where misunderstanding occurred, and participants came and went with serious misconceptions.

NZ VISIT

NZAid, our primary donor, was willing to continue supporting us. Phil Goff, the NZ Minister for Foreign Affairs visited East Timor and wanted to visit Ataúro to see how their funds had been used. I'm asked to accompany him. We went from Dili in a helicopter – this time it was a military one in camouflage colours with an armed soldier at each window. To me, that seemed like overkill, but this was the environment of the times. I'm grateful to NZAid and proud of our program but slightly embarrassed to arrive on the Vila soccer field with all the fuss of INTERFET soldiers and guns as well as a VIP and a lot of dust.

The NZ military man in charge of the expedition told me sternly that the helicopter must return to Dili at 11:50 sharp.

'We must have the minister back here on the field by 11:45,' he says.

I told him that I was not the best person to be timekeeper. 'I'll be explaining things to the minister, I'll be excited, I'll get carried away, I'll also be the interpreter for others who want to talk with the minister and besides, I don't have a watch. I can't be the timekeeper. It'd be better if one of your soldiers keeps an eye on the time and gives me the sign when it's time to move on.' I'm not sure he listened to me.

I outlined our activities: a meeting with Sr Eduardo and the other leaders, a kilometre walk to the Manutasi (Seabird) Kindergarten, some time with the teachers and children there, a call into the library and the clinic, then a morning tea that had been prepared for them by the village women.

Of course, we didn't keep to our time schedule. The minister was personable and interested in everything. He wanted to talk with people and they responded. The children sang songs. He loved the songs and wanted to hear more. The leaders wanted to present their history and their aspirations. When I get the "time to move on" sign from the military, I attempted to wind things up but people didn't want to stop talking. Things got a little behind here and a little behind there. As we walked back towards the beach and the morning tea, the soldier-in-charge came to my side.

'We'll have to skip the morning tea,' he whispered. 'I'm sorry but it's time to go.'

'What? Skip the morning tea? No, that's not possible.'

The women have been up since early morning cooking donuts over open fires, frying bananas and cassava.

'You can't come to Ataúro and skip the morning tea.'

He shook his head. I told him that the morning tea is the culmination of the visit. It allowed people here to show their hospitality, their gratitude, to give something back. This time I deliberately spoke a little louder, so the minister could hear me.

'We'll make time for morning tea,' he says decisively. 'We can make it quick.'

Good man.

And there it was – laid out on an embroidered cloth and borrowed "best" plates: heaps of food, a big pot of weak lukewarm sugary tea. The official party members tucked in and then made a few more quick speeches. I was grateful to the minister. The military man glared at me.

They left late in a cloud of dust and I never did hear that NZ military operations have been inconvenienced by the Ataúro time delay. It was a successful visit and they continued to support us for many years.

PART TWELVE

BALI CHRISTMAS

At Christmas, Ant and I met in Bali. It was a happy time. We stayed in inexpensive homestays in quiet places and did the things we always did: talked lots, laughed lots, loved lots, sang lots, walked on beaches and snorkelled in warm seas on the east coast. Of course, the reefs were not as pristine as Ataúro's reefs and the beaches were not the same; in Bali we are guests of other people, not deeply at home as we were on our other island. Here we ate, walked, slept, sang and swam in a world that was not our world. But being together again felt good and right. We talked about our lives and our work, discussed important and unimportant things at length, listened to each other.

But, in retrospect, there may already have been a niggling new dimension that we both ignored. Although we were overjoyed to be close again… deep down, perhaps, grew a tiny embryo of awareness that we as a couple no longer had a central place in these stories. We were no longer in our world of Ataúro; we were out in the wide world now and times and circumstances had changed.

During the ten days we were together we avoided talking about *what next*. We avoided thinking about *what next*. That was far too hard.

DILI

By December our work in Oecusse was finished and I could start thinking about education work. As Oxfam representative I was invited to education meetings attended by the CNRT Timorese education team, the UN education team, Oxfam, UNICEF and senior Timorese teachers. From the beginning, things did not go well.

Everyone was keen to get schools up and running again: in all the districts, teachers were holding classes under trees outside burnt-out schools. They had no resources but their own enthusiasm, goodwill for their country's future and belief in the importance of education for it. I knew many of the teachers through training work I'd done in Indonesian times; I was often involved in national trainings in those years and had good rapport with senior education department people and primary and early education teachers. But times had changed and it was now Timorese intellectuals, many of them returning diaspora from Portugal or its colonies, that were calling the shots.

I was excited about the possibilities for the education system in Timor; now there was the chance to study pedagogical systems throughout the world and choose the best for this country. There was the opportunity to develop the most appropriate curriculum for the children of this new land. There were funds to resource study trips and education development and plenty of experience and expertise around to inform it. How exciting to be part of this.

In the first education meeting, it was clear that some things had already been decided and were not going to be discussed. The politics of it were very messy. It was understandable that CNRT people wanted to make the decisions but also frustrating that the decisions being made were to me, and others, not wise from a progressive education perspective. The Timorese had to make the decisions – but which Timorese?

Timorese teachers often approached me asking me to represent their views, views based on their experience and their aspirations for a better education system. One of the problems in decision-making was that the returning diaspora have a tendency to ignore the twenty-five years of Indonesian occupation, and to ignore their Indonesian educated and trained countrymen. The "stayers" on the other hand, were in awe of their returning more worldly 'elite' and timid about expressing their own ideas. This caused disconnect and dissatisfaction in the development of many government systems.

When I entered the debate or questioned decisions in those early meetings, I was rebuked by the Timorese education bigwigs but – after the meeting and out of earshot – my questions were strongly endorsed by experienced senior Timorese teachers. Teachers would not speak out in the meetings; Timorese hierarchical thinking didn't allow such boldness and Indonesian-trained teachers saw their position as subordinate to returning Portuguese speaking "elders" who rarely consulted with them.

We, as foreign advisors, had a 'bite-the-tongue' role to play and I was not good at that. When the decision was made that Portuguese would be the national language and the language of instruction in the schools, I was astonished. I love Portuguese, I love Portuguese music and I understood the emotional connection some people have with that beautiful language… but hardly anyone in East Timor in the year 2000 spoke it. How would teachers teach in a language they didn't know? How would children learn to read and write and become truly literate and numerate? I knew how clever many of our young Ataúro students were, what potential they had, and I wanted the best educational opportunities for them. The decisions being made were not my decisions to make but, as someone who loved Timor and Timorese children, they broke my heart.

By the beginning of the year 2000, community organisations (NGOs) were popping up all over the country and one aspect of my Oxfam work was to evaluate them and, if they were genuinely meeting a community need, give or facilitate support. Some were. Many were not. There was so much aid funding about that it didn't take long for enterprising young people to dream up ways to take advantage of it. You could hardly blame them: there was an obvious tiered economic demographic growing in Dili with foreigners on large salaries splashing it about at one end and Timorese on small salaries or without any income at all, struggling at the other. It was a challenge to work through the many applications and assist genuine groups to find support: blatant double-dipping and less than honest reporting that was sometimes comical in its creativity also began to emerge.

ROMAN LUAN

Oxfam had agreed that Ataúro could be one of the focus areas for my education and NGO development work, so I was able to visit often to support the kindergartens and explore other possibilities with the community. We had not yet resolved the problem of how to manage the PPSDM program, now abandoned by the Indonesian university. In February we held a three-day workshop to discuss this with community leaders, teachers and health workers. The facilities the university had left were a sizeable building near the beach, several computers, a photocopy machine and printer, kindergartens in three villages, a library, a good boat and some skilled people. Baptista and Anton had gone, but I was still around to advise and support.

At my suggestion it was decided to start a community organisation to take over where the PPSDM program left off and NGO Roman Luan, Ataúro's own community organisation, was born. The executive team was still to be decided but I, as its official advisor, was to be on it. The name, meaning 'widespread clarity/light' – inspired by its education focus – was suggested by Mariano, a Makili teacher. Ideas and aspirations for further programs were discussed at length, among them was community ecotourism. Roman Luan was a community owned and managed NGO (Non-Government Orgainsation) with its people working in their own community. Exciting.

PARTICIPATORY COMMUNITY DEVELOPMENT PROGRAM (PCDP)

While learning about community ecotourism, we started a program of participatory community development in the remote hamlets of Adara on the west coast and Ilitimur in the mountains. The Ataúro leaders selected these small villages as those most in need of development. One of our stipulations was that a significant number of women have to be involved in the activities. It was a program involving consultation and community review at every level.

Our team, Marcelo, Mateus, Tomas, Duarte, Rosa and I, went in the *Manucoco* to Adara and stayed a week camping in the deserted clinic building. When we arrived Philipe, the Adara conch shell blower, blew on his shell and its deep resonant sound gathered the community to meet under shady trees just above the beach.

Over several months we had many meetings with communites. With them we explored their history. Stretching a brown paper "timeline" between coconut palms and using discussion, drawings and stories they told us their history that ranged from the oldest person's distant memory until the present day. It was fun and fascinating – and, surprisingly, there were no negative stories from the time of Indonesian occupation. We did a similar exercise that assisted people to identify their skills and knowledge, and when and how they learned these things. The results formed the basis for exploring community priorities for development, and identifying community capabilities for achieving them.

We did the same activities with the Ilitimur community. Both villages were far from the nearest primary schools – Anartutu and Atekru – this meant that young children didn't start school at six years but waited till they were older, able to walk the distance twice a day. Both communities wanted a junior primary school in their villages so that when their peers in other villages started school, their children could also start.

Ilitimur's other priority was water storage. Their only clean water was from a trickling spring about 1.5 kilometres from the village. Adara leaders wanted to meet with the dive companies that had started coming from Dili, bringing bikini-clad foreigners to wander on the beach and through the village. Adara's people, of Protestant faith, objected to these brazen new arrivals that had never introduced themselves nor asked permission to visit. Adara leaders were also interested in small-scale community-managed ecotourism for their village.

With local people doing the building and some extra funding we were able to construct classrooms and equip them with basic resources. I trained selected teachers from each community and the schools opened and operated successfully for several years, allowing children to enter age-appropriate classes when they finally went to government schools.

With Ilitimur people, we built a holding tank for their spring water. It was still down in the valley, but at least there was water there when they walked down to it. And in Adara, we arranged a community meeting with the offending Australian dive company and the village leaders explained their concerns and made some demands. Then we assisted the community to build a simple camping ground for the now-more-respectful tourist groups. The PCDP program was rewarding and, along with the communities, our team learned heaps from it.

MAUN-ALIN

There was a desperate need for regular community transport to and from Dili. Apart from our small Manucoco workboat, there were only fishing boats occasionally making the trip, so when we heard about a suitably sized Sulawesi boat on sale in Darwin, we went all out to seek funds to buy it. The newly established British consul agreed to give us half the money and I persuaded our faithful NZ friends to contribute the rest. I flew to Darwin and met Jamie, an iconic Australian boat owner, who agreed to help me fit out the boat with life jackets and other safety gear. He offered to sail the boat up to Ataúro when it was ready and the season was right, and would train our crew to sail and manage it.

Community leaders gave the boat the name *Manu-Alin Ataúro* (Brothers and Sisters of Ataúro) and it served the Ataúro people with regular trips to Dili on Tuesdays and Thursdays for several years before, and even after, the Saturday government ferry service began.

AIRPORT DENPASAR

Anton and Dr Ambar came to Timor to run strategic planning sessions with Roman Luan and some of the other Timorese NGOs. As part of our Oxfam support, I had been asked to find a team to do this and they were certainly the best I could think of. Anton knew Timor and Ataúro, and spoke Tetun, Ambar was a respected university colleague who was now working with Anton in Flores. They both spoke Indonesian and at that time that was still the working and intellectual language of young Timorese.

Because we were working in extreme conditions, Oxfam sent its foreign staff out of the country – to Bali or Darwin – every five or six weeks. I timed my break to coincide with Anton and Ambar's visit and went to Bali to meet them.

As they came through the doors from the wet tarmac, I saw Anton's head above all the others, looking for me. Ambar was squat and walks with short, fast steps to keep up with him. Anton and my eyes met but I sensed that something was not right. From a distance I saw Anton was uneasy. Confused, I took a step back before he reached the door – then stepped forward again to him, reminding myself: this is my Anton, this is my love. A greeting kiss, a scant hug from Ant and I was shaking Ambar's hand and walking out, chatting airport talk – about the place they've left, their journey, their arrival; Anton was avoiding my eyes.

I realised that Anton has not told Ambar about our relationship, and I'm stunned. He's been working and sharing a house with Ambar for six months. During that time our friendship had not changed, we've continued to be in touch with each other, spoken frequently by telephone, regularly by email – but he had not told Ambar about us before this meeting in Denpasar on the way to East Timor. This was confusing and hurt.

We talked. We told Ambar. He was a conservative Javanese

Christian but conservative Javanese Christians are not fools, are more worldly-wise than Anton may think, and he can cope. Before we go on to Timor, Anton and I talked a lot more. I love Anton unconditionally – as lover, friend; in some ways son – so when we talk, I understand what is happening. It hurt, but I did understand. Anton now lived in a different world, a world that is Indonesian. He's a young man; in Indonesia you are a "young" man until you marry and have your own family. Roles are defined and expectations clear. It's not just the expectations of Ant's parents and his extended family that weigh on him now, but those of his peers, his colleagues, his elders and mentors like Ambar. His duty, his responsibility to himself as well as to them, is to marry and to have children. I see that more clearly.

Anton struggled. He loves me. We had shared so much and have been, and are, happy together. He was a strong and good man. But on this visit, I began to realise that I could not give him the life that's expected for him. Perhaps, deep down, the life he expects for himself. We talked, we talked, and he couldn't let go and I couldn't let go so we don't. We laughed again, and we loved again and avoided the deepening shadow falling over us.

AMBON SUPPORT GROUP

Ambon was still under siege, with military-backed troublemakers stirring up and maintaining conflict between Muslims and Christians. Moluku families, Christian and Muslim, have suffered. Ant's sister was studying at Flinders University in Australia and sets up a support group to raise awareness about events in Moluku. The group wanted to put pressure on the Indonesian government to end the conflict.

I applied for membership of the group, volunteering to support it through writing emails, and articles etc. My offer was rejected. I get a response from the secretary saying that I am considered "unsuitable" for membership. This hurtful reminder of Anton's family's deep disapproval shocks me.

SCHOOL FURNITURE

With the exception of Ataúro, most schools in East Timor had been destroyed and classes were being held outdoors under trees. As well as other resources, school furniture was needed. A Timorese friend in Dili and I developed a proposal for the program of local manufacture of tables and chairs for schools. To explore possibilities with carpenters, we visited small Timorese woodworking businesses that were picking themselves up after the September chaos. We believed this would be an excellent and not overly difficult project to set up throughout the country, as most towns and even villages had a skilled woodworker or two. If we had a standard design and could get hold of timber, we could run brief training sessions in the districts and begin work.

The UN has funds for refurbishment of schools. Doing it locally might delay the provision of furniture for a few months, but it would be a positive thing for local communities to set up furniture production for their own schools. With the huge invasion of foreigners, it's a way of putting some responsibility, self-esteem, authority and influence back in local hands. School buildings still have to be repaired or built and, as that will take time, a furniture delay won't matter.

We put in a proposal to the UN for the project, but it was rejected. I was flabbergasted. They have decided to import plastic tables and chairs from the Philippines. We argue strongly for our project for some weeks but eventually have to accept the rejection. Thousands of little plastic tables and chairs come to Timor.

BACK TO ATAÚRO 3

In August 2000 I resign from Oxfam and go back to Ataúro to live and work with Roman Luan. After the first national teacher training run organised and facilitated by UNICEF (my friend, Alison), the CNRT and Oxfam (me) I was clear that I wanted to be away from the centre of things. Too much was happening there that caused me pain.

The teacher training was well planned and teachers from all over the country are selected to attend. They were crying out for support and excited about being with their peers in Dili to discuss education issues and the difficulties they are facing. Alison and I, both experienced educators and creative problem-solvers, were excited about facilitating the training. But there was misunderstanding and conflict between the UN agencies. CNRT, the Portuguese educators and us and we are caught smack in the middle of it. Although teachers have been brought from all over the country and CNRT members have been on the selection panels, the CNRT attempted to sabotage the training. They send word to the teachers who have already arrived in Dili that if they do the training their employment by the future national education department is doubtful.

The teachers were angry. They wanted the training. They stood up to the CNRT. We stood up for them. This got me on the wrong side of the CNRT education people and perhaps put Oxfam's education program at risk. None of this was pleasant and I was not used to being perceived as a pawn. I didn't want to represent anything other than what I believed in, and what the community wanted.

From the teachers' point of view the training was successful and that satisfied Alison and me, but I don't want to take part in the game that's being played around national education. By the end of the training, I had identified my strengths and my weaknesses and decided to go back to Ataúro to work with the community there. Although I was breaking my contract, Oxfam generously offered to support my work by providing me with a volunteer level living allowance for the next two years. I was very grateful and happy to be back.

SEA NOTES: SIX MEN IN A BOAT

This evening at sunset six men pass by me in a canoe; a moving silhouette it is – six heads, six working bodies, four arms paddling, eight arms dragging a net. Six fishermen silhouetted against a darkening lilac sea, a purple sky, six fishermen making ripples and music as they go. I hear their deep voices singing and my heart sings too.

TRINKETS

The sea had once again saved Ataúro, this time from the foreign aid invasion. Even with the helicopters, it was still a remote place; aid workers come but rarely stay overnight. The two UN police and an UNTAET administrator are the only ones who live on the island – making the foreign population, including me, now a total of four. Occasionally well-intentioned people arrive on boats and immediately want to "save" the island people, saving them from what is not always clear.

A young American woman tells me she has come to "get the

women back into their gardens". Because, she explains to me earnestly, they rely on their gardens for survival and since she's been here – two days – she's noticed they're not gardening.

'But I have an idea,' she tells me enthusiastically. 'I've brought gifts and sweets… I'll hang them on trees along the paths that lead to the gardens. That should entice the women back to work.'

She is serious. I conceal my astonishment and point out that the women she's talking about have lived here for generations and know what their lives and their families' lives depend on. They are adults and not children at a birthday party. I also explain that it's not growing or gardening season right now, which is why people are not going to work in their gardens.

'Oh,' she says, disappointed, and goes off to think up another well-intentioned but uninformed plan.

GREEN MANGOES

On the beach, children bring me green mangoes and I eat them there, cutting them into wedges with my pocketknife – pale yellow wedges with green rims of skin. Ripe mangoes are brilliant golden yellow; these are pale and hard, the colour of lemons. I soak them in the sea. I like them tart and salty. When you eat ripe mangoes juice dribbles down your chin, you have to lean forward so it drips on the sand; the stringy bits stay in your teeth. These hard green mangoes, pale and crunchy, are easier to eat but make your lips pucker with their sourness.

THE LIBRARY

At last, we had a community library and activity centre, and it was a good one. We had books in Indonesian and English and were given a large donation of Portuguese language books by the Portuguese government. Local carpenters built shelves, and we painted them in bright primary colours. We put pot plants in corners and woven mats on the floor.

Domingos and Julieta were our librarians and together, learning as we go, we finish cataloguing and arranging books: fiction for all levels, biography, science, mathematics, geography, history, religion, health, music and art. We had picture books and books for older readers. We had encyclopedias and dictionaries, atlases and other reference books and our funding from New Zealand allows us to buy art materials and musical instruments.

We had an official opening with the UNTAET administrator, local leaders, teachers, nurses, the UN policemen… and away we went.

The building was large — we used one room for the books and reading spaces and one for art, drama and music. There was a good storage room and we now had electricity, at night, and working toilets, as long as we have water. We ran information sessions at the library for the primary school teachers, in which we discuss the purpose and uses of a library and how important it was for children to read if they were going to be good readers. We introduced them to the books and invited them to use the library as part of regular class activities. I helped them plan library sessions into their timetables and designed activities for their students. All this as new to the teachers and only some of them were convinced that reading was important for literacy.

Julieta and Domingos, supported by me, ran evening art, drama and music activities that were popular with children and teenagers. It was wonderful and I believed contributed heaps to the education of children in Vila. We later extended books, art materials and musical instruments to remote hamlets, by boat or on horseback. We were told by the Victorian Library Council team that comes to visit, that our library was the best community library in the country and are very proud.

Sadly, A couple of years later when the Italian priests came to live on Ataúro the Catholic Church tossed the library – books, art materials, musical instruments, librarians and patrons all – out of the building. It was not the two good priests who insisted on this but an arrogant Timorese holy man priest who threatened to literally throw everything out into the field if the building was not empty within a week. The Ataúro church leaders who have supported the library since its inception did not object to their treatment. They accepted the decision and the way it was delivered. I was dismayed at the power of the Catholic Church in the new Timor.

We managed to find places for hurriedly packed boxes of books and other equipment in the primary school, empty houses and the ROLU office. Eventually, we were helped with funds by the Victorian Library Fund to build a new, simple library building. The loss of that first library is a big loss for the Ataúro community – a loss never recognised by the church; a library never replaced by the church.

ANTON

The empty space left here by Anton is deep and wide, if I'm not careful I could fall into its depths and despair.

I choose not to despair; every morning, on waking without my mate, I choose not to despair. On seeing the sun on the horizon, seeing the shimmering light it throws on the sea, or seeing storm clouds gather, rain beating on the water, the sea moving in ripples as the tide comes in or goes out, on knowing someone has readied a thermos of hot water for my morning coffee, that my dogs are waiting to be fed, that this morning we have a meeting to discuss kindergartens or horticulture or community tourism… I choose not to despair. And gradually, slowly, the empty space shrinks.

Routines help, patterns form, things fill the mornings, the days, the weeks.

Anton and I talk often. Now, with some effort, I can use a mobile phone on Ataúro – if I walk up a hill, hang by an arm off the side of a cliff or, in low tide, climb out to a particular rock in the sea, I can get a signal from Dili and sometimes reach Anton. When I'm in Dili we talk on the phone and from Dili I send and receive emails. Anton isn't happy in his job. The international NGO that has contracted him is heavy-handed; he tells me they take armed police with them when they go to work with island fishermen in their effort to stop them using destructive environmental practices. This is not Anton's approach. He doesn't believe threats are an effective way of changing behaviour but that education, consultation and exploring alternatives with the fishermen is the way to go. But that takes time, and we are both aware that big organisations with lots of money seldom have the time or the patience to work at the pace required by traditional communities. We talk often about such things.

Ant will not come back to Ataúro and I understand why. And I cannot go to Flores; right now my primary commitment is to Ataúro, and in Labuhanbajo Ant lives a life I know I can't be part of. There he lives in a cos, a shared house, with other young men and Dr Ambar. There, Anton is a young, single man and lives a life that I wouldn't easily fit into, that I would not want to fit into. Even for us to live together would not be right; he is growing comfortable in the life he leads now, a life he knew before Ataúro and one that is again natural for him. We both realise that to live together in the bigger world might just be too hard, might even destroy the love and friendship we have known.

There is no lessening of our feelings for each other. They are embedded in our experiences, in our memories, in our souls, and we have no doubt that we will carry them to our graves. But it's in the shadow of the wider reality now, no longer nurtured by the sacred space of Ataúro, that secluded safe and sunlit other world.

Anton's family continue to remind him of his obligations and their expectations, and this continues to cause him, and then me, great sorrow. That they may be right does not make it easier.

SEA NOTES

Underwater, in the lagoon, there are meandering lanes of rock and coral to explore. Alone now, I swim often along those alleys, following green and purple wrasse through the channels, surprising schools of brilliant blue neon damsels. Spotted black chromis dart about and peer at me from dark holes, hundreds of starfish — soft velvet blue, thorny orange, brown and crimson — scour the sandy bottom; comical tobys peep out from under ledges and puffer fish drift by with serious, focused eyes. Blennies that think I don't see them make me laugh bubbles underwater. A magnificent, elegant scorpion fish passes by.

I float face down in the salty sea, above the channels, out over the reef where big parrotfish swim. I let the currents take me over massive bommies festooned with clinging feather starfish, over fine dancing soft corals and branching corals that are brittle and hard. Bold anemone fish come out to investigate and I am aware of more timid eyes behind rocks, eyes under ledges, eyes through seagrasses, watching me. Floating with the currents, along the coast, past the headland; following the line of Lampia's white beach, I am transfixed. I am transformed. Breathing deeply and rhythmically through my plastic tube, I am absorbed by dancing light reflections, myriads of sea creatures, unimaginable shapes, colours, motion. I am dulled to the above-water world, sharply attuned to the underwater one; I don't miss a flash, a gleam, a spiky fin, a colour change, a sandy slither. I breathe deeply and rhythmically, borne along on the warm currents of silky sea. And this becomes my afternoon meditation.

Over several years of snorkelling along the reef with my slate and my pencil, checking with fishermen and books, I identify 408 different species of fish in this stretch of sea.

TUA KO'IN

Roman Luan, the Ataúro community's NGO, in partnership with Australian Volunteers International and funded by AusAID, took up the challenge of introducing tourism to the island; we built a simple ecotourism resort.

Knowing how tourism can be destructive of a culture and to a natural environment, I had been concerned that it would be thrust upon the inexperienced Ataúro people before they could make any decisions about it. I believed passionately that they need to know how it might affect them and how they might direct it. We heard rumours of casinos and luxury hotels, golf courses and the like, being built here. This was an island surrounded by pristine and beautiful reefs which could well be up for grabs to the highest bidder. I feared that people here could be swept along without knowledge of what could happen to their world. I talked lots about it until they agreed we should do it ourselves.

We proposed an experimental and experiential project that respected culture and the environment, and through which the community could learn about ethical community tourism. We succeeded in attracting support and funding from AusAid, and Tua Ko'in Eco-Village and its education program were developed.

The project was multi-layered. There was a trip to Bali with me for four community representatives; people who have never been out of Timor before. There, we saw examples of good and bad tourism; we meet Balinese people who regretted the way tourism had gone on that island and were attempting to develop true ecotourism that benefitted the community and the environment. We met Balinese people who had been disempowered by mass tourism – selling their lands, being rich for a short time and then becoming landless servants and beggars to tourism. That was an eye-opener for the Ataúro group.

Roman Luan partnered with the Australian Conservation Foundation which assisted with training and brought a Coast Care team and a Marine Management team up to work with Ataúro people. It was all exciting and new, and the training relevant and solid.

Marcelo, Duarte and I designed a simple but comprehensive community education program around tourism that was taken to every village and hamlet. There were meetings and discussions everywhere to talk about tourism and listen to each other. We discussed the challenges that come with tourism – waste disposal, water use, maintaining environmental, cultural and social integrity. We selected a team of local builders, and design cabins and other facilities with them. As much as possible, we used building materials that were produced on the island – various types of bamboo and grass for thatch, cement blocks made here and rendered with local clay. We ran hospitality and management training.

The facility was opened in 2002 and became a model for community ecotourism throughout the country. It was a very successful economic venture for the community; people become skilled and Tua Ko'in soon became profitable. Several Ataúro people were earning regular, modest salaries working there;

fishermen, chicken owners and vegetable growers have a new market, people with boats earn money taking tourists snorkelling or bringing them to the island, guides take people hiking up the mountain or to visit other villages, carvers and basket weavers sell their products. We supported the formation of a local singing group that regularly entertains visitors.

For over ten years Tua Ko'in ran successfully, managed under Roman Luan's supervision by Ataúro people. Community groups from other districts came to train with us, the tourism department used us as a model for community tourism, foreigners working in Dili came for rest and recreation, it was promoted in the Lonely Planet Green Guide, holidaymakers from Australia and European countries began to hear about it and came to stay. AKTOMA, the Ataúro Island tourism association was formed.

Tua Ko'in had a touch of magic, it was a place that was authentic Ataúro. But conflict over land arose and greed and corruption raised their ugly heads. Ataúro people are determined and can be stubborn and stonehearted and, after eleven years of successful operation, the resort was closed down. Even though it had been held up as an example of successful community enterprise, no people in higher places seemed willing to mediate. And Tua Ko'in Eco-Village disintegrated for want of any apparent means of resolution.

ADRIANO CRIES AT THE GATE

Adriano is a man of few words. He seldom smiles but when he does his face is a flash of white teeth and warm, crinkly eyes, revealing a gentle and sensitive heart. Adriano's is a smile that makes you smile. Adriano has the air of someone brought up to think they are inferior. He's never been to school and, around here, he's the one who gets little attention, acknowledgement or praise, except from me. He's not included in conversations or consultations. He rarely asks questions.

Somehow his branch of the family sits at the bottom rung of the social ladder; he lives, with his wife Rosaria, three tiny children and sometimes his or her very old parents, in a small dirt-floored bamboo and thatch house across the road from the PPSDM office.

He was our gardener, cleaner and "security", locking windows and doors at night. His thumbs were green and produced leafy vegetables, eggplants and, in the right season, tomatoes from the tired, dry, sandy soil beside his house. There were bananas and papayas in the garden too, and once he had a passionfruit vine that produced sweet, seedy fruit but died after just one season and he hadn't kept seeds.

Most nights when I was up late working in the cool of the veranda and everyone else has gone home, Adriano came quietly out of the dark and sat with me. We share *kretek* (Indonesian clove cigarettes). We hardly talk. Occasionally he made a comment… about the weather, the sea, a workmate, the garden. Sometimes I asked him a question about the weather, the sea, his family, the garden. Mostly we just sat in silence.

One day, it was a Friday in June of the year 2000, Adriano cried. He cried very, very loudly. Adriano stood at the Roman Luan gate and cried so loudly that people put their heads out of doors, people started running onto the road to see what was the matter. He sobbed so noisily that people thought someone had died and his wife, Rosaria, a tiny, feisty woman, tried to make him stop. At first, she comforted him, then she yelled at him, and finally she started hitting him about the shoulders and head. It was embarrassing having her husband stand at the gate and cry like that and people coming from everywhere to watch. But Adriano kept crying till he could cry no more and then he went home and washed his face with water from the bucket and dried it on a thin grey towel.

That night he came to sit with me as usual. His eyes were swollen. It was a while before he spoke.

'I cried today,' he said.

I'd been away in Makili Village that day and had heard the story from others when I got back in the late afternoon.

'I heard that,' I said. 'People told me.'

'I cried a lot. I cried loudly. Everyone heard me.'

We sat in silence, thinking about him crying. I'd heard several different stories but this was the important one: his version. I waited while he sucked on his cigarette then, finally, I asked, 'Why? Why did you cry?'

He thought about it for a while. He shuffled his feet and sniffled, coughed. It was a few minutes before he finally replied.

'I cried because Guido talked to me like a dog.' He stared out into the night. I could feel his hurt. He took a deep breath. 'I don't like being treated like a dog,' he said. We sat in silence. Feeling the terrible pain of his powerlessness. 'Guido often treats me like that.'

It was true. I think tears rolled down his face again and I could feel my own eyes welling up.

'Nobody likes that,' I said. 'Nobody likes being treated badly. What happened?'

Adriano looking at the floor began his story. 'I'd finished work and was having lunch. Rosaria had cooked cassava and I was sitting under the tree to eat it when Guido shouted out to me. From across the road, he shouted my name... he shouted loudly so that everyone could hear...'

It is impolite on Ataúro to shout at people or call to them from a distance. When you want someone's attention you clap your hands or go closer to them. Guido had shouted from the office veranda, across the yard, across the road and into Adriano's house compound. This was a public breach of courtesy that embarrassed Adriano so he decided, in a moment of uncharacteristic assertiveness, to ignore the shouting and continue eating lunch.

Guido shouted again. Loudly. Angrily. Adriano's children and their friends ran in from the road and told him that Guido had a visitor, the *Malae Metan* (Black Foreigner), who was the UN delegate and temporary administrator of the island at the time, and both men were standing on the veranda across the road, waiting for him to come.

That all the neighbours and the neighbours' children could hear the shouting was bad enough, but that Guido had a visitor with him made matters even worse. Adriano shifted further out of sight behind the tree to finish his lunch – although by then, he had little appetite for it.

When the UN man left, Guido finally stopped shouting and Adriano went to him. Guido ordered him to go to Antonio's house to get the key to the cupboard. In it might be the report that the Malae Metan needed in a hurry. Guido's voice was not so loud now but it was still harsh. Adriano went to get the key, and when he came back with it, he cried. He handed Guido the key and began to cry. He went to the gate and stood there crying. He'd had enough, that's all.

'Nobody likes to be treated like that,' I said. 'It's awful. Nobody should talk like that to another person. I'll talk to Guido about it, if you like.'

Adriano, staring out at the night, nodded.

The next day Guido told me his version of the story. 'Adriano cried yesterday, Ibu…' he began. 'He really cried. Loudly. I think it was because of me.'

He explained that the *Malae Metan* (UN Administration) had come to the office to ask for a report on our activities because he needed to send it to Dili. This Black Foreigner was a big man who walked with a swagger and his nose in the air.

The man told Guido he needed the report urgently because District Office was waiting and Guido, new at being head of an organisation and not understanding his rights and obligations, was confused. I was at the kindergarten in Makili Village and he had forgotten where the report was, but thought it might be in the locked cupboard. Antonio had gone home for lunch and taken the key.

The Black Foreigner had become annoyed then which flustered Guido. He shouted out for Adriano because he needed him to go and get the key quickly. The UN man was impatient. Guido shouted again but still Adriano didn't come. The UN man said that Guido should have better control of his staff and they should come when they're called. Guido was embarrassed and called again. Finally, when the *Malae Metan* stomped off telling Guido to get the report to him as soon as he could, Adriano came out and went to get the key. But when he came back he started crying and couldn't stop. He stood at the gate and cried loudly till everyone in the village, or at least the Tolorica part of it, came to see what the matter was and Rosaria tried to stop him by beating him around the head and shoulders, but he just went on crying until finally he stopped of his own accord.

'He said you treated him badly,' I said. 'He told me you shouted at him from across the road. He didn't like that. Would you?'

'It was the UN man, the foreigner, Ibu. He made me feel bad.

He said I should have the report to give him. He told me I wasn't a good boss... I wanted him to see I was the boss and had control.'

Guido was still learning how to be boss of a new community organisation, learning how to manage people and programs and resolve the many big and little problems that came with trying to do something innovative in your own community. He had no idea yet how to juggle local politics, culture, criticism, suspicion, jealousies, his own doubts, his ambition and pride in matters of his ability.

In Dili the following week I met the bigger boss, the UNTAET District Administrator. She was European; her big breasts in a low-cut silky blouse, large bangles, beads, jangly gold earrings and high heels were incongruous with her environment; a bare, burnt-out shell of an office. She asked me how the temporary administrator on Ataúro, "her man", seemed to be getting on.

'He's a bit of a bully,' I told her. 'He hasn't any right to demand things of our organisation, has he? Surely, he can't demand our program reports and use them as his own. I've told our director, Guido, that he doesn't have to hand them over at all, let alone be bullied into it. We'll cooperate and give him reports to inform him of what we're doing but surely, it's not his right to demand them.'

She laughed a throaty, dismissive laugh. 'Oh, you mean last week,' she said. 'Those reports! I did put pressure on him to get me some reports, any reports, because he hadn't sent in anything, and I needed some idea of what's happening on the island. I told him he had to get something in by the end of the day...'

She laughed and her bangles jingled and her earrings danced. 'I was getting calls from New York,' she explained reverentially.

Ah, so now I saw the chain of it – top dogs in New York put pressure on UNTAET Dili district administrator who put demands on The Black Foreigner – a possibly incompetent big fish in a small pond – who put demands on Guido – a new, unsure of himself community organisation boss – who put demands on Adriano who stood at the gate and cried his heart out.

SUNDAYS

On Sundays I walk on the beach where children play and this is what I see:

... five naked bodies clinging to a log; shining, singing, shouting naked bodies. I see ten legs kicking up chains of silver spray, five smiling faces, sea-sparkling hair, ten thin brown arms waving to me; bob, bob, bob go five girls on a log.

... six boys on a boat – leaping, glistening bodies, out of the water up onto their dugout canoe, running sure-footed along its length then shouting, jumping, splashing into the sea – aaaaah-heeeeee! Aaaaah-heeeeee! One, two, three, four, five, six little boys in turn... leap, run, shout, jump, SPLASH. Aaaaah–heeeeee! Repeat: Boy One, run and splash! Boy Two, run and splash! Boy Three, run and splash! Boy Four, run and splash! Boy Five, run and splash! Boy Six, run and splash! Aaaaah–heeeeee!

.... a coconut shell on a string pulled along the water's edge – a coconut shell boat skimming the waves; a plastic water bottle boat bobbing on a string, its top a bright blue dot in the foam; a lump of driftwood dragged on a string, waves licking away its bumpy trail. Three little boys, three toy boats on strings: bottle boat, coconut shell boat, yellow driftwood boat.

And... a decorated sand village: broken shells, rusting tins, sticks, rocks, plastic, the rubber of old thongs; and its seven small creators smiling wide sandy smiles at me.

The sun shines.

LOBSTER FISHING

There was no Anton to swim with now, but some afternoons Vasco and I went lobster hunting together. When he said the time was right, we'd wade into the lagoon wearing masks and snorkels, carrying a lidded basket for the catch. We dived down to likely rock shelters. We knew them well. I was good at spotting, seeing the feelers gently moving, a black eye staring out. I gave them a thought-warning, – 'Go, go, go little lobster, go,' – but Vasco, following my finger, was on to them, tipping the rock, reaching down… and into the basket they went! We never took many, just enough for our afternoon meal.

They're delicious, these fresh lobsters. At the back of his place or mine, we cooked them straight over the flames of a fire till their shells changed colour and their flesh was thick, warm and white. Sometimes we squeezed limes over them, sometimes we'd eat them straight, tearing at the shells and sucking them dry. *Oh dear lobsters, you are perfect with palm wine and you melt in our mouths.*

Serious lobster hunters sought them out on the reef, down in their dark holes under big rocks. Serious lobster hunters could hold their breath, go deep and bring up bigger, fatter lobsters. Vasco could. But together we got the smaller ones in the lagoon, just a few, and share the meal.

TURTLE

Vasco was wide-eyed with the story he had come to tell me. It was late at night and I was working on the veranda. Vasco was very black and so is the night; I was always startled when he came up the path and appeared before me.

He sat on the wall to tell me the story of a recent dream, a dream about a turtle that came to him in the night. He used his hands to shape his story, his eyes to emphasize its importance. The turtle in his dream two nights ago was a big one that left the sea and came to him as he slept. When she was close to him – inside his house and near his bed – the dream turtle changed into a woman with strands of wet hair hanging down her back and water dripping from her dress. She asked Vasco to help her, and he saw that around her neck was a thick rope, heavy with barnacles and other sea things. She begged him to cut the rope with his knife and when he did, she was grateful to be free of it. She thanked him and returned to the sea.

'Perhaps,' he said, 'she was a mermaid.'

Before I had a chance to ask questions about the dream, he told me the turtle has returned. He gestured towards his house across the road. 'She's there,' he said, 'waiting. Come and see. This time it's not a dream. She needs our help.'

We went across the road into his yard. The village generator had gone off and there was no light except for the dull kerosene lamp he had hung from the fig tree. By its yellow light I saw the shape of the turtle. It was huge and had a thick rope tied around its neck. I stared at the turtle, amazed by her size, and the terrible rope around her neck. She stared at me with a round black eye.

'We have to cut the rope,' said Vasco, taking his knife from its scabbard. 'Help me turn her over and keep her still.'

It was no easy task to turn this huge turtle and, as we struggled with her, she continued to stare at us. She was calm, dignified. Vasco sawed at the thick, shell-encrusted rope and I attempted to soothe her with reassuring words. I had never been this close to a wild turtle before; in the sea there was always the safety of water between us, and they quickly disappeared into the deep. Now, I was close enough to touch her leathery skin and her horny shell, to feel her vibrations, to look into her strong, unblinking eye. I felt like a child in the presence of a graceful, ancient crone.

Vasco and I thought she was female… we didn't really know, but for us there was the strong connection with the woman in his dream. We thought she might have come to the beach to lay her eggs, become disoriented and wandered across the edge of Vasco's dream to seek help.

Vasco told me that before letting the turtle go, he wanted to write a message on her shell. He didn't tell me what or why, just asked if I had a permanent marker that would do the job. I went over to the office, found a torch and searched in likely places but couldn't find one.

We were sitting with the turtle discussing what to do next when a bright light shone in on us from the road and a deep foreign voice said, 'Excuse me madam but what is going on here?'

It was the new UN police, two of them on some kind of security patrol – hardly necessary on Ataúro but they're probably still looking for a purpose to be here. We explained about the turtle, but not about the dream, and Vasco told them he needs a permanent marker to write his message. I translated.

'Is this man of sound mind?' they asked me.

'Yes, yes, he's my neighbour,' I told them, as if that proved his sanity.

'This turtle must go back into the sea,' they said.

'Of course,' I told them. 'But Vasco needs to write a message first.'

'What kind of message?'

'I don't know… it's personal and important to him.'

They shrugged. It started to rain lightly.

'Do you realise it's past midnight?' they asked as if that's relevant. 'The turtle must go back to the sea. Please tell him that.'

'Look,' I said, 'this is his island and he knows the turtle belongs in the sea.' It's Bikeli people who eat turtle. 'He doesn't want to harm it. He wants to write a message on it. But we don't have a pen. Do you?'

The policemen looked at each other with a "they must be crazy" shrug.

'You know a pen won't last long in the sea,' said one.

'That doesn't matter – as long as she takes the message out there.'

They mumbled in Italian and then, to my surprise, one of them said, 'I'll go get a pen.' He headed up the road with the torch while we waited silently in the rain, beside the turtle.

Vasco wrote his message and "Isle de Ataúro" and the date on the shell of her belly, and we asked the policemen to help us turn her back over.

'Gently,' said Vasco, 'we must be careful with this lady. She's a friend.'

I translated, and the policemen shrugged and helped us do the turn. The turtle was confused and disoriented, and we had to direct her towards the beach and keep her great body lumbering down towards the sea. Once we had her facing in the right direction, the policemen took on the job of keeping her going and did it carefully and respectfully. Vasco and I walked behind them, he as supervisor of the process, keeping his cigarette alight in the rain and talking about turtles and dreams.

The rain stopped and a half-moon shone a light on the sea for her. She plodded along slowly, the policemen turning her when she we went off course. But closer to the water there was a change in her; she paused, raised her head, picked up speed and started to run on her heavy flippers. She knew exactly where she was now and lumbered down the sand, plunging into the sea.

We four watched her in silence as she followed the moonlit path, making her way out over the waves with Vasco's message. 'Goodbye turtle,' I whispered, my cheeks damp with tears and rain.

SEVEN DAYS

Anton and I knew, and finally accepted that our relationship would never be the same as it had been. Over time apart, we had learned that ours was a love made in and for Ataúro, the world that nurtured and blessed it. The bigger world was a different place and we were different people in it. In the wider world, our ages did matter, our families mattered in a different way, our cultures mattered. How we chose to spend our time was not the same and this was a truth that ached in our hearts.

We had lived together for four years and now, had been apart for nearly two. Hesitantly, we decided to accept our new reality and go our different ways. Ant's way was perhaps clearer than mine but it was clearly not mine. Neither of us could simply say goodbye and separate just like that; we agreed we needed time, time to be together again, time to try and unravel some of the intricacies that bound us, to adjust to separation. Together, we had to work out how we were going to do this huge thing, how we could do it while continuing to value and honour the special relationship we had shared.

We gave ourselves a week in Bali to make the difficult transformation. Just being together was as exciting as ever, but for the recurring stab of awareness that this was the last time. Sometimes in the joy of that week, it was impossible to believe. We could forget it momentarily, but never entirely. Sometimes we had to remind ourselves, and each other, that the purpose of this time was to embrace our separation, not to forget it.

We hired a small car and headed off with our Bali travelling music – music we could sing to: John Denver, (alone and, with Placido, *Perhaps Love*), the Everly Brothers, Scorpion, Beatles, the Jersey Boys, Ambonese love songs – our masks, fins and snorkels, our sketch pads and pencils. Best friends, we had a lovely time.

Watching Ant do ordinary things: bathing, sleeping, eating, drawing, walking, swimming, looking at me, pretending he doesn't know I'm watching him – still gave me great pleasure. Ever since I spied him in the garden that early morning long ago and became aware of the lankiness of his limbs, his elegant movements, his thorough attentiveness to what he's doing, Anton-watching had always delighted me. Now it took on a painful poignancy and I savoured the last days of simply being able to be with and look at this man.

One day, in the main street of Ubud, we met Wayan, the spy. An ordinary policeman now in a tight brown uniform, he was directing traffic. We were happy to see each other and almost embraced before he remembered he was in uniform and on duty. We chatted for some minutes. Times had changed.

Sometimes during our last week together, I grew impatient. Like the torturous anticipation of a dental appointment, at times I wanted it over and done with. Sometimes those days of anticipation were too painful, too long. But mostly those last days together were beautiful and far too short.

THE LAST NIGHT

And it came then, our last night.

We ate in a small café and drank beer. We clinked our bottles together and looked into each other's eyes. As far as we were game, as far as we could, we looked deep into each other's eyes.

We walked home along the wet road, avoiding potholes on the footpath. Holding hands.

Our hotel room was cheap and plain, but big enough to dance in. Holding each other we danced. Around the bed and the table, we danced, and in the space by the door. We had our cassette player and music that, though the sound was tinny, to us was good. I felt his skin against my skin and his breath on my neck, the familiar thinness of his limbs against me. It was almost dark in our room but I could see his eyes, feel the heat of him, smell his sweet, soapy fragrance.

We danced. The Everly Brothers sang to us. And Scorpion, *You and I*. All the soft, corny songs we loved.

We held each other and we danced in the half-lit room. I didn't want to let him go. My friend, my brother, my darling, I didn't want to let go. He held me, held me close; me – his sweetheart, his sister, his friend. I didn't let go and he didn't let go. Sometimes we laughed a little and sometimes we cried. We sang and danced until late, until we were finally silent, finally spent, and fell into the hard bed, nestling together like children wary of the darkness of tomorrow.

When the day came, spreading its light through the thin curtains, we rose. We didn't talk much. We drank coffee on the veranda in the sunlight and performed a ceremony: Anton taking the gold ring he gave me long ago – the two hearts entwined with leaves, the symbol of our love – from my left hand and placing it on my right, where it beccame the symbol of our friendship. I cried a little, silently, not wanting to disturb the peace of this morning or feed our pain with sound.

Pak Ali arrived to pick me up and Ant put my bag in his van. As it moved slowly down the long driveway he walked beside us, his hand on the open window, his hand over mine, till we reached the gate. And there, Anton, my love, my friend, stood alone on the street corner; standing tall with head erect, his white shirt bright against his skin. He stood perfectly still, watching us drive away and I looked and looked until I couldn't see him anymore.

FLAG RAISING

UNTAET has fulfilled its task of assisting the country to independence and on May 20th 2002 the Timor-Leste flag is raised. World leaders and VIPs, some of them from countries that have previously supported the invasion and occupation of Timor, attend the grand celebrations in Dili. Indonesian President Megawati Sukarnoputri is there. These are new times, and Timor needs new friends.

On Ataúro, the community gathers in the soccer field. I am here, filming. Everyone who can be is here – Inan Luisa, Mama Maria, Jesuina, Fernando, Domingas, Adriano, Ibu Juliana, Pak Manuel, Freitas, the teachers – all standing behind their village leaders, solemnly facing the mountain and the flagpole. With their backs to the sea, the Ataúro community stands proudly. Since early morning, people have been arriving in boats from coastal villages, on foot down mountain paths; this important day reminiscent of the 1999 gathering for the referendum that chose it.

Inansio and his son, Hilario, in traditional dress, woven tais cloth, flowing feathers, lead Macadade and Makili dancers with drums and gongs dance onto the field. Young men and women from Bikeli and Beloi follow with guitars. There are fine speeches. Speeches about the long struggle, the determination and strength of the Timorese people, the lives lost, speeches about the brightness of their future; high and honourable aspirations, hope, and resolve.

When Marcelo, Zito, and Edegar begin the high stepping, formal march across the field carrying the new flag to the flagpole, there is pin-drop silence. Men, women and children stand in awe; it is such a proud occasion, and the atmosphere is reverent, the joy solemn and deep.

The new national anthem crackles out across the field, following the red, yellow and black flag as it inches its way up the pole, creeping higher and higher to finally dance against the clear, blue skies of independent Timor-Leste.

EPILOGUE

SEPTEMBER 2022

I'd forgotten how at this time of year, fine grey dust hangs in the air coating the leaves of trees and shrubs along the road, how red and purple bougainvillea shine through the dust, neon bright against the hot sky. At this time, before the rains come, the hills are red, the tufty grasses brown. It's already hot and dry, although sometimes in the evenings there's a breeze from the sea.

Indonesia is still using its doomed-to-failure military tactics in West Papua. Its military doesn't seem to have learned from the experience of Timor-Leste.

On Ataúro, things have changed. Development: some call it progress. Hundreds of foreigners have tramped the tracks up the sacred mountain, hundreds have snorkelled and dived on the reefs. Speedboats roar up the coast most days, bringing visitors from Dili to explore the island. They come here for holidays, for diving, for doing holiday things local people don't do. The wondrous marine life of the island – corals, reef fish, dugongs, dolphins, whales – is being discovered.

Trucks, and sometimes cars, now roar along the new roads. Still not many, but enough to fill the air with dust and noise and send children, dogs and chickens scattering. More boats now have motors. The stores have more goods, more soft drink, beer and sugary things.

Some of the noble aspirations of the independence struggle seem to have faded; corruption, even on this island, is rife. The dollar has soared into ugly prominence. 'Time is money,' I hear people say and my heart shrivels. Was time ever meant to be money here? But Ataúro has recently become a municipality and that gives the island more autonomy and, I believe, with the right people in charge a better future.

I left Ataúro in 2008 to be a grandmother in Brisbane but come back to the island and my friends here nearly every year.

The children from those first kindergarten years – some of them now rugged fishermen and women married to their classmates and with babies of their own – greet me with kisses when we meet. They call me Mama, or *Ibu*, the Indonesian word for mother I had when I first came. Their children call me *Avo*, grandmother. Some of our students are at school on the mainland – or at university – and they talk about those early years fondly, nostalgically, as if they are as important to them as they are to me.

I have loved Ataúro. I have loved the people of Ataúro. And what I learned on Ataúro remains an essential part of me. When I come back, the gecko that might be Alu comes to live in my wall and still talks to me.

Sometimes I think there's little evidence of my work here now. The library no longer functions, Tua Ko'in Eco-Village which was an early model of community ecotourism for Timor-Leste and provided work, funds, knowledge and experience to the Ataúro community for over ten years, has disintegrated because of unresolved conflict. That broke my heart. Our kindergartens, now run by the government, are no longer such models of active and exciting early learning, our permaculture gardens are empty and dry.

Perhaps though, remnants from those years of our work with the community remain; perhaps fragments of knowledge and experience, fragments of possibility lie still in the hearts and minds of people here. I'm told our work still inspires many. Roman Luan is still active. Marcelo and Duarte keep it going with environmental programs addressing climate change, and AKTOMA (Atauro Tourist Association) the association we started in 2005 as part of the community tourism program, is stronger than ever. AKTOMA focuses on sustainable and ethical tourism that benefits the local community and guided by Avelino may save the island from tourism disasters.

Perhaps life is better – there are Cuban-trained Ataúro doctors serving their own people now, there are Ataúro businesses and more local employment; some people aren't as poor as they used to be. Filipe, the current Chefe do Suco, runs an impressive community program to conserve water, protect springs and save his island from environmental catastrophe. But I don't think life is better in all ways and certainly not for everyone, and many Ataúro people shake their heads and talk about the good old days.

I rarely hear songs from treetops as men harvest palm wine now, rarely hear songs drifting over the water; there are no big heavy boats to pull up the beaches any more so there are no boat pulling gatherings, no more wild boat-heaving dances and songs on the beach, no more celebratory parties afterwards. Development trade-offs.

Many of my old friends have died: Domingos, Duarte, Chefe Manuel from Bikeli, Antoni Freitas, the shaman and his wife, Senorhina Cabecas, Guido, Mama Maria, Vasco, Eduardo. Soon there may be no old men and women who know the music, sing the chants, tell the stories. Soon there may be no one who can talk with the spirits and guide the living. For how much longer will people remember the dances and the ceremonies? For how much longer will they need them?

In 2018, *Pak* Tobias, an Indonesian policeman and partner of an Ataúro woman before the referendum, was brought to my house by an excited group of Ataúro people. He had come back to her after his retirement and everyone was happy to see him. We talked about past days nostalgically and rejoiced that after so many years, *Pak* Tobias, one of the many good Indonesians had returned.

Last time I was here I had a party for my Makili neighbours; we ate rice, corn and chicken, drank palm wine, sang and danced. I ached to hear traditional Ataúro singing and far into the night it went – loud, mysterious, wild, harsh and beautiful as always.

Anton is married and has children. Before her death, his mother saw him with a wife and family and he is, I think, mostly happy. We keep in touch by email and messenger and Ant still calls me "best friend". I wore the gold ring till it became too thin and I store it now in a small box with other treasures, including a black stone from under an eagle's wing.

I'm glad I lived on Ataúro when I did. I lived and loved here with all my heart and with all my soul. And, if I failed in my quest to understand the mysteries of this island and its people, I'm glad I did. I'm glad the secrets of Ataúro remain safely buried in the crooks and crannies of this land, in its forests and caves, in its deep seas, under its rocks; I hope they always do.

Now, as night falls, sea breezes pass through the frangipani to my veranda where I sit waiting for stars to appear. The faint sounds of my neighbour, Tiu Domingos, repairing his boat in the twilight, reach me; and his children's voices float across the sand. The rust-brown flycatchers that have been busy this evening catching insects in the thatch of my roof, have gone. A canoe glides by with two oarsmen, their song soft and blurred across the sea and I recognise the dense deep voices of Bikeli men going home.

The scent of sea and frangipani, the slap of waves on sand, the distant voices of village children surround me… Pulling Ant's tais cloth around my shoulders, I settle into it and my heart sings.

ABOUT THE AUTHOR

Gabrielle, an Australian, spent twelve years on East Timor's remote Ataúro Island living and working with the island community. *Dancers on the Sea* is about the six years prior to Timor-Leste's independence in 2002. Gabrielle, a writer of fiction and non-fiction, lives on a nature refuge in southern Queensland and still regularly visits the island and people she loves. She writes – mainly short stories – to express and share her wonder and appreciation of people and their cultures. Gabrielle has won prizes for her stories, speaks four languages, has degrees in Anthropology and Education and has worked in Australia, Papua New Guinea, Indonesia and Timor-Leste.

Photo: Sarah Moles

ABOUT THE ILLUSTRATOR

AZYU PEREIRA SALDANHO

Azyu is an Ataúro Island man. Born in Maumeta-Vila in 1985 he attended the village primary school but was always more interested in drawing than in school studies. Azyu was 'in and out' of school but, when he could get hold of art materials, was consistently passionate about drawing.

In 1996 Gabrielle formed a small art group in Vila to provide pencils, paper and encouragement to Azyu and two or three other boys. For a time he studied natural sciences at the island high school but his interest was always diverted to his art. In 2009 he attended the Arte Moris art school in Dili where he developed his skills further and eventually became a tutor for younger Timorese artists. Azyu now lives between his island home of Ataúro and Dili where he has artist friends.

www.ingramcontent.com/pod-product-compliance
Lightning Source LLC
Chambersburg PA
CBHW071228070526
44583CB00017B/2092